THE PLEASURES OF ACADEME

THE
Pleasures of
Academe

A Celebration & Defense of
Higher Education

Withdrawn From
Jackson State Community
College Library

JAMES AXTELL

University of Nebraska Press
Lincoln and London

Copyright © 1998 James Axtell. All rights reserved.
Manufactured in the United States of America

⊗ The paper in this book meets the minimum require-
ments of American National Standard for Information
Sciences—Permanence of Paper for Printed Library
Materials, ANSI Z39.48-1984.

Library of Congress Cataloging-in-Publication Data
Axtell, James
The pleasures of academe : a celebration and defense
of higher education / James Axtell. p.   cm.
Includes bibliographical references (p.) and index
ISBN 0-8032-1049-3 (alkaline paper)
I. Education, Higher—United States. 2. College
teachers—United States. 3. College teaching—United
States. I. Title.
LA227.4.A98 1998 378.73-dc21 97-51865 CIP

Title page illustration courtesy of Graphic Arts
Collection, Visual Materials Division, Department
of Rare Books and Special Collections, Princeton
University Library.

LA
227.4
.A98
1998

For Susan
My greatest pleasure

Contents

In Praise of the University

*There are few earthly things
more beautiful than a college.*
John Masefield

I COULDN'T WAIT TO GO to college and I couldn't stand to
leave at graduation, so I became a professor. In thirty years
of professing at four different colleges and universities, I have
never regretted that decision, even when I had cause.

During that time, but particularly in the late sixties and early
seventies and in the past several years, cultural critics, pedagogical pundits, and even current and former professors have argued
noisily that everyone involved in higher education has—or should
have—abundant cause to rue their complicity. In the sixties and
seventies it was the faculty and administration, supposedly, whose
lives were miserable, made so by the disrespectful Dionysians
who suddenly had occupied the American campus and polluted
the educational fount with their lawless protests and extracurricular preoccupations.[1] In the nineties students and their parents are
allegedly the university's victims—of shocking costs, distended
curricula awash in triviality and political correctness, and over-
paid, underworked faculties more interested in lengthening their
résumés than in nurturing their classes.[2]

As a longtime student (and sometime professor) of the history
of American higher education, I have usually taken these criticisms with a grain of salt. Anyone with a long view will have
seen them all before in one guise or another. Today's critics have
nothing on the agitated graduates who wrote—and continue to
write—letters of admonition and advice to their alumni magazines or the opinionated authors of articles in the nation's general

magazines.³ From Harvard's founding in 1636, Americans have had a love-hate relationship with their colleges and universities, and emotions will only run higher and wider as more of us attend college in the future.

What impels me to stick my own oar in the turbid waters of academic debate is the sheer igorance and unfairness of most of the criticism, particularly of the professoriate, the indispensable head and heart of the university. Most critics, especially outsiders but even quondam professors who should know better, raise atypical anecdotes or events to the level of outrageous generalization and then launch their slings and arrows at the straw institutions they have erected upon these shifty sands. They never consult nationwide surveys whose statistics encompass the attitudes and behavior of the full gamut of American faculty members. And because bad news sells better than good, they seldom temper their attacks with any appreciation of what the university means, can mean, or has meant to American society at large and to its individual students and professors.

In this collection of partly familiar essays, I want to redress the balance by supplying the critics' methodological deficiencies and by bringing to the discussion the unusual perspective of someone educated in English as well as American universities, an athlete as well as a student, an interdisciplinary scholar, and a tenured, even chaired, professor whose insider's love of academe is tempered by familiarity with its long history as well as its current foibles and foolishness. I don't presume to speak for all of the nine hundred thousand full- and part-time faculty members in our nearly thirty-seven hundred variegated institutions of higher education. Pleasure, after all, is an individual's sensation, not a mass emotion.

But I also know that I am not alone in regarding my calling as a happy, if not the best possible, choice. Nationwide, at least 80 percent of my fellow professors are satisfied with their vocation and would choose it again; fewer than 8 percent wouldn't.⁴ Moreover, while my experiences as a student and professor were gained in somewhat "name" institutions—Yale, Oxford, Cambridge, Harvard, Sarah Lawrence, Northwestern, and William and Mary—I am confident, from faithful reading of the *Chronicle of Higher Education, Change, Academe,* and *Lingua Franca,* that they do not differ essentially in kind from those acquired at most four-year colleges and universities. The academic landscape I paint will be familiar to most of its denizens, even if my brushstrokes and shadings are the products of a particular vision.

Although my insider's portrait of university life is designedly lit with plenty of sunshine, readers should know that chiaroscuro is my normal medium and irony my rhetorical mode of preference. I am not blind to the many clouds that hang over academe. But some are strictly ephemeral, and the ones that worry or bother me most are seldom those conjured up by outside critics. While I lose no sleep over the portentous chimeras of tenured radicalism, political correctness, or canon-smashing, I am concerned, to varying degrees, about a number of issues in higher education. I worry that mass education is an oxymoron and that too-large institutions and classes can only process, not educate, their students. I doubt if faculty advising is as sustained and strong as students need to help them choose nourishing fare from the rich aisles of our enviable supermarket curricula. I fear that the costs of many of our best private colleges are beyond the reach of too many lower- and middle-class families and that many of our public institutions are fast becoming so. Like every professor, I'm bothered by students' writing deficiencies, which stem not only from poor preparation but common non-sense and tin ears. I have serious doubts that the computer is a pedagogical panacea and concerns about unequal access to its legitimate uses and a straitened labor market excessively tied to its manipulation. I regret the national epidemic of grade inflation, the lack of academic control over big-time athletics, the skewed values and anti-intellectual propensities of sororities and fraternities, and the excessive vocationalism of students and parents who are blind to the value and uses of liberal education.

On the professorial side, I regret the increasing use of non-tenure-track, part-time faculty, "gypsy" lecturers and instructors who are denied the full range of academe's pleasures and benefits—and responsibilities.[5] By the same token, I fear that the end of mandatory retirement and state stinginess will not allow deserving new talent to enter the profession in a timely fashion. I'm peeved when universities use their graduate students as instructors simply to save money without proper guidance by faculty mentors. I worry that (real) faculty salaries will continue to lose ground to the 1971–72 base, and that federal and foundation funding of scholarship in the humanities will never recoup its recent deep losses. I pity the professors—happily shrinking in number—who have never tasted the pleasures and rewards of research and publication, and resent administrators who put a mindless premium on page counts instead of quality. I worry that threats to academic freedom are caused less by external forces (which still threaten) than by self-censorship to avoid hypersensitivities and by the subtle intolerance of groupthink. And, finally, I'm worried that America's best minds and talents are not choosing the academic profession in sufficient numbers.

Having established my critical bona fides (which I will extend in the conclusion), I want to devote the rest of this book to some of the good news about academic life. When Henry Rosovsky, former dean of Harvard College, published *The University: An Owner's Manual* in 1990, he told an interviewer, "what's most distinctive about my book is that it is optimistic and positive. I think it may be the most positive book that's been written about higher education in 25 years."[6] My book is at least the second most, and I fervently hope not the last. I would like the university's acidulous critics to realize that they have largely got it wrong (though I don't expect any public recantations), professors and future professors to know just how right they've got it, and the tax- and tuition-paying public to regard higher education not only as the *best* investment they can make in our national future but one of the *safest*.

Preface

Five of these essays resulted from invited lectures (chapters 2, 4, and 8) or from attempts to make some sense of two of my earliest academic pleasures (chapters 6 and 7). The rest were written especially for this volume, three with my left hand (without footnotes) in a quiet island cottage on the Maine coast. I count the writing of and the freedom to write each of them among the sovereign pleasures of academe.

Chapter 1 is aimed at legislators, editorial writers, and other uninformed critics who feel that professors on the whole do not work very long or very hard at their calling, and who therefore blithely suggest that faculties should spend more of their "free" hours in the classroom teaching more undergraduates in order to relieve the pressure on state budgets. It's a relatively complete accounting of a typically active professor's multifarious duties and activities around the academic calendar, based largely on national statistics and partially on mine as recorded in a daybook for several years.

Chapter 2 was delivered at a meeting of ninety-some professors whose chairs are endowed by the William Rand Kenan Jr. Charitable Trust of Chapel Hill, North Carolina. It analyzes, from a personal and historical perspective, the large and small changes that have affected the doing of scholarship since 1963 when I began graduate study at Cambridge. It was first published in *The Modern University: Its Present Status and Future Prospects: Papers from the Sixth Kenan Convocation, April 22–24, 1993* (Chapel Hill, 1994) and has been updated.

Chapter 3 attacks hard and head-on the false dichotomy between teaching and research, and argues for "habitual scholarship" by the faculties of all but two-year colleges and the least ambitious liberal arts colleges and comprehensive universities. I intend to give overt aid and comfort to chairpersons and deans who want to inspire their faculty members to pursue meaningful scholarship outside as well as in their classrooms. It was published in the *Journal of Scholarly Publishing* (October 1997).

Chapter 4 is my acceptance speech upon receiving the 1992

Loyola-Mellon Humanities Award from Loyola University of Chicago. My thoughts on the need for education in "otherness" were prompted by the concatenation of the Columbian Quincentenary (in which I was heavily involved) and the Los Angeles riots following the police beating of black motorist Rodney King, but they obviously have relevance to the whole modern global village in which we live. They also speak indirectly to recent overheated exchanges about multiculturalism and the (perennial and modest) reconfiguration of the so-called "canon" in various humanities disciplines. An abbreviated version was published in the *Queen's Quarterly* (autumn 1992).

Chapter 5 considers, in light of our national infatuation with university rankings, the criteria we *should* use to assess true academic excellence, whether they are quantifiable or not.

Chapter 6 probes the benign pathology of one humanist's love affair with books. It first appeared in the *Virginia Quarterly Review* (winter 1988).

Chapter 7 views academe from the unusual dual perspective of a scholar-athlete and traces the choices he (or she) must make if he wishes to cultivate both talents to their fullest. It suggests that the collegiate mind/body problem need not result in conflict. It, too, was published in the VQR (winter 1991) and was listed in "Notable Essays of 1991" by Robert Atwan in *The Best American Essays 1992*, edited by Susan Sontag (New York, 1992).

Chapter 8 is essentially the paper I gave in Rome in October 1993 at the invitation of the U.S. Information Service to explain to European scholars of America how I became an ethnohistorian and what that interdisciplinary denomination means in terms of international trends in history and the social sciences. It suggests that working between disciplines, while fraught with intellectual, social, and political hazards, is well worth the risk. It was published in Italian in Daniele Fiorentino, ed., *La storia americana e le scienze sociali in Europa e negli Stati Uniti* (Rome, 1996).

Chapter 9 suggests that classroom teaching is but a part of the teaching that many professors do, and that over a lifetime they may reach more "students" outside the classroom than in. It draws on my experiences as an expert witness in an Indian land claims case in federal court, museum designer and writer, media consultant, public speaker, television and radio commentator and interviewee, and publishing scholar.

Chapter 10 describes the numerous social, economic, aesthetic, and cultural advantages—and a few of the drawbacks—of quintessential college towns (and some college neighborhoods of larger cities), such as Princeton, Ann Arbor, Berkeley, Chapel Hill, Hanover, Providence, Cambridge (England and Massachusetts), Oxford (Ohio, Mississippi, and England), and New Haven.

Chapter 11 narrates the somewhat wacky timing, aims, and itineraries of one family's professorially driven vacations, reflected largely in the bemused and often chagrined looks of his children and spouse.

The conclusion distinguishes the real problems of American higher education from the major misunderstandings and calumnies that critics, largely nonacademic conservatives, have perpetrated about and against the professoriate. It argues that there is no "crisis" in higher education and that the commitment, talent, and hard work of the nation's faculties make our system of higher education the world's largest, most diverse, and best.

The pleasures I have enjoyed as a student and professor will not, of course, be identical to those experienced by other academics, young or old. And the number and range of pleasures I've taken may not be as extensive for others. But anyone who has willingly stayed the course through four years of college, graduate school, or a career in college teaching has known at least some of the pleasures I describe in the chapters that follow.

Whatever else they are, colleges and universities are institutions designed and sustained by society primarily for *intellectual* purposes: to increase the knowledge, understanding, and mental prowess of their students and, at the same time, to increase knowledge and (ideally) wisdom for the greater good of society and humankind through the published research and scholarship of their faculties. The essential life of the university, therefore, consists of "the long quest and slow discovery, the quiet expanding influence of personality upon personality, of mind upon mind, the silent interdependent growth of knowledge and power and spirit, the slow, unconscious advance towards maturity, from day to day, in both teacher and taught."[7] It is at heart the product of the intellectual and imaginative synapse between professors and students in the classroom, office, library, and lab.

Thus it is no coincidence that the academic pleasures I have discovered relate primarily to the central mission of higher education: reading and writing, teaching and learning, stretching and growing, both intellectually and humanly. There are more, certainly, some of which arise from the intense social and emotional interaction that also defines a college or university. But I have focused on the "community of scholars" which includes but transcends our individual campuses. In that international, mutual-aid society of lifelong learners I have found the most pleasure and nourishment outside my own home. I hope this book will encourage others to join its ranks, give current members added reason to enjoy their affiliation, and give outsiders some inkling why anyone would do either.

Acknowledgments

The last thing that we find in making a book
is to know what we must put first.
Blaise Pascal

W RITING THIS BOOK has been an unalloyed pleasure. Not only was most of it written during summer vacations, when I could play occasional hooky from Indian studies with only small pangs of conscience, but all of it was inspired by the colleagues I have enjoyed—students, faculty, and staff—since I entered Yale College in the autumn of 1959. I would never have thought of writing it had their company not constituted, for all its human shortcomings, a real and open community of scholars.

Writers tend to be inveterate readers, and I would like to acknowledge three books that have served as models of eloquent and perceptive writing on the modern university. My copies of J. Douglas Brown's *The Liberal University* (1969), A. Bartlett Giamatti's *A Free and Ordered Space: The Real World of the University* (1988), and especially *Ever the Teacher: William G. Bowen's Writings as President of Princeton* (1987), lovingly dog-eared and ardently annotated, are always near at hand.

I am also grateful to Staige Blackford for publishing my initial attempts at familiar essaying in the *Virginia Quarterly Review*. To the William Rand Kenan Jr. Charitable Trust I am beholden for a wonderful chair of humanities in which to write about modern education as well as colonial history and for the opportunity to talk with my Kenan colleagues about the evolution of scholarship in our lifetimes. Edward Holley, one of those colleagues, applied a deft editorial pencil to the manuscript before publication in the

convocation proceedings. Thanks, too, to Boris Castel for re-
questing a version of chapter 4 for a special issue of the *Queen's
Quarterly* and to Sandra Meadow for accepting chapter 3 for the
Journal of Scholarly Publishing.

The staff of William and Mary's Swem Library, particularly
John Lawrence and Wendy Webb-Robers of Interlibrary Loans,
have gone out of their way to satisfy my at times insatiable need
for obscure and fugitive titles; I consider it my second home. For
two weeks in the summer we make ourselves at home in Northeast Harbor, Maine, thanks to the longstanding sufferance and
kindness of the Eliot clan. As we play "Fictionary" with an 1850
lexicon inscribed by the author to Charles W. Eliot, president and
prime mover of modern Harvard, and savor the view from the tall
southern windows built for the Studio's presiding genius, Charles
Hopkinson, portrait painter of New England's academic aristocracy, it is difficult not to feel educationally engaged, if not collegially challenged.

To a more intimate group of academic friends I owe a great
deal, not only for careful readings of assorted chapters, but for
sustained scholarship and sustaining friendship of the best kind.
Rolena and David Adorno (formerly Princeton, now Yale), Tim
Breen (Northwestern), John Thelin (formerly William and Mary,
now Kentucky), Larry Wiseman (William and Mary), Bill Taylor
(formerly University of Virginia, now Southern Methodist), David Weber (SMU), Ted Ziolkowski (Princeton), and Alvin Kernan
(formerly Princeton, now Mellon Foundation) make it easy to
idealize the academic life because they are so good at what they
do and make no effort to hide their pleasure in doing it.

I am also grateful to William Cain of Wellesley College and
Neil Whitehead of the University of Wisconsin-Madison for
timely and instructive readings.

Finally, my family has given me myriad pleasures well beyond
the academic. They have also and always allowed me my academic
enthusiasms, though not without considerable cost to normalcy

Acknowledgments

and a retaliatory dose of raillery. My now-grown sons Jeremy and Nathaniel—despite their own graduate degrees, bookish tastes, and writerly habits—won't let me forget precious vacation time lost in bookshops and museums, the precipitate conversion of their abandoned bedrooms to study annexes, or two favorite Christmas presents entitled *At Home with Books* and *Library: The Drama Within*. Fortunately, their mother, Susan, while equally amused and bemused, is more tactfully tolerant. Her ubiquitous grace, high intelligence, focused energy, and devotion to her own (three-year-old) students are a daily inspiration. She more than doubles my academic pleasures by sharing them with me.

ACADEMIC

CHAPTER ONE

(Mis)Understanding Academic Work

The layman doesn't know what
professoring really is.
Carlos Baker

ERIODICALLY, American politicians, pundits, editors, and writers of letters to editors feel compelled, qualified, and entitled to take our colleges and universities to task. The causes of these spasms of pedagogical pique are various. Sometimes the extracurricular behavior of the students is the target, whether goldfish eating or rioting in the streets. At other times the faculty is on trial—sometimes literally—for expressing or merely being suspected of holding allegedly dangerous ideas and opinions, thereby corrupting the tender minds of America's youth. More recently, cost-conscious legislatures, faced with mounting demand for affordable state institutions, have taken aim at higher education's rising price tag. In their search for politically painless ways to trim state budgets, politicians often target higher education first on the assumption that most students don't vote, professors are too few and too pointy-headed to worry about, and most voters are neither college graduates nor the tuition-paying parents of current students.

Usually these reductions in higher-education budgets are simply mandated across the board, leaving the stricken institutions—often on very short notice—to allocate the cuts and control the damage. But occasionally legislative committees or gubernatorial commissions stage hearings to rationalize the proposed cuts, at least politically and in the myopically short run. On such occasions, particularly in recent years, the vox populi has been heard to express newfound concern about "efficiency" in our public colleges

3

and universities. Knowing that universities are labor-intensive and that their budgets are therefore dominated (about 70-80 percent) by relatively inflexible wages and salaries, politicians have been suggesting that the route to "fiscal responsibility" lies in getting more pedagogical bang for the public buck. "Instructional technology"—TVs and computers instead of people—is a venerable panacea, but increasingly popular in the most recent populist climate are calls for more work—more classroom teaching of more students—and less research from the pampered professoriate. The implication behind these proposals is that professors as a class do not work very long or very hard at their highly paid jobs.[1] The perhaps apocryphal story of a midwestern legislative committee interrogating a professor from a large state university underlines the point. One member of the committee asked the professor how much time he spent in the classroom. When the professor answered "Nine hours," the legislator looked pleased and acknowledged, "That seems like a good day's work."

The joke, of course, is that most professors at four-year institutions today teach *in the classroom* between five and twelve hours a week. About half of the faculty members of universities, public and private, teach between five and eight hours; in public universities, nearly twice as many professors teach nine to twelve hours as teach one to four hours a week.[2] But where is the humor really? Such a joke makes sense only to academics who know, first, that *any* statistic about classroom hours is meaningless in isolation; second, that politicians would be apoplectic at such an answer if they understood the weekly (rather than daily) reference; and, third, that even college-educated politicians and voters are woefully ignorant of what constitutes academic life and work.

If politicians and the public have no idea about how and how hard professors work, we needn't be surprised. Where could they find out, except perhaps by having one born or marry into the family? Although there are some 550,000 full-time faculty members in the United States today, they leave far too many families bereft of their personal instruction in the mysteries of academic life.[3] There are no TV sitcoms, series, or dramas starring college professors. Academic novels and films are of little help because they tend to focus on the usual fictional themes of greed, sex, and power, with only a vestigial collegiate setting to support their heavily satirical, romantic, or cantankerous treatments. The majority of Americans who have never attended a college or university, of course, have had no opportunity to observe the faculty species at close range. Even college graduates are rarely informed about the work habits of their professors because the great majority of students seldom see more than one of their teachers' multiple roles performed and have little contact with professors outside class and occasional office visits. A number of authors of recent book-length critiques of higher education are or have been professors—the rest are hostile and uninformed strangers—but their concerns are less with the lackadaisical schedules of professors than with their alleged moral cowardice, intellectual bankruptcy, or ideological obtuseness.[4]

How, then, can we ever explain what it is that professors do for a living or why simplistic calls for more pedagogical "productivity" are infeasible and largely undesirable solutions to constricted state budgets? There are only two reliable sources of such information. The first is representative statistics on the behavior of the national professoriate as a whole. We have three rich sets of them, which are consonant with many earlier studies. In 1988 the U.S. Department of Education polled over eleven thousand faculty members at 480 colleges and universities.[5] A year later, and again in 1995-96, the Higher Education Research Institute at the University of California–Los Angeles surveyed some thirty-five thousand professors at nearly 400 institutions.[6] The institutions in both studies were carefully chosen to represent every locus of higher education, from multipurpose two-year community colleges to elite private research universities—our Princetons, Yales, and Stanfords. The other source is the articulated personal experiences of working professors, which lend specificity to the broad generalizations of the national statistics. While we have a handful of articles on the subject,[7] I have drawn mainly on my own experience as a full-time professor over thirty years in four different institutions, the last six years recorded briefly but faithfully in daybooks. Although my experience was gained in somewhat atypical "name" institutions, three private and one public (Yale, Sarah Lawrence, Northwestern, and William and Mary), it does not differ markedly from that of tens of thousands of my colleagues across the country in virtually every kind of four-year institution.

Let's begin with the easier question of how long professors typically work. According to the Department of Education, professors in all institutions work an average of fifty-three hours a week. Those who teach in two-year community colleges, where long classroom hours are the norm, work the shortest though by no means the easiest week—forty-seven hours. Professors in public research universities, such as the multiversities of Minnesota, California, and Virginia, put in fifty-seven-hour weeks.[8] These are averages, of course; half of the professors work longer, half work shorter hours. Virtually no one works as few as forty hours, which constitute the standard American workweek. A similar study in Great Britain recently found that while all faculty members worked an average of 53 hours a week, as in the United States, senior professors put in 59 hours and female professors a prodigious 64.5 hours.[9]

These last statistics remind us that professors, like members of other learned professions, make careers in stages, which must qualify any statistic or generalization about the profession as a whole. To judge by my colleagues over many years, instructors and assistant professors tend to put in extra long hours finishing their dissertations and first books, writing their first sets of lectures for new classes, and overextending themselves in committee work, conference-going, and other pre-tenure paths to academic success. With a few publications, initial drafts of lectures and class notes, and tenure under their belts, associate professors can begin to devote slightly less time to career and slightly more to postponed personal lives or families. Then, as they gain seniority, responsibility, and perhaps eminence as full professors and children grow up and away, faculty members are likely to be consumed again by heavy professional demands.

Granted, professors seem to put in long hours during the school year, but we all know that academic calendars look nothing like those of most American workers or even of other learned professionals, such as lawyers, physicians, and engineers. What about those long, lazy summer vacations that professors get every year? I know of only one small statistical survey to answer that question. I also know from personal experience and observation that while professors' contracts are written for only nine or ten months, their paychecks are commensurately and proportionally smaller than those of other professionals who spent no more and probably fewer years acquiring their qualifying degrees. This leads a goodly number of them to teach one or both sessions of summer school for absurdly low stipends. Most of the rest, I would hazard, take short personal or family vacations and then spend most of each sunny day and many nights reading or rereading for next year's classes, pursuing research in the library or lab, or writing up its results for publication. If they teach at a research university, they will also continue to advise and read the ongoing work of graduate students, whose calendars also contain precious few holidays. A few lucky professors will take off for foreign parts to gather visual, scientific, or archival data about their subjects, but most will stay home, putting in only marginally fewer hours than they did during the school year but with more concentration on fewer duties, chosen and scheduled with greater freedom.[10]

Since professors are in their classrooms only a few hours a week during the academic year, we can be excused for asking just what they are doing the rest of the time to clock such lengthy workweeks. The Department of Education gives us a rough idea of the breakdown of professorial activities, to which the UCLA studies add several refinements. In all colleges and universities, 56 percent of the average professor's workweek is devoted to teaching and its preparation, 16 percent to research, 13 percent to administration and committee work, and 15 percent to a category called "other." These figures, of course, smooth out several significant differences between types of institutions. The faculties of community colleges, for example, spend 71 percent of their week in teaching and only 3 percent on research, whereas professors at public research universities devote 43 percent to teaching and 29 percent to research.[11] Both groups, it should be noted, work in accord with the specific missions, constituencies, resources, and traditions of their respective institutions. With nearly thirty-seven hundred institutions of striking variety, American higher education serves the diverse needs of more than 14 million students of all ages with considerable efficiency and surprising quality. America's professors display as much variety and versatility as do their institutions.[12]

These figures are of some help, but the categories of analysis — teaching, research, administration — are still too broad to give us a clear picture of the work life of a modern professor, a new age Mr. Chips. I happen to know one well, so I will borrow from his experience without further acknowledgment in an effort to provide a realistic notion of how professors work under considerable (if self-inflicted) pressure at complicated (if largely self-scheduled) jobs. The *quality* of what they do is an extremely complicated question best left for another occasion; here we are interested only in the magnitude and range of their efforts.

While scholarly research is the most mysterious aspect of professorial life, teaching may be the most misunderstood. Since most of us have been the sustained object of teachers in primary and secondary school for thirteen years of our lives, we easily fall into the trap of thinking we know what teaching is all about and that, in a pinch, all of us could do it. If we are parents, we do teach our children on a daily basis, sometimes by precept but more often by example. But teaching young (and increasingly older) adults in colleges and universities is quite different from teaching children. First, to prepare them for the independence of adulthood, college students are placed under very little constraint—option-rich degree requirements, few parietal rules, perhaps an academic honor code. Unlike in school, their relationship with teachers is largely voluntary and self-motivated. They are free to tune a professor out, ignore his office hours, rate him poorly on a course evaluation, or simply vote with their feet, often well into the semester. Second, in higher education, professors no longer concentrate on the inculcation of basic cultural values, the necessary information for good citizenship, and the rudiments of learning, but on introducing students in a thorough way to the various liberal and professional *disciplines* (as opposed to mere "subjects") and on teaching them to think *critically* for themselves, to become their own producers of knowledge and values. Both of these conditions make college teaching a different and no less difficult challenge. Professors must not only show their students the extent and depths of their disciplines, they must do so in a way that wins and nourishes their attention and their respect if not enthusiasm for the subject. Thus, no matter what subject they teach, professors must master both its science—its constantly evolving disciplinary codes, literature, and methodologies—and the art of teaching it effectively and memorably.

Just where and how often this kind of higher teaching is done obviously affects a professor's workload. A typical college semester consists of about thirteen or fourteen weeks of classes and a few days of "reading period" to prepare for about two weeks of final examinations. (Quarters, three of which constitute the academic year, are substantially shorter—as few as nine weeks of classes.) Most courses meet either twice or three times a week for a total of three "credit hours"; language and lab science courses, which meet more frequently, are the major exceptions. A credit hour lasts fifty minutes in order to allow students time to travel between classes. Classes convene in a variety of settings. Much college teaching, particularly on large campuses, takes place in lecture halls where, as in Puritan churches, a speaking aristocracy dictates to a silent democracy. But today's lecture course is often punctuated by student and professorial questions and discussion, cut and thrust, which are the staples of the small-group seminars, labs, office visits, and after-class hallway encounters where teaching also transpires.

The variety of teaching venues and the different styles of teaching required by them demand considerable versatility and extensive preparation from the professor. So do the different levels of students he teaches, from confused freshmen who require clarity and breadth of knowledge to advanced graduate students who seek expert depth. Which is why the mere number of hours professors spend in the classroom and the size of their classes are less indicative of their workload than are the number and variety of class preparations they have each week. In research and doctoral universities, the normal teaching assignment is two or three courses per semester, which usually means between four and nine class preparations a week. About half of all professors at four-year institutions spend between five and twelve hours a week preparing to teach or seventy-five minutes preparing each fifty-minute class; another 30 percent prepare between thirteen and twenty hours a week.[13] Seminars take considerably longer than lectures to prepare because the teacher must reread the assignment, no matter how many times he has already read it, for in discussion command of fine and fresh detail is essential. A book a week for each class is not unusual at better colleges. And regardless of how many students a class has—lecture or seminar, tutorial or lab— the professor's preparation for it entails the same commitment of time, energy, and discipline.

Virtually all of the above figures on preparation are for teachers who have taught their courses at least once, having constructed the syllabi, read the required reading, and written the initial set of lectures or questions for discussion. They obviously do not include the months, often years, of focused reading in general and specialized fields that are necessary to the shaping of any course and syllabus. Unless professors continue to teach only the first courses they fashioned as newly minted Ph.D.s, from the same books and lecture notes and in the same way, they must constantly, throughout their careers, read widely in their own and cognate disciplines (and today fruitful ideas and theories come from surprisingly numerous and unpredictable places) and read deeply in their specialties (most of which are growing exponentially, thanks to more numerous, more prolific, and better-connected colleagues and a plethora of specialized books and journals). To avoid early obsolescence, mental fatigue, and sheer boredom, every course must be continually updated, reconfigured, and rejuvenated to take into account new theories and approaches, new audiences, more relevant or engaging data, better audiovisual aids, new pedagogical twists and assignments, and more probing exam questions. Like research, this kind of steady, extensive reading takes time—time that to busy outsiders looks suspiciously like recreation or escapism. Small wonder that in active America, with its persistent streak of anti-intellectualism, adults who read for most of their living are misunderstood and distrusted.

Despite appearances, teaching and its preparation require much more than a little talking and a lot of reading, which explains why Mr. Chips and most of his colleagues find that when classes are in session, research often gets pushed to a back burner until vacations begin. A course begins at least three months before the semester, when the required books and "course paks" of xeroxed articles have to be ordered from the college bookstore. This means that the professor has read them in advance and has chosen them from the alternatives that are still in print, usually paperbacks to save student pocketbooks. A week or two before classes begin, the professor drafts and reproduces his syllabus and puts his required reading on reserve in the college library. In Mr. Chips's university, this entails not only filling out a form and looking up the books' call numbers but going to the stacks with a library cart to carry the volumes to the understaffed reserve book room, a healthy if humbling exercise for some dons. Also well in advance professors who use audiovisual aids in their teaching— and their numbers seem to be increasing—must order and sched- ule films and videos and have slides shot and processed, preferably by the college's audiovisual lab. Professors like Mr. Chips who regularly use slides to capture and assist students raised on tele- vision and video games and to convey unfamiliar material spend considerable time researching, labeling, filing, and refiling them, not to mention hauling projectors and screens back and forth if they are not built in. If audiovisuals are not to be used for merely decorative or time-filling purposes—and so (dis)regarded by the students—they must be integrated into teaching as thoroughly and relevantly as any spoken or written words, such as primary documents, maps, and other handouts.

Teaching exists only to facilitate learning, and learning must be focused and evaluated by regular testing. After preparing classes, the professor's most demanding and time-consuming ob- ligation is the evaluation of students' progress, typically through quizzes, exams, exercises, and essays. The size of a class contrib- utes to the professors' workload less in preparation time or effort than in the evaluation process. Especially if the essay assignment or the exam questions are the same for every student, reading a hundred or two hundred responses is much more onerous in both time and mental numbness than handling thirty or fifty. Some professors, like Mr. Chips, prefer polished and type- or com- puter-written essays on different, largely elective subjects to blue- book answers scribbled under pressure of the clock. If they assign three or four essays of varying lengths in a semester and require frequent rewrites, they take on a substantial burden of home-bound reading and annotation. Fine-toothed editing of a three- to five-page essay takes at least twenty to thirty minutes, after which detailed notes on each essay's strengths and weaknesses must be made for the record should the student someday ask for a letter of recommendation or question his or her grade.

In smaller classes, student-led discussions and presentations can be effectively used for evaluation and for gradually liberating learners from the dominating authority of the teacher, every true teacher's goal. As Erasmus, the sixteenth-century humanist, observed, "the best way to separate what you know from what you think you know is to teach."[14] This mode of teaching, however, requires of the professor plenty of advance consultation with the student teachers to discuss the goals, substance, and pedagogy of each class. Teaching for independence is always harder and more time-consuming than pontificating ex cathedra to captive if restless audiences, but it carries its own rewards.

Keeping tabs on classroom hours is doubly meaningless because a great deal of college teaching goes on in a professor's office during and outside scheduled office hours. Faculty offices are the locus of individual or small-group conferences (Chips has only three extra chairs) with student teachers or students who want or are required to rewrite their essays, who seek an explanation for low grades, a topic for a research paper, or bibliographical suggestions, who need a favor, a letter of recommendation, or approval of a class schedule, or who want to discuss career options or a personal problem. In Chips's department, each professor is encouraged to schedule as many office hours a week as he spends in the classroom. The more individualized work he assigns and encourages, the more numerous will be his drop-in clientele. The more visitors he has during office hours, the more time he must spend at home or in a library carrel preparing his classes and grading exams and papers.

The two classes of students who take greatest advantage of

professorial office time are undergraduate honors students and graduate students, neither of whom is ever visible in the teaching stereotypes of college critics. At a few colleges, most notably Princeton, all juniors write a major research paper and all seniors a thesis, which means that every faculty member has at least a few if not several students to guide through fifty- to one-hundred-page productions. At most institutions, however, departmental honors students, one or two at a time, add to the hidden workload of professors who are seldom given official credit for supervising them. In terms of faculty time invested, senior honors theses are virtually indistinguishable from M.A. theses by first- or second-year graduate students, with the exception that honors theses have draconian deadlines, followed by one- or two-hour oral defenses with a faculty committee. Getting any red-blooded undergraduate who's carrying three or four other courses to research, organize, write, and rewrite ninety to one hundred pages is not a job for anyone short of stamina or office hours.

For reasons that are not difficult to understand, graduate students per capita are the biggest consumers of faculty time. They are closer in age, they identify professionally, and they are less deferential, so they do not hesitate to pop in a professor's door, open or closed. To leave the 2 million graduate and professional students (14 percent of the total) out of the picture of academic work is a serious omission.[15] Nearly everything about graduate teaching—knowledge, concentration, standards—is on a higher level than that of undergraduate teaching and the faculty's workload is commensurately heavier. Virtually all graduate classes are seminars, intellectually freewheeling and often student-led, requiring advance planning with the professor. Assignments are longer and more demanding of both faculty and students; with more flexible deadlines, written work comes over the faculty transom at all times of year, "vacations" definitely not excluded. Requests for letters of recommendation—for the next stage of graduate work, prizes, fellowships, first and subsequent jobs—are frequent and nearly universal. For many a Mr. Chips, summing up and selling honestly a young person's whole academic past and promise in a two- or three-page letter is one of their most trying and sensitive duties.

Graduate school hurdles, while negotiated by the students, constantly have to be erected and maintained by the faculty. At Chips's university, all graduate students must pass a foreign language exam, administered by one of six departmental members twice a year. Every M.A. student is put through a thesis and a one-hour oral comprehensive exam; doctoral students endure sixteen hours of written comprehensives and a two-hour oral to qualify to write a dissertation, which must be defended during a two-hour oral from five inquisitors. In any graduate department, serving as an advisor or even reader of theses and dissertations is a major commitment of professorial time and focus. Because they may take as long as six or more years to complete and the candidate is usually in a hurry to obtain his or her degree, the reading of draft chapters and finished products takes on an urgency that often clashes with the professor's best-laid plans for a little research of his own or innumerable other obligations. Once the degree is awarded and often before, the advisor and most readers are asked to help the new doctor secure gainful employment, which in today's bearish market requires a blitz of finely honed and tuned letters to one's colleagues or nonacademic employers with jobs to share. The word processor has made the repetitiveness and individual tailoring of this long-term process somewhat less onerous, but it has not reduced the fundamental obligation or its professional seriousness for both writer and subject. Nothing a professor writes, except his scholarly publications, reflects as accurately and importantly on his and his institution's professional standing as his letters of recommendation, and most professors in Chips's acquaintance approach them accordingly.

One final faculty responsibility toward graduate students is to prepare them, and to oversee their initiation, as college teachers.

Probably most graduate students, in the liberal disciplines at least, serve at one time as teaching assistants to professors in large lecture courses, leading discussion groups, grading, and giving occasional lectures. The supervising professor meets weekly with his TAs to discuss teaching and grading philosophy, pertinent points for discussion, appropriate paper topics, and anything else related to the conception and operation of a typical college course. In some universities, the best advanced graduate students are allowed to teach their own courses, either a seminar in their specialty or a smallish introductory course. In this event, their advisor is called upon to oversee their whole performance, from syllabus to final exam. In the midst of his own busy courses, he will visit two or three classes and then discuss their strengths and shortcomings with the junior professor, as he will the student evaluations when the course is completed. If in his own classes he hasn't practiced what he preaches, these discussions are well designed to raise his consciousness.

As that suspicious-looking category in the national statistics called "other" suggests, the work of most professors can never be encompassed fully by describing their curricular duties alone. Many professors give part of their long workweeks over to hybrid forms of teaching that defy easy categorization; some might as easily be classified "public service." How else should we describe talks or lectures addressed to new students, parents, departmental majors, and alumni? Or farther afield, Scout troops, school assemblies, Elderhostels, Daughters of the American Revolution, and preschool classes preparing for Thanksgiving? One of Mr. Chips's most amusing chores is to respond to requests from high school term-paper writers and curious citizens for "everything you know about ——, or, if you're too busy for that, a list of all the books on the subject."

Far more rewarding and common but also more time-consuming is service on editorial boards of scholarly journals or publisher's series and as readers of manuscripts for both. Somewhat rarer is the chance to advise and write for TV, radio, and now

CD-ROM producers or for museums in search of expert help. The opportunity to reach audiences infinitely larger than, if not as concentrated and sustained as, one's classes is seldom rejected by tried and true teachers. Giving inservice workshops to museum staffs and guest-lecturing at other universities, here and abroad, similarly extend a professor's pedagogical reach while supplementing his abbreviated income.[16]

* * *

If college teaching is now a little less misunderstood, we have only to unwrap the mystery of scholarly research to reveal fully the heart and soul of a modern professor. In some ways, the academic imperative to "publish or perish" is easier for the public and politicians to understand because many of them harbor a similar, perhaps romantic desire, to be published authors if not daily writers. And since most Americans can read and write, they feel that writing a book or an article is not above them, although most of them would not feel equal to performing open-heart surgery, building a bridge, or arguing a case before the Supreme Court. What most of them forget when they take aim at our colleges and universities, however, is that the long-established social function of higher education, particularly in North America, is to *advance* knowledge as well as to sift and recycle the accumulated wisdom of the ages in transmitting it to new generations. Too much of the gross national product—about a third—depends on new knowledge not to involve our premier brain factories in the search.[17]

Even if academic research were not so vital to our national progress and quality of life, professors would still be drawn to and do well to pursue scholarship, to make it a major component of their jobs. There are at least twenty-five reasons for professors to publish, half of which relate to their teaching function.[18] To generalize, scholarly research crucially informs college teaching by keeping the teacher not merely abreast but on top of his constantly evolving discipline and specialties. Teaching is most effective when professors serve as active models of the life of learning, when they are as intellectually engaged and alive as they hope their students will be, certainly by the end of the course. Ideally, research for the classroom and that for scholarly publication are one and the same. Even if they are not, the *process* of discovery, its intellectual rigor and the moral discipline it demands, redounds to the quality of the whole professorial performance. Rather than conflicting, teaching and research are deeply symbiotic, for a good scholar shares with a good teacher five key attributes: enthusiasm, authority, rigor, honesty, and humility.

Furthermore, we should not lose sight of the fact that publication of scholarship in books, articles, and other media *is* a form of teaching in itself. A good book (or CD-ROM), accessible to students as well as colleagues, reaches and therefore teaches, in a concentrated, polished form, far more students than the author's evanescent lectures will ever reach in a lifetime. Its knowledge is diffused geometrically through other professors' lectures and writings and through course adoptions to thousands of students all over the country and perhaps the world, not just to the students who happen to enroll in the writer's local classes. Since all higher education depends on books, publishing professors repay their calling in kind, ensuring its future and progress. Many professors, Mr. Chips among them, are rewarded simply by returning to the classroom upon publication the scholarship directly inspired by the needs of their own classes.

On campus, research begins with the sedulous search for books and other sources of information, a process that is never finished because of the diverse modes and uses of scholarship. Most professors accumulate sizable working libraries of their own, but all of them have to and are happy to resort frequently, sometimes daily, to their college libraries. The periodical shelves have to be swept every few months to keep up with professional and pedagogical journals, which is no short task in university libraries that often receive five thousand to thirty thousand subscriptions. In lieu of a general sweep, many dons opt for more focused searches via specialized bibliographies, footnotes, reviews, and electronic indices. If their library is reasonably large, say, at least a few million volumes, they might be able to find most of what they need locally. But few faculties are blessed with such resources, so they must locate and request books and copies of articles from other institutions through interlibrary loans. Computer linkages and cooperative associations of libraries have speeded up this process in recent years but it still takes time and patient foresight. More unique materials—museum collections, archaeological sites, scientific experiments, manuscript collections—are still accessible largely through personal visits to distant locations, though CD-ROMs and laser discs are beginning to capture some.

In all but the largest research libraries, whose ample budgets and trained acquisition librarians ensure the prompt purchase of most of the world's best scholarship, faculty members are intimately involved in the budget-minded selection of library acquisitions. If the library has an automatic ordering system for a tailored profile of university presses, departmental representatives every few weeks must choose from the shipments the titles most useful to their present and future colleagues and students. Titles that do not fit the profile or are published by other presses must be ordered by individual professors on short departmental budgets, which entails frequent searches of new and used book catalogues and the general and specialized review literature. Several weeks or even months (for foreign orders) may pass before the professor is rewarded with notification from the circulation desk or with lucky dibs on the new-book shelves. Again, patience and plenty of alternative employments are essential for scholarly results.

Once his materials are well in hand and often before, to help collect them, the scholar needs to secure financial support from his own institution or from some Maecenas, mostly to buy release time from teaching to think and write. When every serious author knows that writing books is a full-time job, it is small wonder that a full-time teacher is seldom able to write them satisfactorily or promptly enough in the narrow interstices of his semestered life or even during his extended, unpaid vacations. If his own college does not have a semester leave or summer research program or its award schedules or resources do not coincide with his needs, he will be forced to submit lengthy, time-consuming applications to government agencies, foundations, research libraries, and other centers for advanced study. These invariably require letters of recommendation from several experts whose cooperation is always endangered by untimely or too-frequent requests. Fortunately, the favor is usually returned sooner or later and the circle of academic amity remains unbroken. Perhaps the best outcome is a grant that allows the scholar to remain at home, where he must learn to ignore his importunate phone, colleagues, and students and relearn the difficult art of total concentration and disciplined productivity. If he does not mind losing weeks of work in packing and relocating his kin and kaboodle to another site, he will probably be rewarded by the change of scene, conducive working conditions, and stimulating new colleagues.

Alone or in collaboration, the informed and funded scholar then faces the proverbially dreaded void on his computer screen (or, in Chips's case, on his yellow legal pad), which *dares* him to sing his scholarly song on key. While not every author feels with veteran wordsmith Gene Fowler that "writing is easy; all you do is sit staring at a blank sheet of paper until the drops of blood form on your forehead," the public of would-be authors grossly underestimates the time and tension involved in putting words on paper in cogent order with suitable style.[19] For most scholarly writers and even for many professional hands, two to four double-spaced pages a day would be more than acceptable, and not every day can be fully devoted to writing, what with the attendant duties of thinking, organizing, and procrastinating.

Scholarly publication takes several forms. Trial balloons for larger ideas are often sent up as twenty- or thirty-minute presentations of papers at specialized conferences and annual meetings of professional associations, which are also attended three or four days at a time to confer with colleagues, peruse exhibits of the latest books, cultivate publishers, listen to other papers, and renew faith in one's calling. Invited lectures at other universities or colloquia at one's own serve the same purpose. These short versions, if not completely deflated by their sharp-minded audiences, often metamorphose into journal articles. Getting them accepted usually requires revisions, sometimes substantial, after critiques by editors and anonymous experts in the field. Then, after correcting and returning page proofs, the new author gets to admire his creation briefly before sending out inscribed offprints to a select list of friends, benefactors, and indulgent relatives.

Many professors like Mr. Chips find that longer, more sustained pieces of argument and proof in book or article form are best tackled during winter and summer vacations with their longish stretches of concentration time. Books are especially difficult to write on an academic schedule; one every five years would be prolific, and volumes of ten years' gestation are not uncommon. Even when the professor manages to turn out the requisite two hundred or eight hundred pages of acceptable prose, he must obtain a contract from as prestigious a publisher as possible with a lengthy proposal and outline, a search that may take several attempts. Again, after in-house and outside readings, revisions, and final acceptance, the author may wait an antsy year or more before receiving his page proofs and a request for their return—and shortly an index—which invariably conflicts with several other obligations. But before the grand denouement, the author must have received written permission to quote at length from manuscript and copyrighted material and to publish illustrations, which he must also obtain, often at considerable personal expense. He must also have filled out a long publisher's information form for jacket copy and publicity purposes, usually with suggestions for appropriate publications of review. Then he is finally ready to receive with mixed emotions the ten complementary copies of his shining opus, whose critical fate he must now anxiously await. No matter how it is received, he can know immediately the secret pleasure of adding an important line to his curriculum vitae.

The research cycle is completed when the author-professor is asked to review his peers' manuscripts and publications. Writing thorough, fair, and constructive reviews of scholarship is as time-consuming as it is crucial to the knowledge industry. Because it is usually unpaid, it must be a labor of love undertaken out of a sense of professional pride and duty. A book review of only four hundred to a thousand words often takes an interrupted week to write, and many published professors are asked to write several every year. It is another hidden facet of academic work that is seldom recognized or rewarded even by the academy.

Reviewing is only one of many examples of how research, like teaching, easily spills over into a hybrid rubric of "professional service." In addition to writing recommendations for scholar-friends and acquaintances (often younger) applying for grants, fellowships, and jobs, professors are frequently asked to evaluate the vitae and scholarship of colleagues standing for promotion or tenure at other universities; answers require reading the candidates' published work and, with delicate honesty, assessing its merit relative to that of their peers. Similar, though less thorough, evaluations of one or several applications are requested, usually unannounced, by institutes for advanced study, research libraries, foundations (including the mysterious MacArthur, whose "genius grants" are the not-so-secret envy of every academic), and government agencies like the National Science Foundation and National Endowment for the Humanities. If a published professor has gained a certain reputation in his field, publishers will importune him to write book-jacket or advertising blurbs for new books by friends or younger scholars. For the same reason, he may be asked to fill out long biographical forms for educational and professional directories, such as the *Directory of American Scholars, Contemporary Authors,* or *Who's Who in America.* With less fanfare or reason, his own administration will require him annually to update his vita for the dean's merit evaluations and perhaps for the university's annual list of faculty publications, grants, and other kudos. All of these requests take time to fulfill with little tangible reward, but they fuel the engine of scholarship that has always operated on internal combustion.

With 70 to 80 percent of the professor's work life accounted for, we have only to see what he or she does under the categories "administration" and "other." Since universities are largely governed by their faculties and not by professional administrators, considerable faculty time must go to service on departmental and college-wide committees. Between advising and registering freshmen, graduate students, and departmental majors each semester and serving as advisors to a variety of student organizations, such as departmental clubs and honorary societies, professors attend at least monthly department and general faculty (or faculty senate) meetings, each of which, in obedience to Parkinson's Law, invariably expands to fill two hours. In most departments, professors typically serve on at least one working committee, which may meet frequently during periods of heavy business and sporadically thereafter; several colleagues will perform heroic, unpaid service as department librarians, newsletter editors, budget directors, and schedulers while a few receive extra compensation and course reductions for chairing the department and directing graduate and undergraduate studies, all with formidable bureaucratic loads.

Some committees are voracious for faculty time, often at peak periods in the teaching cycle. Among the most demanding college committees are those on educational policy (which oversee curricular standards and changes), faculty research (which award summer and semester grants), and promotion, retention, and tenure (which usually must act on all cases before decanal deadlines early in the second semester). Every ten years most colleges must submit themselves to an extensive self-study for accreditation purposes. The hefty document that results from this one- to two-year-long process consumes vast amounts of faculty time for each of its chapters, written by representative university committees.

At the department level, two committees especially are fiendish eaters of faculty time at certain periods: the graduate program committee (which oversees curriculum and admissions) and the appointments or personnel committee (which selects new full-time faculty and temporary replacements). Both committees—often working at the same time—must read literally hundreds of applicant folders and then endure prolonged, often evening, meetings of intellectual agony (and political jostling) to cull from the mass the best candidates. In faculty hiring, several candidates will be interviewed at an annual professional convention, after which three or four will be flown to campus for extensive interviews with administrators and "teaching talks," public lectures, tours, receptions, and meals with department members. No one outside academe can appreciate how much pressure professors feel to act as responsible citizens of their academic republics while trying simultaneously to fulfill their primary obligations to their students and to scholarship. Especially in the second semester, professors never have enough hours in the day or week to do conscientiously all that is asked and required of them, a conflict that is painful to most.

Although last and probably least, we should not ignore some of the "other" components of the average professor's fifty-three-hour workweek. A certain amount of time inevitably goes to walking around extended campuses, from parking lot, departmental office, and classrooms in other buildings to library, dean's office, faculty club, and bookstore. The rituals of morning arrival have been elaborated by the need to acknowledge voice-mail messages on the phone and by the advent of the computer, which waits impatiently to unburden itself of sometimes staggering bytes of e-mail messages from colleagues around the globe and fellow subscribers to specialized mailing lists on the Internet. Even without these, the U.S. Postal Service does its part to tie up the time of the community of scholars, which is still bound with chains of paper. Some professors, particularly in the professional disciplines, spend time off-campus consulting with government and industry; museum-rich Washington is a favorite destination, as it is for liberal artists and scientists called in as selection advisory panelists by the national endowments. Other faculty members devote themselves to professional improvement by attending pedagogical or administrative seminars, computer workshops, language institutes, and National Endowment for the Humanities Summer Seminars for College Teachers. Much less serious and perhaps more enjoyable, professors at institutions where classes are small enough to foster student-faculty friendships have been known to attend plays, sports, dance recitals, and concerts in which their students are performing. By the same token, they attend the lectures of visiting scholars and the colloquia papers of local colleagues and graduate students. In the unlikely event that the faculty should ever have time on their hands, the weekly calendar of any university or sizable college offers ample fare for every professorial palate in search of extra-curricular nourishment.

* * *

Our close attention to the details of academic life and work will not, I hope, blind us to two broad conclusions. First, most professors are convinced that they have the best job in the world, a closely guarded secret they don't want to get out. They feel privileged to interact with eternally young people in attractive settings, to have daily commerce with great minds and important values and ideals, to be paid for reading books, and, perhaps most of all, to exercise unusual control over the disposition of their time. At the same time, the life of a professor, as Dartmouth's president James O. Freedman has so clearly recognized, is difficult and often lonely, carrying substantial costs. The first cost is "the continuous struggle to learn afresh what remains fundamental about a discipline that is always evolving, while bringing that knowledge to life in the minds of new students." A second cost is "the struggle to compress a host of protean and unruly tasks into a single day. In the absence of a clear boundary separating vocation from avocation, teaching from scholarship, creative effort from routine chores, no block of time can be protected from a flood of conflicting but equally legitimate demands." While the professor largely controls his own time, the amorphousness of his schedule constitutes a persistent pressure that is seldom or never fully relieved. The third and final cost is "the responsibility to create new knowledge." "Because the search for knowledge is open-ended, there can be no point of conscientious rest."[20]

In short, as ethicist Peter Markie has remarked, "being a professor is an ideal we pursue rather than an activity we simply perform."[21] No amount of description of that activity should obscure that fundamental truth.

CHAPTER TWO

Scholarship Reconsidered

In scholarship as in all phases of life
it is more blessed to be
hopefully on the way than to arrive.
Herbert Eugene Bolton

S CHOLARSHIP IN AMERICA has undergone substantial—
some might say revolutionary—changes in the past thirty
years. What we do, how we do it, and with whom we do it
have all changed markedly since the mid-sixties. In recent years,
media pundits and cultural critics have taken aim at just a few of
these changes, usually to deplore or ridicule them along with selective alterations in the classroom. But no one to my knowledge
has tried to view the process of scholarship as a whole and from
the inside. The cohort that entered graduate school before most
of these changes occurred—some 40 percent of today's faculties—
is well placed to put them in perspective because we experienced
the before and the after, the contrast between the calling we entered and the vocation it has become.

As a member of that cohort (just under the wire) and as an
historian, I naturally gravitate to a chronological approach, based
roughly on the stages of development through which we and most
scholars have passed. Most of us are not born but become scholars
through the apprenticeship of graduate school, we must buy or
earn time off from our other duties to pursue our scholarship, we
choose subjects within or between disciplines, we collect data to
test hypotheses and to frame scholarly arguments, we interact
with and rely on colleagues and peers, we publish our results, and
if we are fortunate we reap rewards for our efforts. What kind of
changes have we seen in each of these seven stages?

* * *

Becoming a scholar today is a process substantially but not radically different from the transition we made thirty-some years ago from studious students to fledgling professors. Somewhat atypically, I went from all-male Yale to largely male and strictly segregated Cambridge for graduate work, having experienced scholarship mostly as men's work, conducted in semi-monastic settings reminiscent of the medieval university. But I was enough a creature of the early sixties to realize that monasticism, especially the vow of celibacy, though less so the vow of poverty, was no longer a prerequisite for the scholarly life. This was a happy discovery of my senior year, when I not only took a graduate history course in which some members were female scholars-in-training but also met my future (and current) wife, who agreed to assume the long-term burden of a scholarly spouse and to accompany me to England.

At Cambridge I encountered virtually no women among the graduate students—most of whom were foreigners seeking the still un-English Ph.D.—but even at home I would have met only one woman in nine at a convocation of the national doctoral population.[1] Beside the lazy Cam we shared labs and seminars with a goodly number of students from the declining British Commonwealth, but back home people of color were nearly as rare as women. Foreign students took home nearly 15 percent of the doctorates in the early sixties, but American minorities earned less than 9 percent as late as 1976.[2]

Because Cambridge admitted doctoral students mostly on sufferance and the assumption that they were autodidactic self-starters, we tended to finish our degrees, and in relatively short order. Attrition was very low (in my fading memory), partly because we had no formal requirements other than to write a publishable book, partly because we usually had reliable sources of external support for the two or three years of research required.

The situation back home was quite different. The median time between the B.A. and Ph.D. was eight-and-a-half years, somewhat lower in the sciences (where dissertations ran just over a hundred pages on average) and somewhat higher in the social sciences and humanities (which produced on average 225- and 285-pagers, respectively). Not surprisingly, some 40 percent of all doctoral students never got their degrees. While nine out of ten doctoral students had some form of financial support, such support often ran out before the dissertation was completed. This forced them to rely even more — as one wag put it — on "the sweat of their fraus." The longer the dissertation, the higher the attrition. But science students finished in greater numbers also because they enjoyed more outright fellowships without teaching duties, closer faculty and peer relations in labs, and a less bewildering choice of methodologies.[3]

Some trends in American doctoral work could be seen best in hindsight. For example, the growth in numbers of Ph.D.s awarded annually and of doctoral programs and the shift in fields and foreign language requirements were hard to recognize in 1963. But by 1970 it was evident that in just ten years the production of Ph.D.s had tripled to some thirty thousand a year, thanks largely to the national demand for college teachers, Vietnam draft deferments, and increased federal support. Likewise, between 1958 and 1972, the number of doctoral programs doubled; in the latter year these new programs produced about a quarter of all degrees.[4] The increase in degrees was fairly proportional across fields, but by the late eighties it was clear that Ph.D.s in the arts and sciences, the humanities in particular, were becoming increasingly scarce. Whereas the share of degrees taken in the arts and sciences was 40 percent in 1971, it had dropped to 25 percent by 1985. Doctorates in the humanities had fallen to thirty-six hundred in 1988, only 11 percent of the total.[5] Perhaps symptomatically, even in the early sixties the traditional language requirement of French and German was giving way to other languages and to the substitution of statistics or quantitative methods for one language.[6] In unknowing tune with the times, I took Dutch to complement my undergraduate French, not because Cambridge required it but simply in order to pursue my research on the intellectual history of seventeenth-century Europe.

After two years in England we came home to the other Cambridge to enable my wife to finish her Wellesley degree, to revise my dissertation, and to find a job. Fortunately, Yale asked me back before I could even begin to fret about the job market. But I don't remember much worry about employment on the part of my graduate cohort; we simply relied on the proverbial, undoubtedly biased but reasonably efficient "old boy network" to secure our first rung on the academic ladder. Most of us seem to have gotten jobs because undergraduate institutions were also proliferating and growing all through the sixties and early seventies, creating a steady demand for scholar-teachers. In 1970 nearly 80 percent of the Ph.D.s in history had a job in hand by commencement.[7]

How markedly different the graduate experience looks in the nineties. The doctoral population today is increasingly female — nearly 40 percent in all disciplines, nearly half in the humanities. Nearly a third of all Ph.D.s now go to foreign nationals; American minorities (Indians, blacks, and Hispanics) earn only 8.3 percent while Asians take home another 13.4 percent.[8] The number of doctoral programs has leveled off at around 350, and the top forty still produce almost half the degrees, but a third of all degrees emanate from the programs inaugurated since 1958.[9] For the forty-two thousand new Ph.D.s each year, however, fellowships are harder to come by, teaching assistantships and loans have increased, and the median time-to-degree has stretched to nearly eleven years accordingly. Half of all candidates never get the degree, and of the graduate scholars who do, fewer than half are sure of a place to exercise their newfound skills.[10] The only consolation for the rest may be that the vast majority of job searches are nationally advertised and conducted — theoretically — according to nondiscriminatory standards. That most of the unplaced can ill afford to wait for the predicted spate of faculty retirements between 1997 and 2005 drives them into nonacademic employment, where more than half of all Ph.D.s now go.[11]

* * *

As soon as we new professors began to exercise our calling in the classroom, we turned some of our attention to our ongoing scholarship and how to find time for it and finance its pursuit. Twenty-five years ago most of us taught in colleges and universities that did little to promote our research until we received tenure, unless we were scientists. We taught at least three courses a semester, summer research grants from the college were rare or nonexistent, and sabbaticals were reserved for tenured professors. And our salaries were not so munificent that we could afford out of pocket to fly off to the archives in the summer unless we taught a session or two of summer school. Yale was certainly no different during the six years I taught there, save that it had a competitive fellowship year for several junior faculty, which I was lucky enough to win in the middle of the research for my second book.

In the intervening years, however, the picture has changed considerably. Teaching assignments have dropped in most four-year institutions. In 1996, 43 percent of their faculties taught *fewer* than nine hours a week; 80 percent taught twelve or fewer.[12] More colleges offer competitive summer research grants and semester leaves, financed often by the overhead from federal science grants. Many institutions enable their scholars to maximize their research opportunities by "topping off" the grants or fellowships they get to equal their regular salaries. Because the (mostly quantitative) standards for tenure have been ratcheted up, some universities feel compelled to offer competitive research leaves for junior faculty in their third or fourth year. And since 1967 the National Endowment for the Humanities has annually awarded upwards of two hundred summer grants, making it easier for young professors to devote themselves to their scholarship than to (grossly underpaid) summer school teaching.

But the warm climate for summer support has turned cooler in recent years for scholars seeking subsidies for research during the school year. In 1989 nearly 60 percent of a large faculty sample from four-year institutions told the Carnegie Foundation for the Advancement of Teaching that financial support for work in their discipline had become harder to obtain during the past two or three years; only 15 percent said it hadn't. When asked if they had received research support from the federal government in the past twelve months, only 18 percent of all the faculty surveyed said they had; in 1975, 30 percent had. Another 41 percent had received institutional or department funds for the same purpose, down 11 percent from 1984.[13]

The problem seems more serious for scholars in the humanities. Federal appropriations for the National Institutes of Health and the National Science Foundation increased 157 percent between 1980 and 1992; the budgets for the national endowments for the humanities and arts rose just 15 percent. Scientists and social scientists, therefore, could not only dip into federal pools well over 11 *billion* dollars deep (minus administrative costs, of course), but they also enjoyed application success rates between one in two and one in five. Their poor cousins from the arts and humanities scrambled for only 352 *million* federal dollars, and only one application in seven succeeded. In national competition as a whole—including NEH, the American Council of Learned Societies, Guggenheim, and the National Humanities Center—the award ratio in the humanities climbed to one in eleven and a half.[14]

More disturbing perhaps is the rapid erosion of support for the humanities. Between 1983 and 1991 the total number of fellowships and the total expenditure increased, but so did the number of applicants and inflation. Campus-based humanities centers sprang up to help compensate for the 20-percent decline in the number of fellowships awarded by national programs, but their awards were much smaller, nonportable, half-reserved for local faculty, often restricted to prescribed themes, and prey to recessionary cutbacks. And in constant dollars each award was worth six thousand dollars less than it was ten years before. Less than twelve thousand dollars from a humanities center and twenty-two thousand dollars from a national program will not enable most scholars, even the most junior, to take a research leave without hustling for sabbatical or additional fellowship support.[15] The relative threat to so-called "small science" from increased federal outlays for megascience projects and from general cutbacks in basic scientific research may present comparable dilemmas for the nation's scientists.

* * *

The third element of scholarship we might reconsider is our choice of subjects. Without malice *or* forethought, early in my career I seem to have walked on or near the "cutting edge" of a couple of scholarly trends in the humanities and social sciences, probably for the last time. You wouldn't have guessed it from the title of my dissertation: *The Educational Writings of John Locke*, a "dead white European male" if ever there was one. Yet I chose to pursue him, not in Oxford where his manuscripts slept but in less frantic Cambridge so that I could work under the leading Locke scholar, Peter Laslett. Working with Laslett conferred an added bonus: he was in the process of pioneering the new field of English historical demography, an adaptation of a French approach to social history through quantitative assemblages of births, deaths, marriages, bastards, and the like. Such a perspective on the inarticulate "little people" had no discernible effect on my Locke studies, but it quickly informed my approach to the educational history of colonial New England and later the ethnohistory of North America. It prompted me to shift my focus from the "high culture" of elites to the pervasive or "low" culture of whole societies as they encultured their young and acculturated the "others" around them and in their midst, a shift that became known in the late sixties as the "New Social History."

The other feature of the new history that held out bright possibilities to me and many other humanists and social scientists was its interdisciplinarity. If all societies at all levels had culture with a lowercase *c*, the best people to talk to were not intellectual or "high culture" historians but anthropologists, who had spent a great deal of print defining and describing culture as it manifested itself around the world in large societies and small. And if I wanted to learn about the diverse native peoples of the early Americas, the best and most numerous scholars were anthropologists by training, many of whom, by the same token, had once had to acquire historical methods and sensibilities in order to fathom the documentary record of the native past. Ethnohistory is a perfect example of what Clifford Geertz has called "blurred genres."[16] It is a convenient marriage of history and anthropology that worries less about maintaining disciplinary boundaries than solving a common set of problems, most of which straddle conventional frontiers of time, space, and culture.[17]

My experience is not atypical. All of us have had the mixed blessing of living in "interesting" and rapidly changing times, which in turn have imposed themselves on our consciousness and scholarly agendas. As women, blacks, Asians, Indians, gays, the elderly, the poor, the handicapped, and the so-called Second and Third Worlds increased their hold on our daily attention, many of us sought to understand the roots, manifestations, and implications of their various situations. With the exception of the physical sciences, virtually all disciplines expanded to accommodate the new subjects, which of necessity fostered new modes of analysis and new tolerance for the inter- or cross-disciplinarity that the solution of such unconventional problems required. Of course, many of the sciences have gone down the same road in an attempt to save or solve other appearances.

More recently, we have been challenged by the Janus-face of postmodernism, a European import of power as well as confusion. In its primal questioning of our notions of "truth," "intentionality," and "representation," and our distinctions between "text" and "context," "self" and "other," and "center" and "margin," postmodernism has generated a rash of scholarship on the *epistemology* as well as the traditional *content* of our disciplines. It is now possible to receive tenure, fellowships, and fame not only for pellucid work on the killing of cats in eighteenth-century Paris and the developmental psychology of prep-school girls but also for opaque critiques of the very possibility or relevance of such studies. Like it or not, the postmodern challenge has forced us to re-examine our fundamental assumptions and first principles. Ultimately, such close self-scrutiny will serve to restore confidence in, as well as banish cocksureness from, our disciplinary pursuits as soon as the dust settles.[18]

* * *

Finding a scholarly topic in the expanded possibilities of the intellectual present may well prove harder than locating the data to sustain and develop it. I'm referring, of course, to the literal explosion of information that threatens to inundate us and our academic enterprises any day now. A recent database ad tells us ominously that "internationally, about 1000 books are published every day," about 9,600 periodicals are published annually in the United States alone, "more information has been produced in the last 30 years than in the previous 5,000," and the amount doubles every five years. Another flyer warns that "No matter what your specialty, one thing is certain: without up-to-date, reliable information *you risk falling behind.* You need to know what your colleagues are doing. And you need to know about it now."[19]

I don't remember being scared by my cosmic ignorance back in the sixties; perhaps we were too young, too foolish, or too optimistic to feel oppressed by the titanic task of keeping up with the ever-increasing products of cold type and offset publishing. I always assumed that I could never keep up—much less catch up—with all that was possible to learn and therefore chose research topics that were somewhat manageable, intellectually and bibliographically. John Locke and the intellectual history of Tudor-Stuart England were challenge enough at twenty-two, and my reach soon grew toward education and society in colonial New England. By my early thirties I had become firmly entangled in the ethnohistory of colonial North America, where I remain mired, almost submerged by an added interest in the comparative history of exploration, colonization, and slavery throughout the Americas and the Atlantic world.

In 1963 Locke was a good choice: he was intellectually congenial (a nice but not impossible stretch for an ex-philosophy major), his manuscripts were conveniently collected and catalogued in Oxford (reachable by train), and the primary and secondary bibliography on him was still within the reach of an impecunious graduate student who pretended that book-collecting was an academic necessity rather than the telltale sign of an advanced case of bibliolatry. With the help of bookseller friends and a long-suffering spouse, I even managed to put together the world's third largest collection of Locke's *Some Thoughts Concerning Education* (the main text of my dissertation), mostly from ten- and fifteen-shilling copies of seventeenth- and eighteenth-century editions that no sensible collector would want.[20]

Equally inexpensive at home and abroad were Penguin paperbacks, Modern Library classics, and even new university press books. Recent American books were easy to find because the Internal Revenue Service had not yet imposed its anti-intellectual tax burden on publishers' inventories, thereby driving titles quickly out of print. And scholarly journals were many fewer in number and still within the budgets of individual scholars. If any source was hard to obtain, it could be photocopied by the miraculous labor-saving machines slowly making their way into the world's libraries.

How dramatically different is data retrieval today. Book prices and journal subscriptions make it increasingly difficult to form personal libraries, especially for young scholars in and just out of graduate school. Most university libraries have on-line computerized catalogues. Even medieval Cambridge has leaped into the twentieth century by replacing its leatherbound folio catalogues that had the bibliographical strips pasted in, often out of strict alphabetical order because of the unpredictability of book titles and authors' surnames since Gutenberg. Awesome on-line networks link on-line catalogues and holdings of libraries literally around the globe—for example, the on-line catalogue of the Library of Congress. Once a book or periodical has been located on the OCLC terminal, a copy of the chapter or article can often be faxed within minutes; in any event, the delivery time of interlibrary loans can be accelerated because the orders are placed by electronic wire rather than mail. Whole museum, archival, and library collections are now captured on CD-ROMS or laser discs, smaller than the 45-RPM records we used to listen to in our antediluvian youth.

If we want specific information on a topic, we have only to resort to First Search, Internet, Dialog, or some other electronic database search that provides access not only to the OCLC Union Catalog of books but to scads of other indexed collections of periodicals, newspapers, statistics, and government publications. For this chapter I was led by a kindly librarian to ERIC, the disk-driven database of educational articles and reports produced since 1966. With a call number in hand, I then retrieved a microfiche of the report and plugged it into a standard reader. Other references could have come from less direct searches through printed or on-line bibliographies of bibliographies, citation indices, and journals of abstracts or from equally anonymous suggestions found on computer bulletin boards or e-mail networks. Indeed, so many electronic sources of information exist today that there is a lot of loose talk about the possibility, even desirability, of bookless libraries and electronic books, almost all of it, ironically, found not on fluid hypertext screens but in traditionally linear print-and-paper media.

Before we wax too rapturous over the electronic future, however, we should realize that the various disciplines do not seek or obtain information the same way. The happiest customers of the new electronic library are likely to be scientists, who need the latest information, and in volume, from sources that are proliferating beyond human control. After all, the information technology's fundamental design is based on the needs of the physical sciences and engineering. Of the sixty-five hundred computer databases available in 1991, only 4 percent were classified as "humanities."[21] Nor do the minuscule allocations to the humanities of national and university research funds promise much greater access to the expensive services and machines of the electronic information industry.

An even better reason for caution is the research styles of humanists and some of their social scientific brethren. Humanists tend to work alone, relying on individual taste and judgment to select as well as to interpret information. They use more books than articles, and so far books reproduce electronically less well than articles. The process of humanistic research is almost as important as the product, so browsing in the stacks and serendipitous discoveries are highly valued. Because their subjects are usually in the past, humanists rely as much on older primary texts—all editions and states—as on newer scholarship. Since they prefer to write books rather than articles, there is less urgency for humanists to retrieve data than there is for scientists, whose preferred mode of publication is the team-written article that points to the future.[22]

Perhaps most important, humanists seek their information not in vast, unspecialized databases ham-handedly classified and indexed by third parties but from qualitative, contextualized references found in the footnotes of specialized disciplinary literature, bibliographies, and book reviews.[23] Humanists are therefore not interested in all the possibilities of information, just the best or most pertinent ones, for they know instinctively what Northrop Frye discovered long ago, that "scholarship is as much a matter of knowing what not to read as of knowing what to read." [24] Yet the information they require emanates from a greater variety of sources than those used by their colleagues in the other disciplines. While over 70 percent of the citations in the published work of scientists and social scientists typically comes from material in their own personal libraries, humanists find only a shade over a third there and most of the rest in departmental and institutional libraries and in libraries in other cities and countries. [25]

If scholarly research in the future bears any resemblance to that of the sixties, humanists may be largely responsible, for they have firmly rejected the notion of a paperless society in which books give way to computer screens. While they show little reluctance to embrace the Xerox machine, the fax, PCs, e-mail, and even CD-ROMs and laser discs, they will probably remain restrained users of the Web and cling to familiar methods for the mental processing of their newfound facts.

* * *

In the process of choosing disciplines, fields, and subjects, we also select from many possibilities the scholarly colleagues and peers with whom we wish to associate and work. We pick a self-identifying label and cast our lot with a cohort of subdisciplinarians and specialists who we hope will make and not break our scholarly career. We send our work to a certain set of journals and publishers, we attend the annual meetings of particular learned societies and professional organizations, and we rely on a smaller coterie of like-minded specialists for intellectual friendship and criticism, sometimes in our own universities but more often a stamp, phone call, or e-mail message away.

When I came home from England in 1965, I was at some disadvantage in these crucial collegial matters. I was not part of an American graduate network that was launching itself up the lower rungs of the professional ladder. But more problematic, I was shifting my interests from England back to colonial America, as I had planned to do from my junior year at Yale. This meant that while I kept as my scholarly colleagues historians of education, I had to cultivate a new subset of them and at the same time involve myself in the workings of the larger tribe of American colonialists whose intellectual center was in strange and distant Williamsburg.

A few years later, I had to make a more pronounced shift when I transferred my membership from the History of Education Society to the American Society for Ethnohistory. For reasons both field-specific and national, I discovered to my delight and profit that people who studied Indians and other native peoples—mostly anthropologists—were often female. And the deeper I dug into the ethnohistory of the Americas, the more women became my closest colleagues. When I was pursuing the history of education, the best scholars I knew best were men from elite schools in the Northeast. Now, for stimulation and criticism, I write to and hobnob at conferences with nearly as many women as men, from a great variety of institutions—museums as well as universities—all over the country and the continent.

The increasing "democratization" of my academic peer group only reflects a larger national trend, particularly in the humanities and many of the social sciences. Since we began our careers thirty-odd years ago, the number of colleges and universities has grown to nearly thirty-seven hundred and we now have more than nine hundred thousand colleagues in higher education, many more of whom are women and minorities.[26] Nearly 40 percent of all faculty members are women (though only 17 percent of full-time full professors are) and the trend is upward.[27] Our learned societies are much larger than they have ever been, and many more special-interest groups exist to welcome the erudite and recondite. The American Historical Association has grown 68 percent since 1963 to some sixteen thousand individual members today. Thanks largely to the buyer's market of the late seventies and eighties, the best scholars are no longer the monopoly of elite "name" universities; they are also found in small liberal arts colleges and comprehensive public universities. Certainly, professional organizations, conferences, and journals have responded to the forces of change by opening their memberships, governing councils, editorial boards, and panels to the new scholars. And virtually all journals of worth now select their articles through blind refereeing so that the race, gender, and home institution of the authors play no part in the decision. University presses still lag behind, partly, I suspect, because it is difficult to exorcise such signs from a large book manuscript.

While our professional colleagues have changed considerably in hue, background, and gender—bringing to our scholarly fields different, revitalizing perspectives, assumptions, questions, needs, styles, and schedules—we have as a national cohort, surprisingly, come closer together in our scholarly expectations and performances.

When we were starting out and for some time after, we were told that 10 percent of the nation's faculty published 90 percent of the books and articles and that an embarrassing number of faculty published nothing during their lifetime.[28] The implication drawn from these findings—which misleadingly included faculty from two-year community colleges—was that "the tyranny of the research model" should be broken and teaching effectiveness should be the primary, if not sole, criterion for faculty advancement. The "ascendant model in academe, positing what faculty *should be doing*," argued Everett Ladd as late as 1979, "is seriously out of touch with what they *actually do* and *want to do*."[29]

That is no longer the case. The artificial conflict between teaching and research is fast becoming an artifact of the past, as the 1989-90 Carnegie and 1995-96 Astin surveys of American faculty make very clear. First, a growing percentage of faculty in four-year institutions are, as a behavioral fact, researching, writing, and publishing in addition to their teaching. More than half have published at least one book, 87 percent have published at least one article, and 57 percent have published six or more articles. Eighty-four percent say they are engaged in scholarly work they expect to publish. Seventy-six percent attended a national professional meeting in the last year. More than half spend five hours or more a week on their research and writing; 21 percent spend thirteen hours or more.[30] And these figures, of course, do not account for the three-plus months of (unpaid) vacations we all receive for recharging our scholarly batteries.

And why do so many of today's faculty put so much effort into scholarship? Because their personal goals and the professional ethos of higher education motivate them to do so. Virtually all faculty still view as their primary obligation and goal to be good teachers. But nearly two-thirds also feel that their most important professional goals include engagement in research; only slightly fewer seek, as a personal goal, to become authorities in their fields.[31] One reason for the increase in scholarly activity up and down the institutional scale is academic expectations. More than three-quarters of the four-year faculty agree that in their departments it is difficult to get tenure without publication; 80 percent think that the *number* of publications is important. Sixty-three percent think that getting tenure is harder now than it was five years ago.[32]

But has the new interest in scholarship taken its toll in the classroom, as many critics charge? In 1975, over 70 percent thought that the pressure to publish reduced the quality of teaching at their universities; in 1990, only 46 percent thought so. An almost equal number felt that it hadn't. And more than two-thirds saw *no* conflict between institutional demands for research and their *own* effectiveness as teachers.[33] For a substantial and growing majority of faculty, teaching and scholarship do not compete in a zero-sum game. While the biggest source of stress in faculty lives is time pressures in general, more faculty feel that household responsibilities, teaching load, and institutional "red tape" are more stressful than research or publishing demands.[34]

Nor do those who publish regularly shortchange their students: they spend as much time proportionately preparing, grading, and advising as do their less productive colleagues, though they tend to teach two fewer hours a week. Nor do they skimp on administrative or service duties; the extra time they devote to scholarship comes out of their private or family time.[35]

In short, scholars today have a much larger and more like-minded cohort of colleagues who not only preach the scholar-teacher ideal but practice it as well. When we take the ill-informed hits of budget-conscious legislators and dyspeptic critics on the Right and the Left for our alleged neglect of America's youth as we chase the Golden Fleece, it should be of some comfort to know that our collective back is very broad and we are well protected by our true goals and behavior.

* * *

Excited by our topics, sated with information, stimulated by our colleagues, we turn to the publication of our work. When I began to publish, I was totally naive about the whole process. Perhaps like most neophyte scholars, I gave much less thought to the "hows" and "wheres" of publication than to the "whats" and "whys" of research. Somehow I placed my first article — researched in Cambridge during a track trip the summer after my senior year — in the stolid and widely unread pages of the *Bulletin of the Institute of Historical Research* of London, which did instill in me a keen appreciation of the offprint as an instrument of communication.

From its inception, my dissertation was aimed at Cambridge University Press, which had published my mentor's model edition of Locke's *Two Treatises on Government*. Needless to say, I was a complete tyro in matters contractual: I received no advance and failed to reserve the film rights, although I did inaugurate a lifetime of meddling in book design by asking that a well-known typographer design the book jacket in eye-catching red. My inaugural proofreading apparently passed muster, but one of the

Times Literary Supplement's infamous unsigned reviews declared that my edition was definitive "save only for a remarkably bad index."

For my own part, publishing hasn't changed much since the sixties. I've published all my books with university presses — Cambridge, Yale, five with the American branch of Oxford, and the last with Louisiana State. I still receive small advances, but I've wised up about the film rights. I haven't had any complaints lately about my indices, and I now design my books from cover to cover. The great majority of my articles and reviews have appeared in scholarly journals, though some are less specialized of late. Perhaps the biggest change in my modus operandi is that in the last few years, particularly since planning for the Columbus Quincentenary began around 1985, I have dropped my bon and scholarly mots in a much wider variety of places than hitherto: on museum labels and walls, in local and national newspapers, in radio and TV interviews, in general humanities magazines and literary journals, and in invited lectures all over the country and in Canada. This has not only augmented my income slightly and compounded my Frequent Flier miles, but it has made me a better scholar and teacher, I think, by exposing me to a wider and noisier spectrum of opinion than I normally find in my classes and by sensitizing me to the difficulties of presenting complex, nuanced ideas to interested parties with made-up minds and selective hearing.

But for younger scholars today, the publishing picture is different. There are now several guides of a general and discipline-specific nature to orient neophytes around the cluttered landscape of scholarly publishing.[36] There are more university presses than ever before — about a hundred — with lists that have grown substantially in the last fifteen years. Because of reduced library sales and increased costs, however, specialized monographs that once sold between one thousand and two thousand copies now sell only five hundred or six hundred and are not being accepted by editors as eagerly as they once were. The number of scholarly monographs has grown considerably since the late seventies but not nearly as fast as the number of new faculty seeking advancement. This means that such works will need greater institutional or foundation subsidies in the future, they will be published only electronically, or certain underpopulated areas of scholarship will wither for lack of publication channels.[37]

The writers of scholarly articles are in a much better position. Since we began scribbling in the sixties, new journals have proliferated like overheated rabbits. On every imaginable topic under the sun, a journal is poised to publish an article; if not, one will start up tomorrow on someone's desktop. Between 1978 and 1988, more than twenty-nine thousand science journals came into being, often at exorbitant prices. When the class of '63 began graduate school, the MLA *International Bibliography* listed some sixteen thousand items; the 1995 edition included nearly forty-five thousand. So many journals exist in the United States—nearly ten thousand at last count—that one dean of library science charges that scholars can get "virtually any manuscript published almost without regard to its quality, if they only have sufficient perseverance."[38] And if the future spawns more electronic journals without editorial gatekeepers, we can expect an even greater glut of bibliographical ephemera.

For all their virtues, the new spirit and productivity in academic scholarship has a triple downside: too many universities are pushing quantity over quality, too many faculty are succumbing by chopping their work into LPUs ("least publishable units"), and too many journals abound to maintain reasonably high standards or to establish a reasonable pecking order among them. The more widely diffused scholarly ethic—the latest and not necessarily more sensible incarnation of "publish or perish"—also has the potential to breed résumé inflation, articular dross, and outright fraud.[39] The best way to prevent these excesses is to emphasize quality by limiting the quantity of scholarly writings that can be submitted for tenure, promotion, or merit, graduated by rank

45

and responsive to disciplinary differences. Presumably, electronic publications will find their way onto these abbreviated curricula vitae if the profession can solve the knotty problems of authorship, royalties, plagiarism, cost, impermanence, and paper bias.[40]

* * *

Finally, we come — or we hope we come — to the extrinsic rewards of the scholarly life. The trend here, as far as I can discern it, is one of a steady but modest increase in prizes, much continuity at the top of the profession, and a generalized decline in mobility below the top. The number of Nobel Prizes has not increased noticeably nor have the restricted memberships in the National Academy of Sciences and the American Academy of Arts and Sciences. Thanks to the recession of the eighties, upward or even lateral mobility has dwindled, save in the rare ether where academic superstars ply their various and newsworthy crafts.

But the learned societies have instituted more prizes, especially for certain categories of meritorious books and for lifetime achievements in scholarship and teaching. Universities and colleges certainly glory in more endowed chairs than ever before. And a few new prizes at the national and international level contribute to the aspiration to honors. The Wolff Prize was established to honor mathematical excellence because the Nobel committee didn't. The NEH sponsors annually the Jefferson Lecturer, who speaks at the Library of Congress and other venues around the land. And we all know — and secretly salivate after — the MacArthur fellowships and the "genius" laurels they confer upon their surprised recipients.

Prompted by Ernest Boyer's 1990 Carnegie report (which gave this chapter its title), a movement is under way to enlarge the circle of scholarly rewards by giving the scholarship of *teaching*, *application*, and *integration* parity with the more familiar scholarship of discovery.[41] Certainly we should recognize meritorious scholarship in all its guises; as long as exacting peer review remains standard in each, few will object to such a sensible reform so long overdue.

But it remains to be seen whether other sorts of scholarship should or will receive ratings and rewards equal to those accorded the scholarship of discovery, which is, after all, indispensable and central to the information—or more accurately, knowledge—society in which we now live. Until the discretionary income of universities dramatically increases, until we find a way to evaluate teaching as easily and effectively as we judge scholarship, and until we can be assured that an expansion of honors will not lead to their devaluation, academe will, I predict, be slow to reconsider scholarship in all the ways Dr. Boyer would have liked.[42]

47

CHAPTER THREE

Twenty-five Reasons to Publish

To have acquired knowledge
without the talent of imparting it is just
as though one had never thought it.
Pericles

AMERICAN HIGHER education is a huge, variegated enterprise whose constituent parts and levels cannot be treated monolithically without prejudice to their distinctive aims and means. This is especially true when we raise the hoary specter of "publish or perish." Unfortunately, far too many institutions and particularly administrators and faculty members of promotion, retention, and tenure committees have contributed to or been seduced by "expectation inflation" when it comes to evaluating the scholarly performance of their colleagues. In the past fifteen or twenty years, since the job market for faculty turned stubbornly bearish, colleges and universities not in the first rank realized that they could, for the first time, command the services of graduates and young faculty from "name" institutions and, simultaneously, ratchet up their own standards for the tenure, promotion, and merit raises of continuing faculty as well as the presumably abler newcomers.

This has led to a lot of harmful nonsense, feelings of betrayal, and institutional hypocrisy. The greatest harm has been done to faculty morale, a crucial ingredient of any successful college. The older continuing faculty, who were hired under one set of expectations, are now suddenly, and usually without consultation, subjected to a new and higher set. And far too often, teaching loads, "service" commitments, salaries, sabbatical policies, and research assistance are left unchanged, leaving the faculty in a frustrating squeeze between unexpanding time and energy and escalating demands.

Another costly casualty is institutional integrity. Of course, any institution has a right and perhaps a duty to improve itself. But such improvement must be substantial, not a cheap grab for un-earned status; it must be gradual and evolutionary, not a pre-emptive strike; and it must be the result of campus-wide consul-tation and consensus-building, not an administrative putsch. If the faculty, trustees, administration, and generous alumni are committed to institutional improvement, there is no earthly rea-son why it should not be attempted.

But when an institution with one kind of mission decides to ape its reputational "betters" of another sort simply by inflating its name and enjoining its whole faculty suddenly to "publish or perish," we know we are in the cuckoo land of Madison Avenue, not in the honest groves of academe. If, in addition, such insti-tutions employ a traditionally narrow notion of scholarship based on typographic tonnage rather than importance of subject, depth of research, quality of thought, felicity of expression, and imagi-nation, they deserve our pity as well as our scorn.

At the same time, genuine scholarship has a vital role to play in the intellectual life of all institutions of higher education, particularly in research and doctoral universities and in liberal arts colleges and comprehensive universities that have collec-tively decided to raise the quality of their overall performance. But the scholarship they promote and reward should be more broadly conceived, perhaps in the manner of Ernest Boyer's 1990 report to the Carnegie Foundation for the Advancement of Teaching, to include scholarship of intra- and interdisciplinary *integration*, of practical *application*, and even of *teaching* as well as the more familiar scholarship of *discovery*.[1] In these select and self-selected institutions, the whole faculty—graduate and undergraduate—should regard the process of scholarship, thus conceived, as an integral part of their job descriptions and profession as higher educators.

Such a mild prescription should come as no surprise to anyone who entered the American professoriate since World War II. To judge by their recent behavior and opinions, a sizable majority of professors in America seem to need no reminding of their scholarly obligations. In a 1989 Carnegie Foundation survey of nearly ten thousand faculty members at 306 colleges and universities, 77 percent of those teaching in four-year institutions agreed that it was difficult for a person to achieve tenure in their department if he or she did not publish. Eighty percent felt that the *number* of publications for earning tenure in their department was important. Only 13 percent had never published an article in their careers; 57 percent had published six or more articles. Fifty-one percent had published at least one book or monograph. Eighty-three percent were currently engaged in scholarly work that they expected to lead to publication, exhibition, or performance.[2]

Yet other attitudes suggest that many professors are dissatisfied, not with their careers in general—only 7.6 percent said that if they had it to do over again, they would not become college teachers—but with the scholarly side of their academic lives. Forty-seven percent believed—rightly or wrongly—that at their institutions publications used for tenure and promotion were merely counted, not qualitatively measured. Seventy-four percent agreed that their institutions needed better ways, besides publications, to evaluate the scholarly performance of the faculty. And while 64 percent of the professors declared their major academic activities to be both teaching and research, 45 percent felt that the pressure to publish reduced the quality of teaching at their schools, more so at research and doctoral universities.[3]

In addition to statistics, anecdote and personal experience tell us that scholarship is regarded by many professors neither as a source of pleasure nor as a palatable duty, certainly not as an academic habit to be cultivated. We have all heard the delicate rationalizations of "dedicated teachers," many of them stuck as tenured but unpromotable associate professors or at wan salary levels, who year after year choose to teach summer school rather than apply for a research grant, or to travel, garden, and play tennis rather than engage a long- or short-term piece of scholarly work. We probably also know able men and women who dropped out of graduate school after eight or ten years because they could not bring themselves to complete their dissertations, having developed a paralyzing distaste for their subjects, their advisors, or the whole process of scholarly research and writing. We certainly know victims of "publish or perish" who lost one tenure-track appointment after another or ended up driving a cab.

There are many reasons to account for the professorial resistance to habitual scholarship besides the basic human instinct to avoid hard work. What they all have in common, however, is a focus not on the difficulties or unworthiness of scholarship—which commands ready lip service—but on the higher claims of nonscholarly pursuits on the professors' limited time and energy, especially teaching. One reason for this state of affairs, I suspect, is the academy's traditional equation of scholarship with monographic or periodical publications of (usually small) discovery, many of them produced not in an air of intellectual ferment but in a funk of pedantic lamp smoke.

Another reason, which may loom as large, is that most colleges and universities do a perfunctory or slipshod job of explaining to their students, alumni, and faculty members—new, old, and potential—why the *process* of scholarship is important to the continuing vitality and integrity of their particular institution and of higher education in general. They expend more effort fashioning carrots and sticks to induce young faculty to publish the minimum to satisfy deans and tenure committees than giving them compelling reasons to pursue active lives of scholarship throughout their careers, with or without external reward. This kind of instrumentalism is no different or better than the student ethos that prefers cramming for grades to sustained study for understanding and mastery; indeed, they may be causally related.

Perhaps the best, or at least the heaviest, counterweight to the prevailing professorial resistance to the life of scholarship is a lengthy set of arguments in its favor, as inclusive as possible. After a far from exhaustive search, I have managed to find twenty-five reasons to "publish," which is simply shorthand for the habitual pursuit of the diversified scholarship advocated by the Carnegie Foundation. I have lumped instrumental with idealistic, personal with professional arguments in hopes of enticing every doctorate-bearing professor who plies his or her calling at a four-year institution onto the scholarly hook, and letting none off. Like the late Jacob Viner, Princeton's great economist and teacher, I want all Ph.D.s "put under some pressure or seduction to be also scholars."[4]

The first eight arguments are professional in character and speak to the duties and enduring mores of the professoriate.

1. The advanced degree required for virtually all faculty positions in higher education, the Ph.D., is essentially a research degree that puts a premium on extensive knowledge of a specialized field in a learned discipline and the writing of a major research dissertation.[5] It is meant to prepare the recipient for a lifetime of scholarship as well as of teaching, to some extent in fields besides the field of specialization. The great majority of those who have completed the doctorate consider the most valuable and enjoyable part of their doctoral work, not the courses nor the language, comprehensive, and oral exams, but the research for and writing of the dissertation, the last act of their lives as dependent students and the first step toward their intellectual independence as professors.[6] "At the very least," says Theodore Ziolkowski, Princeton's former graduate dean, "the dissertation as an exercise should prepare the new Ph.D. to organize his or her first college course and to appreciate what it takes to write a good book."[7]

2. Higher education is the only learned profession that requires no recertification at suitable periods after the award of the terminal degree and no regular upgrading of skills and knowledge. Without habitual scholarship and the peer review of publication, professors make a mockery of their honor system of self-recertification and expose the profession as a whole to charges of malpractice.[8]

3. Advances in knowledge account for about one-third of the increases in the gross national product, and have since the mid-1960s.[9] Most of that knowledge is the product of research conducted in colleges and universities by professors, who therefore serve a vital national function. Faculty members of all but the smallest and poorest colleges have access to libraries, financial support, and laboratories—their own institutions' or those of others—with which to pursue scholarship of potential value to the national culture or economy. The pace and depth of scholarship will undoubtedly vary greatly from institution to institution, but the existence of national interlibrary loan services, computer networks, photocopying, research and travel-to-collections grants, fellowships, exchange programs, and summer institutes does much to equalize the resources available to the nation's faculty.

4. Colleges and universities are meritocracies, not unions, that apply qualitative standards of excellence to themselves as well as to their students. Over many decades, the professoriate has decided, in the words of a Yale report, that "original scholarly work is the surest proof of intellectual distinction and the surest guarantee that intellectual activity will not cease" with the granting of tenure or promotion to full professor.[10] Even the least prestigious institutions hire the best dissertation writers from the best research universities they can on this premise, even if they are primarily seeking teachers rather than productive scholars. For they believe, as did J. H. Hexter in his feisty 1969 defense of "publish or perish," that a professor's "mere research and schol-

arship" provides the most reliable measure of his or her worth as a teacher.[11] Graduate students who can, in a small number of years, work their way through an enormous secondary literature, master an imposing mass of primary sources, organize the latter into a new pattern while paying due attention to the former, and express their conclusions with force, clarity, cogency, and style are assumed—with good reason—to be capable of mastering any teaching fields they are assigned as professors and presenting them comprehensively and imaginatively after a reasonable amount of preparation.

Teaching experience, particularly before the Ph.D. but even after, is regarded as a much less reliable guide to future intellectual vitality and durability. Most graduate students serve only as teaching assistants or discussion section leaders in lecture courses taught by their elders. Even when they are favored with their own courses, they are assigned either smallish introductory survey courses (which perhaps only senior professors of wide reading and long experience should teach) or small upper-class seminars in their specialty (which they are better qualified to teach)—neither of which poses the challenge of most bread-and-butter mid-level courses that bite off sizable chunks of the subject or discipline and demand a considerable grasp of the primary and secondary literature.

5. The academic meritocracy believes that peer review by fellow professors is the only reliable and justifiable way to evaluate its activities. Since teaching is inherently personal and difficult to assess by standard criteria, professors understandably prefer to rely on assessments of a colleague's published scholarship as the best indicator of intellectual and pedagogical excellence. Student and even alumni evaluations of teaching are regarded with suspicion, though they are given grudging credence when different kinds of evaluation are added to those of faculty members who have seen and heard their colleague talk, teach, and interact with students.

6. American institutions of higher education and their professors are expected and duty-bound to *advance* knowledge, not merely to preserve and recycle existing knowledge. Jaroslav Pelikan, former dean of the Yale Graduate School, contends that "publish or perish" is "a fundamental psychological, indeed almost physiological, imperative that is rooted in the very metabolism of scholarship as a vocation."[12] American society, more so than nostalgic alumni, students, and fee-paying parents, expects college and university faculties to contribute to the production and dissemination of new knowledge, only some of which consists of rethought and reconfigured inherited knowledge. Faculty who do not contribute actively to the search for new knowledge can, in some sense, be regarded as "parasites" (as a former Princeton president uncharitably put it) who do not carry their full load and can expect few rewards.[13]

7. Dean Ziolkowski has persuasively argued that "it is ultimately the principle of scholarship and research that unites an otherwise disparate faculty" in today's complex institutions of higher education. As fields of knowledge, physics, economics, and literary history are poles apart. "But the process of discovery in those fields, their intellectual rigor, and the moral discipline that they demand is remarkably similar. It is the similarities among the disciplines, produced by scholarship, that justify the Romantic ideal vision of the university as a unified universe." Above all, "it is the dedication to scholarship and research—the commitment to the *process* of knowledge rather than merely to its product—that contributes the intellectual tension and excitement to life in a university."[14]

8. As Logan Wilson pointed out as long ago as 1942, the professional status of a teaching professor is much lower than that of a publishing or research professor. First, there is no systematic basis for recognizing good teaching as there is for determining good scholarship. Second, the teacher's status is exclusively local, unlike the scholar's, which may be national or international.

Scholars belong to one of the three gown-wearing vocations, a calling that has always transcended institutional and political boundaries; they belong to international disciplines and the "community of scholars." Third, the chief acclaim of the teacher "comes from below," from his social "inferiors," who are not capable of raising his status. The prestige of the teacher is "primarily dependent on his students, that of the scholar is independent of his students" and therefore "relatively independent of the institution that supports him." "The commodity market for teaching skill," in short, "has no international currency."[15] Published research, on the other hand, is currency that can be weighed and evaluated across institutional and even national boundaries.[16]

Professional status is one thing, tangibles are another. The next two arguments speak to the economic or instrumental rewards of scholarship.

9. Since the 1930s at least and perhaps the 1890s, published scholarship has been the common currency of academic achievement. All the official and unofficial perquisites of academe flow from scholarship and publication: tenure, endowed chairs, merit raises, reduced teaching loads, distinguished lectureships, summer and semester research grants, election to learned societies, appointment to editorial boards, faculty awards, fewer or powerful committee assignments, honorary degrees, and mobility. While all of these incentives to productivity may be viewed as unseemly and extrinsic to the true life of the mind, they do palliate the long, lonely process of scholarship and fuel the aspirations of those mortal professors who do not burn with a hard, gem-like flame.

10. Publications of the right sort and a reputation based on them can also lead to extra income, wider audiences for one's ideas, and opportunities to travel to other cities, countries, and institutions. Books—textbooks, syntheses, casebooks, readers, and even monographs—almost always provide royalties. Periodical articles suitable for classroom use earn reprint fees from publish-

ers of college readers and course paks. Institutions, organizations, and conveners of meetings, foreign and domestic, that want scholarly authorities pay honoraria and travel and living expenses. More rarely but more lucratively, participants in lawsuits need expert witnesses to bolster their cases. Granting agencies and foundations—NEH, NSF, ACLS, the Social Science Research Council, Guggenheim, MacArthur—rely on published scholars, not mere teachers, to help them disburse their funds—and pay their expenses if they need to convene in Washington, New York, or Chicago.

From practical arguments we move to more personal reasons to cultivate the habit of scholarship.

11. When "mere" professors retire, they often find themselves at loose ends without an audience, the applause and responsiveness of a class, or the daily routine of teaching, however much they may have complained of the "rat race" during the school year. Habitual scholars, by contrast, make easier transitions because they always have their reading, research, and writing which, if arteriosclerosis doesn't set in prematurely, should be as good as, or better than, the work they produced on the job. Although Samuel Eliot Morison lived to an exceptionally healthy eighty-eight, he wrote more histories—many of them superior to his earlier efforts—after he retired from Harvard in 1955 than he did before, and he was extraordinarily prolific before.[17]

12. Before and after retirement, scholarship has the power to confer unique pleasure upon its devotees. "Once the taste for it has been aroused," testified Jacob Viner, "it gives a sense of largeness even to one's small quests, and a sense of fullness even to the small answers to problems large or small which it yields, a sense which can never in any other way be attained, for which no other source of human gratification can, to the addict, be a satisfying substitute, which gains instead of loses in quality and quantity and in pleasure-yielding capacity by being shared with others—and which, unlike golf, improves with age."[18]

13. Books, like progeny of a human sort, are a lease, however small, on immortality; they are not only tombstones that the authors get to script and carve themselves before death, they often survive well beyond death and remaindering. "Professors are lucky," said a faculty wife in Carlos Baker's *A Friend in Power*. "They can write their own monuments and people will always read them."[19] Maybe not always, but they do bequeath to their living authors "the subtle rapture of a postponed power," Oliver Wendell Holmes Jr. called it, "the secret isolated joy of the thinker" who knows that after his death men and women who never heard his name will be "moving to the measure of his thought."[20] The nonpublishing professor takes his hard-won and extensive knowledge to the grave. In some sense, "results unpublished," Logan Wilson contends, "are little better than those never achieved."[21] The publishing scholar bequeaths a rich legacy much before death and continually adds to the principal.

* * *

The greatest obstacle to habitual scholarship is the perceived tension between it and teaching. Although folklore—faculty, student, and administrative—asserts a strong correlation between teaching and research, positive and negative, the tests that have been devised to establish such relations have largely failed to confirm any statistically significant correlation, except a small positive one.[22] Teaching and research seem to be independent variables, at least as far as the test makers can tell. But common sense tells us three things. One, teaching is such a personalized activity of infinite variety that no one has devised a reliable instrument for measuring successful teaching that does justice to its variety and goes much beyond the useful, though limited, evaluation by students who are immersed in the teacher's course. Two, *teaching* is not synonymous with *learning*, which is even more difficult to measure and ultimately of more importance. Three, we recognize in a general way that many of the qualities of a good scholar constitute some of the qualities of a good teacher. Intuitively, we un-

58

derstand, as did Princeton president Robert Goheen, that re-search and teaching are "two ends of the same bow," neither of which "has much force without the other."[23] Thus, we can safely enumerate a dozen reasons why teachers must be scholars, even if those reasons can never be quantitatively calibrated by educa-tional test makers.

14. "Research," noted Henry Rosovsky from the vantage point of the Harvard dean's office, "is an expression of faith in the possibility of progress," a form of "optimism about the human condition." "Persons who have faith in progress and therefore possess an intellectually optimistic disposition—i.e., teacher-scholars—are probably more interesting and better professors. They are less likely to present their subjects in excessively cynical or reactionary terms."[24] In other words, good professors know something about the power of positive thinking, even if they are trained to be critical of received opinion and are seldom Pollyannaish.

15. One key element of a good college or university is a faculty consisting of convincing exemplars of the life of learning. Stu-dents should get an early sense of the scholar's seriousness and personal devotion to the subject. They should see that a profes-sor—an adult—is also a lifetime learner, someone for whom the payoffs of serious study arrive with regularity. They need to see, through living example, that education is a continuing process. "It is therefore necessary," argued Harvard president Nathan Pu-sey, "that the professor be a scholar, that his scholarship shall have brought him a secure knowledge of his subject, that his knowl-edge be his own—alive and growing, and not a textbook's infor-mation—and that he have some ability, some method or artistry, to communicate both his learning and his enthusiasm for the field of his inquiry and his sense of its importance, to younger minds finding their way into that world illumined by intellect where his own chief pleasure is found."[25] Even Ernest Boyer, author of the Carnegie reports *College: The Undergraduate Experience in*

America and *Scholarship Reconsidered*, believed that "all faculty, throughout their careers, should, themselves, remain students. As scholars, they must continue to learn and be seriously and continuously engaged in the expanding intellectual world." This is essential to the vitality and vigor not only of the research university, he argued, but of the undergraduate college as well.[26]

16. Habitual scholarship is the healthiest, most efficient, and most academically acceptable way to prevent the burnout that threatens every thirty-five- to forty-year professorial career. A research-oriented faculty is simply less likely to be the home of intellectual deadwood. Once departmental teaching assignments and "turf treaties" are made, course syllabi set, and lectures written, teaching tends to take on a comfortable sameness year after year. Students remain the same age and arrive with the same expectations, preoccupations, talents, insecurities, and naïveté. Over the long haul, while the professor ages and matures in knowledge, that is, "gets better," his or her students can seem to "get worse," or at least no better. To avoid mid-career plateauing and late-career depression, therefore, professors should have scholarly projects that hold their interest and renew their enthusiasm for their subjects and disciplines. (Needless to say, they should also have projects for teaching renewal—new courses, textbook writing, articles on teaching, exchange teaching, interdisciplinary or team-teaching—many of which will require a good deal of scholarship.) As a good decanal economist put it, "The essence of academic life is the opportunity—indeed, the demand—for continual investment in oneself. It is a unique chance for a lifetime of building and renewing intellectual capital," an opportunity that should never be squandered.[27] "If research had no other value," Louis B. Wright concluded after nine years dispensing Huntington Library fellowships, "its service in keeping professors alive and interested in their fields of knowledge would amply justify it."[28]

17. A good scholar has five crucial attributes of a good teacher:

enthusiasm, authority, rigor, honesty, and humility. If professors are to be convincing models of the life of learning, they must first exhibit genuine *enthusiasm*, however low-key, for their subjects and disciplines. Many students will soon forget the details and even general themes of their college courses, but few will forget the passion with which their professors approached the subject day after day or the inspiration they gave them to think the subject important and worth pursuing, at least for a semester. Teachers who have no living traffic with their knowledge cannot quicken or inspire their students, which is nearly as important as the transmission of knowledge itself.

"The purely inspirational teacher," as Louis Wright called him, "the man who never goes to the springs of knowledge, presently runs dry. He may whip up his zeal by reading secondary books, but soon the most callow students can see through his devices. When he has exhausted his original capital"—banked in graduate school—"he has nothing to fall back upon." But "honest inspiration" in a teacher has its source "in knowledge and in the enthusiasm that comes from discovery. The teacher who is a discoverer of truth . . . will be able to transmit to his students some of his own enthusiasm. Teaching then becomes part of an adventure in which both professor and student share."[29] Even among Harvard students, Dean Rosovsky noticed, "intellectual excitement is enhanced by contact with people who have written books."[30]

18. Scholarship also invests teaching with direct and convincing *authority*, based on firsthand discovery of the knowledge being retailed in the classroom. Professors must have something to profess. They can pass on someone else's discoveries and hard-won knowledge at second or third hand—which all teachers must do to some extent—or they can present their own data, syntheses, and ways of viewing the world, gained by wrestling with the primary sources of the subject. To profess is to maintain a continuous search for new knowledge and to teach others not only what one has learned but how to do the research itself.[31] In the presence

of personal authorities on their subjects, students are confident that they are getting their money's worth, even if the teachers' skill in presenting their accumulated knowledge is not equal to the inherent value of the subject.

19. Ernest Boyer reminded us that "while not all professors are likely to publish with regularity, they, nonetheless, should be first-rate *scholars*" who stay abreast of their disciplines and know the evolving literature of their fields. "Scholarship is not an esoteric appendage," he said; "it is at the heart of what the profession is all about."[32] It is essential that a professor's scholarship shall have brought him "*secure* knowledge of his subject" and that his knowledge be "his own—alive and *growing*."[33] The best teachers are those who are actively engaged in the pursuit of fresh truth, not those who simply report as convincingly as they can what has already been found to be true by others. A lecture course can and should be a *re*thinking of a whole field, however small. If it does not encompass the whole field and its latest as well as its older critical perspectives and insights, it will shortchange the students. Only broad, substantial scholarship enables professors to encompass the known structure of a whole field and to learn afresh, in James Freedman's words, "what remains fundamental about a discipline that is always evolving."[34]

20. But reading and research are not the same thing.[35] According to Webster's dictionary, the aim of research is the "revision of accepted conclusions in the light of newly discovered facts." Reading in and around a field can be haphazard, aimless, and whimsical unless it is keyed to the deepening of the primary base and the broadening of critical perspective. Even teaching that consists primarily of passing on an intellectual tradition, usually to underclassmen, requires a firm grasp of the potential pool of candidates for canonization, the various principles for including and excluding titles ("Books should not only procreate," says Jacques Barzun, "but also kill off one another"), and the critical

approaches to all of these works and questions.[36] Since we, too, are part of the intellectual tradition, we must publish our own contributions to the canon so that future generations of students and scholars can argue about our relative worth.[37]

Habitual scholarship is certainly needed for the teaching of more advanced courses. Only someone deeply knowledgeable about the whole field, the essence of the discipline, and the evolving literature of both can pick and choose wisely among the latest knowledge, even in fields they have not personally researched in depth, deal with student questions and objections, present their own ideas and interpretations, and provide spontaneous examples from their own research experience and familiarity with the primary sources.[38]

Dean Pelikan argues convincingly that every undergraduate major should provide the opportunity for "disciplined research, to give students a taste of participating in the expansion of scholarship rather than merely receiving the results of such expansion; for in many ways," as for the faculty themselves, "the process is more important than the results."[39] Only professors who have done and continue to pursue their own scholarship can reliably lead advanced students into the scholarly thickets. Those who direct honors or senior theses must certainly be so experienced.

Similarly, graduate teaching is less an extension of a professor's undergraduate teaching than of his or her research.[40] This is a key reason why, even in major research universities, not every member of the teaching faculty is allowed to teach graduate students and to claim membership on the graduate faculty. Those who have written their own books are best qualified to guide those who are writing their first book-length studies. Certainly the recruitment of graduate students is facilitated by the well- and widely regarded books of graduate faculty, which may have been encountered in undergraduate classes.

21. Many proponents of habitual scholarship affirm that, while

publication of scholarly discoveries is important for many reasons, it is of incidental value; the more fundamental value is the influence that the search for the material for those books and articles has upon the men and women who write them.[41] The scholar is called to a *process* of research, an attitude of curiosity, and one of the several benefits of such a process is the transfer of disciplinary *rigor* to his or her teaching.[42] Here the peer review of scholarship pays pedagogical dividends. All Ph.D.s are soon removed from the regular rigor of the graduate school classroom. The sharply focused, sometimes painful, but usually salutary feedback a graduate student receives from professors and classmates in seminars and on oral presentations, papers, and dissertation chapters is not available to the teaching professor in his or her own classroom. Peer review of one's knowledge and performance as a teacher is, for all intents and purposes, nonexistent, mostly because, for reasons of "academic freedom," we do not allow our colleagues, administrators, or anyone other than bona fide students into our classrooms. Thus, it is all too easy, when the bittersweet memories of graduate school begin to fade, to let down our guard and standards in class, rationalizing that "they are, after all, just kids who don't know any better." If we expect to bring any rigor to our teaching—what we present, how we present it, and how we evaluate our students' attempts to learn it—we can be helped enormously by maintaining the kind of rigor we once knew in graduate school by habitually subjecting ourselves to the rigor of peer review of our own scholarly efforts.

22. Peer review has two other major benefits. One is that it helps to guarantee professorial *honesty*. Since scholarship can be evaluated in a way that teaching cannot, only by insisting on the regular peer review of our scholarship can we be confident of the quality and integrity of the *teaching* process.[43] If we are slipshod with our evidence, slaphappy with our generalizations, and gas-

eously irrelevant with our illustrations and asides, our published scholarship will expose us much sooner and more starkly than our closeted classroom behavior, for most students are not qualified to catch vices of this sort, and precious few colleagues ever read our student evaluations or visit our classes.

23. The second pedagogical result of subjecting ourselves to the intellectual scrutiny of scholarly peers is *humility*. Along with quiet confidence, the true scholar possesses unfeigned humility in the face of enormous and acknowledged ignorance. Gilbert Highet calls humility the second principle of scholarship (the first being devotion). It is based on the Hippocratic aphorism, "The life so short, the craft so long to learn." Indeed, notes Highet, the problems that scholars study would be difficult enough "even if they remained static; but they grow, and change, and interact, so that only a very immature or conceited scholar can now think of 'mastering the subject.'"[44]

But in teaching academically if not intellectually inferior undergraduates year after year, professors can easily slip into arrogance, wrapping themselves in the mantle of imaginary omniscience. The best cure is a humbling dose of peer review—a curt rejection notice from a professional journal or university press, a fistful of steely-eyed book reviews, or the apathetic response of a scholarly audience to one's carefully polished pearls of wisdom. Even a dismal course evaluation from one's students does not carry the salutary sting that can be administered by scholarly peers. It is therefore desirable for professors who judge their students to have the tables turned and to acquire the humility and the sense of humor that comes from being judged themselves.[45]

24. Professors who struggle habitually with their own writing are better prepared than nonwriting teachers to deal sympathetically as well as critically with student writing. Moreover, the students can read some of the professor's best literary efforts to see

if he practices what or as well as he preaches. By the same token, the scholar can have no better practice for writing books for a nonspecialized audience than undergraduate teaching.[46]

25. Finally, one fact that is always lost in the fractious turf fights between teaching and research is that publication of scholarship in books, articles, and other media *is* a form of teaching in itself. A well-conceived, well-written, well-distributed book reaches and therefore teaches far more students than the author's evanescent lectures will reach in a lifetime.[47] Its knowledge is diffused geometrically through other professors' lectures and through course adoptions to thousands of students all over the country and perhaps the world, not just to the students who happen to enroll in the writer's local classes. Moreover, as Derek Bok has emphasized, published scholarship represents "the ultimate expression of a [teacher-]scholar's powers, intellectual labor brought to its highest, most exalted state."[48] Classroom lectures seldom achieve the same degree of polish and perfection.

Most of the teaching and learning we do in higher education depends on books. One of the final goals of a good teacher—the better, more charismatic, more authoritative he or she is, the more difficult it is to accomplish—is to wean students from the teacher's authority by showing them how to ask important questions and how to approach if not answer those questions with the full array of disciplinary resources available, including critical approaches to the best books in the field. By contributing published materials to their discipline, teachers repay it in kind for their own education and facilitate the timely independence of their students.

The academic demands of teaching and scholarship are not a zero-sum game, even in the least selective four-year institutions. According to the 1987 Department of Education survey, teaching faculty at four-year institutions average about fifty-three hours per week working at their professional calling. Very few professors teach in the classroom more than twelve hours a week; the average is between seven and ten hours, depending on the institution. Even with preparation and grading thrown in, some 51 percent of their workweek is spent on teaching, while 19 percent is devoted to research or comparable scholarly activity. It is equally evident that those faculty who have published eleven or more articles in their careers (45 percent) and are considered "publishing leaders" do not shortchange their students by stealing time from teaching preparation for their research. While they do teach an average of about two hours less than the other 55 percent of the faculty, they spend exactly the same proportion of time preparing to teach and evaluating their students as do their colleagues. There is therefore no evidence that frequent publishers take their assigned teaching responsibilities any less seriously than anyone else in academe.[49]

Richard Mandell, keen-eyed and sardonic student of *The Professor Game*, contends that "rate-busting scholars" who habitually publish more than their colleagues tend to be "rate-busting teachers" as well, "who do far more than the minimum on all counts." He suggests that professorial go-getters labor to "maintain their self-respect" as scholars by minimizing their summer school teaching with "a little domestic belt-tightening" and by "circumscribing their golf, television, lushing, fretting, procrastinating, and companionable analyzing of colleagues that absorbs the discretionary time of almost all of their associates." Even the collegially safe but ambitious goal of an article a year and a book every five (recommended by Professor X in the 1973 classic *This Beats Working for a Living* and seconded by Mandell) would entail, Mandell estimates, only a hundred pages of finished prose a year, which amounts to no more than two pages a week or, alternatively, twenty-five to thirty pages for each month of the professor's free summers.[50] No matter how burdened and preoccupied professors are or feel when classes are in session, they still have the opportunity and obligation to use their three- to four-month vacations for the pursuit of, and to renew the habit of, scholarship.

For most professors, there is no doubt that research and teaching (preferably undergraduate teaching) belong together—"not always for anyone," says Dean Pelikan wisely, "not at all for everyone, not in the same proportion for every university," but definitely in symbiotic tension if not harmony.[51] "Do you want your teachers to be imaginative?" Alfred North Whitehead asked. "Then encourage them to research. Do you want your researchers to be imaginative? Then bring them into intellectual sympathy with the young at the most eager, imaginative period of life." In the muddled modernity of higher education, where complex charges daily test the tensile strength of institutions and faculty, it is refreshing to have the great philosopher re-explode one of academe's most cherished and false dichotomies with ruthless simplicity by reminding us, who so badly need reminding, that "a university is imaginative or it is nothing—at least nothing useful."[52] Perpetuating the artificial animosity between teaching and scholarship is perhaps the least imaginative and least useful thing we could do.[53]

CHAPTER FOUR

Encountering the Other

No culture retains its identity in
isolation; identity is attained in contact,
in contrast, in breakthrough.
Carlos Fuentes

W HEN AMERICAN historians look back, 1992 will be
memorable for two apparently unrelated events. One
is the quincentenary of Columbus's fateful voyage to
the Caribbean. By effectively lashing the world's major continents
to each other with nautical lines, he set in motion the greatest
movement and mingling of peoples in history. Asians, Africans,
and Americans were quickly thrown together by and with Europeans in what Quincentenary organizers astutely dubbed the
"Columbian Encounter."[1]

The personal modifier is apposite because, in his own voyages of discovery, Columbus encountered a dazzling mosaic of
peoples: legendary Asian moguls and actual Mediterranean pi-
rates, African slaves, Canary Islanders, Icelandic fisherfolk, and
American Indians, as well as humble family weavers in his native Genoa and, in his adopted Spain, Italian financiers, fervent
Catholics, Moors, Jews, and the king and queen themselves. And
not least important for his education in diversity, he married a
Portuguese lady of noble extraction and had an illegitimate son
by a Spanish peasant.

Five hundred years later, in a West Coast city whose angelic
name would have resonated for the devout Columbus, riots ig-
nited block after block of black-, white-, Hispanic-, and Asian-
owned real estate and a nationwide debate about the past, present, and future of race relations in America. Sparked by the

acquittal of four white policemen charged with using excessive force to arrest a black speeder, the conflagration instantly produced an array of angry, hurt, and defensive responses in California and across the country.

At the heart of this national debate was a question unwittingly posed by Columbus and his European successors when they invaded the inhabited islands and mainland of the "New World": can people of different colors and cultures create a society of legal equality, economic opportunity, and mutual respect? In the "Old World" the answer seemed to be "no." But America offered rich new possibilities and a fresh start, at least for the invaders. That the question is still being asked—with periodic urgency—five centuries later speaks volumes about the enduring worth of its informing vision and the clipped coinage of our social inheritance.

Both these events—the commingling of the world's peoples in the wake of Columbus and the resulting racial tension and cultural conflict—make it clear that a major key to social peace and progress is universal education in the toleration and appreciation of "otherness." Of course, public and private institutions, some of them international in scope, must play prominent parts to ensure equal justice and to provide economic opportunity for all inhabitants of the "global village" we now share. But mutual respect can come only when people learn to regard all other human beings, singly and in groups, as both *different from* and *equal to* themselves, to understand them as much as possible in their *own* terms. This is a task for every educational institution: the family, schools, churches, mass media, and colleges and universities.

Yet higher education must bear the lion's share of responsibility simply because of the psychodynamics of human development. Most of us are much too busy before our late teens and early twenties trying to fashion and shore up our self-identities; we don't have much time or talent for serious and sustained attention to "others," except the occasional "significant" one. Only in college do we normally have at once the need, the opportunity, and the curricular encouragement to confront otherness on both a personal and a philosophical level. Only there do we have the leisure and license to cultivate the degree of cultural relativism and disinterestedness needed to navigate the polychromatic world we inherited from Columbus. For in college, if we've gotten our money's worth, we come to understand the central paradox of a liberal and humane education: namely, that to discover others is, in the end, to discover ourselves, by contrast, comparison, and reflection. True identity is found, oddly enough, when we lose ourselves. Like happiness in living and good style in writing, a strong identity generally comes, if it comes at all, only when we are preoccupied with something or someone else: if we deliberately go after it, we will probably not get it.[2]

From birth we gradually, fitfully, and with considerable reluctance grow out of our extreme egocentrism, our boundless fascination with our own bodies, feelings, and thoughts. Never without a struggle, we learn the difficult arts of recognizing, tolerating, and even loving other human beings. For the longest time, those so favored by our magnanimity fit within the neat little circles in which we happen to circulate: first the family and then the neighborhood, perhaps the church, and the school. But even in those circles, we tend to cleave to those most like ourselves in age, color, class, and gender because those who are different are perceived by our unsteady, inchoate selves as threats. Only slowly and at some risk do we discover that others are not necessarily better or worse, more secure or less, but simply different from and possibly equal to ourselves and our carefully chosen reflectors.

The personal discovery of otherness constitutes a small but significant step forward in human evolution, and we like to think that most adults have taken it with only an occasional stagger or stutter. But to judge by the tragic backwardness of human history—the wars, the ethnic and religious violence, the xenophobia that confronts us every night on the evening news—tomorrow's adults must be much better equipped to deal with their global counterparts if they hope to improve the human lot. And they can be best equipped *philosophically* because the personal experience of the vast majority will never be extensive, intensive, or non-threatening enough.

In order to gain what Reynolds Price calls "the most beautiful and fragile of our birth-gifts . . . accessibility to all other members of our species," we must acquire an uncommon pair of intellectual tools.[3] The first I might call ontological humility—the recognition that everyone else in the world is and feels as much a first-person subject, an "I," as we do. As John Updike put it so succinctly, "billions of consciousnesses silt history full, and every one of them the center of the universe."[4]

The second tool is a measure of cultural relativism, the acknowledgment that, while our own beliefs and values are worthy and ought to be defended with reason, not mere habit or prejudice, the beliefs and values of other people are equally deserving of respect and explicable in their own terms. By sublimating our trigger-happy tendency to judge others—usually negatively—by our own standards, we should discover that no race has a monopoly on beauty, intelligence, or strength.[5] We could do worse than recapture the insight of Montaigne who, after closely observing and speaking with a Tupi war captain from Brazil in the 1550s, recognized that "each man calls barbarism whatever is not his own practice." "Barbarians," he warned, "are no more marvelous to us than we are to them, nor for better cause."[6]

College is the best place to develop an understanding and appreciation of "the other" for two reasons. First, college is an intense, voluntary field of personal and cultural encounter. For at least four years, students are thrown together in close quarters with several thousand self-selected and usually friendly "others" in a relatively safe environment where speech and thought are ideally free and intellectual stretching is encouraged by parents, faculty, and society at large. And second, most of the stretching done in college is — or should be — philosophical, the product primarily of the humanities and certain social sciences. Indeed, William Bowen, former president of Princeton, is correct in thinking that "an appreciation for 'otherness' is central to the very idea of liberal education."[7]

A few disciplines are more likely than others to teach us to imagine what it is like to be human in situations very different from our own.[8] History, anthropology, and literature spring to mind because they deal directly and accessibly with otherness in its temporal, cultural, and imaginative manifestations. Students of these disciplines become connoisseurs of "alien turns of mind," as Clifford Geertz has termed them, philosophical explorers who regularly seek contact with "a variant subjectivity."[9]

Novelists introduce us to people and parts of the contemporary world we are unlikely to imagine by ourselves; by taking us deep into their characters' minds, hearts, and skins, they transport us out of ourselves to alien turf where we can make safe if disturbing contact with plausible others. Ethnographers do much the same thing by translating for us, with many of the novelist's techniques, their personal encounters with peoples and cultures far distant and different from our own. They know that, while we global villagers don't have to love one another, "we must know one another, and live with [and by] that knowledge," Geertz has argued, "or end marooned in a Beckett-world of colliding soliloquy."[10] And to escape our temporal parochialism, we turn to history to illuminate the human condition from the witness of memory.[11] The past is filled with myriad examples of other human beings trying to make sense of the world they inhabited. Because they are now dead, we can view the whole course of their lives in perspective — their goals, the choices they made and rejected, their successes and failures, and how they felt about the lives they led.

To witness lives preserved in the amber of the past gives an enormous advantage to people still swimming in the murky but fluid possibilities of the present, if they but seize it.

In fact, the main purpose of the study of otherness in all its curricular guises is to give us concentrated doses of vicarious experience to supplement our own limited supplies of personal experience. But these supplements will do us little good unless we recognize and assimilate the others they present. This requires the cultivation of two attitudes. One is openness to change, for "seriously to study another way of life," as philosopher Peter Winch observes, "is necessarily to seek to extend our own—not simply to bring the other way within the already existing boundaries of our own."[12] The other requirement is empathy. "The encounter with others presupposes and requires that we place ourselves 'in abeyance,' as if in parentheses," counsels Henri-Irénée Marrou. "We must forget for the moment whatever we are, so that we may be openly receptive to Otherness."[13] With these attitudes in place, a college education has some chance of becoming the "self-inflicted, passionate, and collective contamination of strange and different wisdom" that Afro-American scholar Gerald Early knows we must have for a better future.[14]

All this is well and good, but how exactly do we make contact with others? How can we penetrate their strange and scary difference? For that matter, how can we understand or come to know anything about other human beings? How do we plumb their full humanity so as to add to and define our own? How can we possibly discover what's in their heads and hearts, what they believe, feel, value, aspire to, and fear?

While tough, questions such as these are not unanswerable. A moment's reflection will suggest that for all people, living or dead, the evidence comes from three basic sources: their own *words*, particularly those uttered in unguarded moments or under oath; their *actions*, including their cultural products; and the testimony of *contemporaries*, preferably eyewitnesses.

All of these sources are problematical, though not fatally so. Take words, for starters. It seems simple enough to listen carefully to a stranger speaking and to figure out the meaning of his speech. If the speaker has been articulate and apparently honest, we feel justified in thinking that we have plumbed some of his depths, gotten a fair bead on his true identity. But *are* we justified? Even assuming that we speak and think in the same language and dialect, is speech so transparent a medium? Clearly not, for speech is saddled with several limitations.

One limitation is what is *not* said, for language is always bounded by what Ortega y Gasset called "a frontier of ineffability," of silence. "Each society [makes] a different selection from the enormous mass of what might be said in order to succeed in saying some things."[15] Much is left unsaid because the speaker chooses not to say it, because it cannot *be* said, or in the interests of economy, wherein the speaker assumes that the listener can and should intuit the missing thoughts or add them to the conversation himself.

Another difficulty is that the articulation of words does not constitute meaningful language until it is completed by vocal modulations, facial expressions, gesticulations, and the total posture or "body language" of the speaker. Think what a difference in meaning is given to the same words—"My sister is an attractive girl"—by various vocal inflections and a wink, the fanning of a hand bent at the wrist, a rolling upward of the eyes, or a blush. Think how differently an Italian woman, an English lord, and a Zulu orator would say the same thing. Those of us who try to understand otherness primarily through the written word, shorn of its expressive context, should therefore be duly humble about our prowess in retrieving the meaning of alien texts, for the written word is a substitute—"a miserable Ersatz," Goethe called it—of the spoken word.[16]

Indeed, we should be doubly humble because the texts we read also omit the social context in which they were originally produced. Humans usually speak or speak out in answer to other interlocutors in an ongoing dialogue, whether written or conversational. Therefore, the isolated texts we inherit give us only half the conversation, leaving out the questions or provocations to which they are replies.

Finally, even when we stand face-to-face with the other and speak the same tongue, we confront the ambiguity and equivocality of verbal meaning. Words constantly evolve and change meaning; word order and authorial intention make sentences madly difficult to read. Sentences make little sense outside the larger context of oral or written paragraphs and pages, chapters and conclusions. Is irony detectable? Did you catch the wicked wit, the playful pun, and the veiled insult? How serious was the speaker, or was satire his game? Since words always say both more and less than the speaker intends, the student of alterity should be on his mettle if he expects to fathom "alien turns of mind" with them. It's not that they can't be fathomed; it only means that we must use every trick of the verbal trades—hermeneutics, semiotics, common sense, whatever works—to snake through the opacities and obstacles of language to the otherness within.

If the other's words are hard to read, his actions are equally so, even though the repertoire of physical movements is considerably smaller than the potentialities of language. Like language, actions have their own grammar, their own code of signification, which is culture. Since cultures differ one from the other, the meaning or social message of the same actions performed in two different cultures will be different, sometimes embarrassingly so, as any naive traveler can attest. If we wish to converse with and learn from the members of other cultures, we cannot simply interpret their actions according to our own behavioral logic. We must learn to decode or reconstruct the particular cultural context in which their actions occurred. As a growing tribe of anthropologists and historians have demonstrated, this is not an insuperable task because the expectation of the actors was that their actions could be and would be read and understood.[17] Once we break a stranger's cultural code, we break through his difference and otherness. As Clifford Geertz has written, "understanding a people's culture exposes their normalness without reducing their particularity. It renders them accessible: setting them in the frame of their own banalities, it dissolves their opacity."[18]

Rendering the opaque actions of others clear and comprehensible sounds manageable enough, until we realize that even micro-events, such as Balinese cockfights or horse races and court days in colonial Virginia, derive their meaning from larger as well as immediate social contexts. To reconstruct the whole culture, we must not only relate the micro-events to each other, but situate each event or action in the ongoing, long-term processes of social, political, and economic change.[19] This will enable us not only to navigate between the twin shoals of radical relativism and historical determinism, but to understand the extent to which others are limited and free to act at all.[20] "To understand all" does not mean that we have "to forgive all," but any understanding of the cultural constraints under which people act should make us less prone to snap, negative judgments of strange behavior.

To take an historical example, the opening acts of the Columbian Encounter in North America brought together two sets of equally opaque strangers. On literally every beachhead, the European invaders were greatly outnumbered by the native Americans. Moreover, the Europeans were at a severe tactical disadvantage because they did not know the local terrain, they were usually short of food, and they could not understand the Indians' tongue. By the same token, the Indians could not match European weapons and horses, and they could not fathom the intruders' strategic objectives because they, too, were ignorant of the "other's" language. The scene was set for misunderstandings galore and the eruption of violence in every first encounter from 1492 well into the eighteenth century.

Yet nearly every documented first encounter in North America was peaceful. How was this possible? How did total strangers arrive at enough understanding of one another to effect a nonviolent modus vivendi, at least in the short run?

First of all, being human and recognizing the other's humanity, they immediately established communication through sign language and elemental trade jargons or patois, mostly of native origin. Through facial expressions and gesticulations, they signaled their peaceful intentions, their mutual welcome, and invitations to exchange food, gifts, and hospitality. After all, smiles, a hand over the heart, and gentle touching translate reasonably well around the world.

But not unexpectedly, the newcomers were initially nonplussed by a few native customs. In the 1530s, a western village of Indians greeted a small Spanish party "with such yells as were terrific" and "striking the palms of their hands violently against their thighs," behavior that was easy to misinterpret.[21] All over North America, Europeans learned to suffer various forms of adulation by smoke and tobacco, which the Indians considered sacred. A French missionary in Louisiana had smoke blown up his nose, as if it were incense, he guessed, not incorrectly; other Frenchmen in the Great Lakes region were "smoked like meat," they said, or had tobacco ground into their foreheads. Yet it was always clear from the social context that the Europeans were being honored rather than prepared as the main course of a savage meal, so they were not afraid and allowed themselves to be fed such local delicacies as *sagamité* (cornmeal mush seasoned with fat) and roasted dog.[22]

For their part, the hospitable Indians had their understanding and good will tested by certain European practices and products. Eskimos on Baffin Island were obviously surprised when Captain John Davis stuck out his hand in greeting in 1584; one man kissed it instead. At least one Indian thought he had been poisoned by the large spoonful of mustard he was offered by a French commander in Alabama, until a swig of brandy brought relative relief. A few years earlier, a French soldier had overloaded a musket in

order to upend a curious Indian marksman; the victim's tribesmen had nothing to do with guns again for two weeks, though
they did not withhold their company from the French gagsters.[23]
And when Chief Donnacona of Stadacona (modern-day Quebec
City) asked Jacques Cartier to demonstrate his weapons, Cartier
obliged by firing a dozen cannon into the woods. The Stada-
conans were "so much astonished as if the heavens had fallen
upon them, and began to howl and to shriek in such a very loud
manner that one would have thought hell had emptied itself
there."[24] Again, social intercourse was not interrupted by this
awesome display.

The second vehicle of peace was the natives' adoption ceremonies, whereby they sought to incorporate the still-unpredictable,
potentially dangerous, and strangely hirsute newcomers into their
society as honorary Indians. And for their part, the wary Europeans allowed themselves to be incorporated because they quickly
realized that refusal was not only a breach of local etiquette but a
virtual declaration of war. So they accepted—with as good grace
as they could muster—the feasts, gifts, names, adopting families,
and female partners (some meant as permanent wives, others
as temporary hostesses) that the natives offered, and submitted
themselves, sometimes none too patiently, to the long calumet
ceremonies that gave them an inviolable passport through even
hostile Indian country. Only later, when they had gotten a secure
foothold in the new land, did the Europeans develop equivalent
ceremonies to make natives into temporary military or trade allies
(rather than permanent relatives) through the giving of feasts,
gifts (regarded by the givers largely as bribes), medals, flags, and,
occasionally, military ranks.[25]

The third source of information about other human beings, the
testimony of contemporaries, has its own limitations, as anyone
who has ever heard court testimony and cross-examination will
know. The most reliable sources, of course, are those who know the
subject personally—family, friends, acquaintances, and enemies—

and those whose job it is to know him—teachers, psychiatrists, parole officers, and priests. But all informants, without exception, have blind spots and biases that render their individual portraits of the subject necessarily incomplete, pointed, not rounded. This is not a lethal liability by any means because, as Barbara Tuchman noticed, "bias means a *leaning* which *is* the exercise of judgment as well as a source of insight."[26] We can escape the bias of single informants by paying attention to others, as many as we can find, so that we triangulate the subject, much as a surveyor would. While memoirs by and about the subject in their angled particularity often make interesting reading, good biographies usually do better service because they see the subject whole and dissect his or her otherness with as many probes as possible.

The search for otherness is further complicated when we turn to the past for heuristic examples, as we must sooner than later. History is an indispensable form of human self-knowledge, and one of its social functions is to correct the myopia of present-mindedness by communicating some sense of alternative ways of looking at and living in the world.[27] But we gain access to these different perspectives only through evidence that is fragmentary, flawed, fugitive, and fragile.

Our best evidence about human history, people's words, have almost wholly vanished into thin air because they were spoken and not written down. The fortuitous fragment that did reach paper has suffered from the cruel and largely random action of vermin, dampness, heat, wars, fires, floods, rebuilding, stupidity, venality, absentmindedness, acid paper, taste, and fashion. The record that survives is often seriously flawed and one-sided. Institutions, the literate, and the upper classes leave the heaviest documentary tracks. And most written documents were produced by myopic, careless, self-interested, or insensitive observers or by indifferent factota in great impersonal bureaucracies. Nor are the records of the past equally accessible. One-of-a-kind books, manuscripts, and paintings are buried in exclusive libraries and private collections; governments, heirs, and principals restrict access and use; fads and fashions of scholarship consign whole genres of documents to limbo until the winds change. And if the ravages of the past were not enough, the record is continually being lost: archaeological and historical sites are bulldozed for condominiums and parking lots; frescoes are flooded, paintings slashed or stolen; documents are burned or shredded; languages die out with native speakers; stone monuments disintegrate from auto emissions and acid rain.[28]

Moreover, our most familiar historical sources—words—are now inert but were fleetingly alive in the mouths, ears, and memories of past performers. As historians, we have to work with "those painfully retrieved words," in Inga Clendinnen's phrase, "pinned like so many butterflies to the page, remote from their animate existence." It is difficult but necessary to keep in mind "their flickering variability, their strenuous context-dependence, in life." And even when the words come through loud and clear, we need to guard against taking them for the easy truth. Not only do words weakly register people's moods, emotions, and sensibilities—"the distinctive tonalities of life"—but the temporal and cultural distance at which we read them can lend "a spurious simplicity and clarity which denies the rich muddle of a more local view."[29] In short, there's nothing easy about the search for otherness, and perhaps the only thing that impels us to undertake it in the face of its manifold difficulties is its absolute indispensability to our own identities and education as human beings.

Although the personal and cultural rewards to be gained from encountering the other are both considerable and real, we are obligated to ask if the attendant obstacles can ever be overcome and, if so, how. In truth, some difficulties cannot be overcome. Unless psychic research takes a quantum leap in the near future, for instance, we are unlikely to plumb the wordless silences of the other. Until the world's languages, and body languages, dissolve into transparent *lingua francae*, we will be forced to translate, decode, and interpret our way into otherness. Unless the lost voices of the past can be captured on three-dimensional videodisc, we will have to be content with the halting, incomplete testimony we do have.

But there is a great deal that we can accomplish: while "the other" is not an open book, neither is he a lost edition of the Cabala. To crack him, to get past his difference to his redemptive humanity, we must hone three human faculties or qualities, and the college curriculum should do its part.

The first aptitude we should cultivate, and perhaps the last as well, is *understanding*. This may sound terribly obvious, but it is seldom the first response we make when we encounter the other unexpectedly or even in familiar surroundings; defensiveness, fear, and denigration are more typical. Once we establish that the stranger poses no physical threat — and in the imperfect world where we live that is all too often a real concern — we should quickly sublimate our basest instincts in order to deal rationally with more benign but equally inhibiting attitudes. Our goal should be the ability to say, with Spinoza, "I have laboured carefully, when faced with human actions, not to mock, not to lament, not to execrate, but to understand."[30] It is so easy to disparage or, what is no better, to pity and condescend to others of different color, culture, or circumstance. We are never sufficiently understanding because we would rather pass judgment, a natural tendency but one that ought to be postponed at least until we have extended ourselves to decode and appreciate the other's different humanity.[31] As a counsel of patience, the fictional advice given in 1555 by a seasoned Franciscan missionary in Peru to a Spanish newcomer makes good sense. "Have nothing to do with the things of this land," he said, warning the neophyte not to attempt to reform Inca customs, "until you understand them, because they are different matters, and another language."[32] The same counsel applies equally well to those who deal with, or merely contemplate, the inhabitants of the world's inner cities, "pagan" Africa, or rural Appalachia.

The second vital quality we need, not only for our approach to otherness but to life itself, is what some might term objectivity but I choose to call *disinterestedness*, neither of which stands in particularly good odor in the postmodern demimonde of campus intellectuals. Fortunately, the less precious world of workaday stiffs and quotidian scholars rates this intellectual goal a great deal higher and seems to know it when it sees it. I am not suggesting by this term any sense of passionlessness, indifference, or neutrality, which belong more to Matthew Arnold. What I have in mind instead is, in Thomas Haskell's words, a form of "ascetic self-discipline that enables a person to do such things as abandon wishful thinking, assimilate bad news, discard pleasing interpretations that cannot pass elementary tests of evidence and logic, and, most important of all, suspend or bracket one's own perceptions long enough to enter sympathetically into the alien and possibly repugnant perspectives of rival thinkers." This kind of conscious detachment enables us to develop more inclusive, less egocentric views of the world and helps to "channel our [ubiquitous] intellectual passions in such a way as to insure collision of rival perspectives."[33] For reasons such as these, George Whalley, one of the best minds in North American education, regarded disinterestedness as "the greatest instinct a university can encourage and the greatest contribution it can make to society."[34]

Yet understanding and disinterestedness alone, even in combination, will not enable us to approach and appreciate the other without a third ingredient: *imagination*. "People only exist for us in our thoughts about them," Logan Pearsall Smith wrote Virginia Woolf. "They float like slow, strange fish in the . . . aquarium tanks of our imaginations."[35] The trick is to make our conceptions of others approximate as closely as possible the rounded reality and self-image of the others themselves. This calls for *exact* imagining, for "only the painstaking exercise of discipline illumined by imagination, and of imagination channeled by discipline," notes Jaroslav Pelikan, "can lead to the rediscovery of an authentic humanism."[36]

Imagination is the wellspring of empathy, which enables us to imagine ourselves in the head, heart, and place of others. It is possible through disinterested understanding to learn the external facts about others, traits they largely share with other members of their culture, but only imagination can take us beyond the surface into their human uniqueness. Likewise, when we look to the past for exemplary others, the most useful faculty we can possess is imagination. Since we can gain access to past people only through the piecemeal evidence they left, we must use our imaginations to reanimate the known facts and restore them to life, to fill the holes in our evidence with informed guesses, to reestablish, in the face of hindsight's certainties, the choices that the dead once enjoyed in the past, and to discern the larger forces that transcended and patterned the individual lives of our subjects.[37]

Ideally, the home of the imaginative acquisition of knowledge, knowledge of nature, self, and others, is the university.[38] Said Bart Giamatti, who ran a great one before turning to baseball, the university "nourishes at its core the humanizing and spacious acts of the individual imagination," which play such a large role in the lifelong process of liberal education. He also knew what we in higher education must remind ourselves frequently, that a liberal education is "an intensely practical act of self-fashioning," but one that proceeds in large measure through the discovery of other selves.[39] For like Columbus five hundred years ago,

> *We shall not cease from exploration*
> *And the end of all our exploring*
> *Will be to arrive where we started*
> *And know the place for the first time.*[40]

CHAPTER FIVE

What Makes a University Great?

True excellence knows no external
standards, only the inner drive.
Eugen Weber

IN HIGHER EDUCATION, September is the serious season. The return to official business after the summer hiatus
launches the academic year on wings of clear purpose and
firm resolve. Healthy undergraduate faces and the unfurrowed
brows of graduate students and faculty members signal a time of
fresh starts, new curiosity, and better game plans. For those not
yet admitted to higher education's privileges or for those seeking
a change of educational venue and fortune, September is also the
month of the great educational sweepstakes. That's when *U.S.
News and World Report*, *Money*, and a host of other magazines
and guides hand out grades to America's institutions of higher
education in the form of rankings or *Guide Michelin*-like starred
assessments.

Although the assessors purport to be interested solely in giving
consumers—mostly the college-bound and their parents—a rational basis for individualized choice, the news media and particularly academics are intensely interested in the "winners"—the
top-ranked colleges and universities and graduate programs. If
some university knocks Harvard off its pedestal, as both Yale and
Princeton did in the *U.S. News* ranking in 1996, academe is all
atwitter. But even minuscule shifts in rank can galvanize college
admissions and news offices into feverish gloating or administrators and boards of trustees into agonized hand-wringing.

Why are Americans so taken with this peculiar fall sport? Why do they seem to care so much about academic hierarchy, about where colleges and universities stand in the educational pecking order? There are several answers. One is that American higher education at the turn of the twenty-first century is a huge, competitive, and expensive business. With the economic advantages of a college degree steadily rising along with the costs of attending, potential consumers and investors need independent standards and comparative rankings by which to judge the twenty-two hundred four-year institutions making frequent and often inflated claims of academic excellence and trying mightily to attract students, faculty, and funds.

Second, Americans are a competitive bunch and have long looked to rankings of academic quality to help them sort out the best from the good, the good from the rest. The U.S. Bureau of Education launched a four-"class" sorting of institutions way back in 1870, but scientist James McKeen Cattell made the first numerical ranking in 1910.[1] The mass media's interest in the game began in 1983 when *U.S. News* began to publish its annual "Best Colleges" issues and books. *Money* magazine added a new twist in 1990 by ranking "Your Best College Buys," based on a mysterious compound of academic quality and price tag.

A third reason we love academic rankings revolves around college car decals and sweatshirts: alumni, students, parents, and even academics all want bragging rights by being associated with institutions of "excellence," or at least *reputations* for excellence. If we're not personally blessed with genius or accomplishment, at least we can bask in the reflected glory of our larger, brighter alma mater.

Finally, colleges and universities, as intensely (if not purely) meritocratic institutions, should practice what they preach: they should hold themselves to the highest standards, just as they subject their students and faculties to regular merit evaluations. Comprehensive self-studies every ten years or so are a first step toward accountability, but outside accrediting agencies must hold institutions' feet to the fire to ensure rigorous appraisals. Annual rankings by the mass media, while seriously flawed, do much to save leading institutions from complacency and to inspire competition.

The core and quest of most rankings is reputation. As Clark Kerr, former president of the University of California, has said, "A reputation, once established, is an institution's greatest asset. Whatever may be the sources of the reputation to begin with, they will mostly continue to support the reputation."[2] Since 1906 the list of the fifteen top-ranked universities hasn't changed much: three came on, three dropped off, but not very far. Moreover, they belong to a very select group—the 200 research and doctoral universities, according to the Carnegie Foundation's classification, out of the country's 3,688 two- and four-year institutions of higher education.[3]

Like most students, faculty members, and alumni of "elite" or "selective" colleges, I took considerable pride in my various associations with Yale, Oxford, Cambridge, and Harvard, and still do, particularly when we discuss them in my seminars on the history of higher education. But recently, as an indirect result of those classes and of the mass media rankings, I have come to ask: What are the more or less objective criteria or components that *should* constitute a reputation for academic excellence? What, in other words, makes a university truly great?

We might take some rough clues from Clark Kerr's observation that about half of the nation's doctoral and research universities—about a hundred—exhibit one or more of the following characteristics. These universities were built in

— leading centers of the historic professions (law, medicine, and banking)
— growing centers of progressive economic activity
— larger cities rather than smaller towns
— rich communities with cultured establishments and large, rich states

— areas with effective and committed political leadership and with aggressive industrial leadership

— and areas of great physical beauty and good climate.

Unfortunately, this is not much prescriptive or predictive help, because the other half are flourishing in areas unlike those described.

More to the point, if we seek to establish criteria for academic excellence, we need to keep firmly in mind what a university is essentially and primarily about. A university has two main goals and only two: (1) to preserve, refine, and advance knowledge through imaginative *scholarship*, and (2) to transmit that knowledge to future generations through effective and infectious *teaching*. Our criteria of excellence should therefore focus on these goals and not on the secondary or tertiary tasks that higher education has accumulated willy-nilly in the past century.

From scholarly studies of academic rankings, we know that rankings must exhibit several characteristics if they are to be of real help or have validity. They must

— be multidimensional in what they measure

— be based on whole institutions and not just parts (such as a graduate school) or a few "stars" (whether faculty, student, or alumni)

— measure resources not in the aggregate but per capita

— attempt to measure the educational "value added" to the student between matriculation and commencement

— not only rank institutions on a comparative scale, but measure each against some absolute or external standard of quality.[4]

What, then, are the salient components of a great university?

1. FACULTY. The sine qua non of a great university, above all else, is an outstanding faculty. Attending to the two main goals of any university, faculty members must be hybrid *scholar-teachers*, driven to excel in both endeavors.

How can we determine whether a whole faculty is pedagogically "ept"? We can't really, or we can only with some difficulty and an appreciable expenditure of time. State or national teaching awards to individual professors provide some index, but they don't indicate much per capita, and some state awards rotate among only public institutions or have strict quotas on the number of awards that can be made to any one university; institutional awards, of course, are relative to the institution and might be given as consolation prizes to nonscholars (though in my experience they seldom are). Student course evaluations are also relative and tend to rate everyone "above average"; they also depend on the judgment and acuity of the student evaluators and on their academic experience, which is normally acquired at a single school. Moreover, they concentrate on the professor's delivery and management style rather than the intellectual content and cogency of his syllabus and teaching.[5]

Some rankings try to get at faculty quality *in*directly through faculty quantity: percentages of Ph.D.s on the faculty, student-teacher ratios, faculty teaching loads, class sizes under twenty and over fifty, full-status faculty-student ratios (excluding graduate teaching assistants and other part-timers), and the like. But the method is obviously flawed.

In 1995 *U.S. News* inaugurated a ranking of institutions committed to undergraduate teaching. But commitment to teaching and good teaching are not the same, though there is, we trust, a strong connection. Moreover, the ranking was based on the opinions of a sample of deans, presidents, and officers of admission — people who have precious little to do with actual teaching. In fact, I doubt if faculty members (much less administrators) know anything substantial about the teaching quality of their colleagues, as whole faculties, at *other* institutions, and not very much about their own. We simply don't go into each other's classrooms; and if we did, we would bring to our evaluation very different notions of what constituted effective teaching, each rooted in our distinctive personalities.[6]

A somewhat more helpful measure of pedagogical quality is

the teaching portfolio, which documents a professor's educational philosophy, the way he conceives and structures his courses, and the resulting growth in his students' learning. But there is no way to quantify or rank them, and they effectively filter out the oral tone, body language, and emotional climate of the quotidian classroom that plays such a key role in student attention and reception.

Many faculty members, well-published ones at least, have long felt that the surest way to gauge the quality of teaching—that infinitely individual and personalized act—is by assessing the quality of a professor's published scholarship, as judged by his or her peers, not by relatively inexperienced students. It is assumed—correctly, I think—that if professors can research, analyze, and interpret complex subjects of significance with clarity, authority, and interest, they probably bring those skills regularly to their classrooms.[7]

How can we tell whether a university faculty excels in scholarship? We can look at

— the number of refereed publications (books, articles, chapters) the faculty produced, either per year or over a lifetime, per capita; admittedly, this is a quantitative standard, but productivity correlates closely with quality.

— disciplinary and national prizes for those books and articles or for career achievement, such as the Pulitzer, National Book Award, and the NEH Jefferson Lecture.

— citations of faculty scholarship in the scholarly literature, as reported in the *Science, Social Sciences,* and *Arts and Humanities Citation Index.* This is a raw measure because citations can be favorable or negative and they can be made by scholars of eminence or by novices. Moreover, the indexes do not cull citations from books, only from periodicals.

— nationally competitive fellowships to support research, which are based on peer assessment of past performance and future promise. Those awarded by the Guggenheim Foundation, American Council of Learned Societies, NEH, Social Science

Research Council, Alfred P. Sloane Foundation, and the National Science Foundation are among the most prestigious. The MacArthur Foundation's five-year "genius" grants are noncompetitive but obviously carry enormous prestige.

— memberships in national or disciplinary honorary societies, such as the American Academy of Arts and Sciences, American Philosophical Society, National Academy of Sciences, and Society of American Historians.

— honorary degrees for lifetime achievement (which usually come too late to be of much help in assessing current faculty scholarship)

— and national media visibility as TV and radio commentators, op-ed and magazine writers, book reviewers, and quoted authorities.

Again, all of these measures should be per capita, lest we be dazzled by a few bright stars in an otherwise dim firmament.

2. STUDENTS. Theoretically, it is possible to have a great faculty teaching brilliantly a less-than-great student body and still have a great university. But in practice, great universities tend to have both first-rate faculties *and* students, to stimulate and challenge each other at a companionably high level. And to educate each other—some of the most important learning they do—students ideally should be not only brain smart but emotionally mature, ambitious, motivated, hard-working, multitalented, and, perhaps most of all, diverse—regionally, "genderly," racially, ethnically, economically, and religiously.

To measure just their intellectual wattage, we can look at their credentials before, during, and after college. Before, we have SAT and ACT scores, grade point averages (GPAS) in high school, class rank, National Merit Scholarships, Westinghouse Science awards, and the selectivity of the admissions procedures that chose them. During college we have dean's list and honors graduates (both of which are relative to the school) and particularly the educational "value added" to all graduates. *U.S. News* has tried to establish a method for measuring the educational value of institutions by contrasting their "predicted graduation rates" (which correlate well with SAT levels) with actual rates, which is more than most universities use to measure their effectiveness. Some schools like to measure the GPAs and graduation rates of their Division I athletes against those of the whole student body. This is less an intelligence quotient than a measure of institutional integrity. Postgraduate measures of achievement might include the percentage of students going on for advanced study, their Graduate Record Exam (GRE) and Medical College and Law School Aptitude Test (MCAT and LSAT) scores, nationally competitive fellowships won, and perhaps "successful" careers as measured by peers in their respective fields, though the lag time entailed in such a measure renders it less useful for assessing current university performance.

3. LIBRARY AND LABORATORIES. President Garfield once said that the ideal college was Mark Hopkins (the president of Garfield's alma mater, Williams College) on one end of a log and a student on the other.[8] But even in Garfield's halcyon days, the locus of teaching was bigger and more sophisticated than a mere log. Without excellent lab facilities for scientists and an excellent library for humanists and social scientists, a university can hardly be considered great.

Labs must have state-of-the-rapidly-changing-art equipment, large research funds for materials, personnel, and technicians, and flexibility to accommodate new interdisciplinary studies and fields; the best will pursue Big Science in teams (with cyclotrons, accelerators, and atom smashers, for instance) as well as small, more individualized science.

Libraries, "the humanists' workshops," should be large, open-stacked for maximal access, capable of seating a good percentage of the student body (the American Library Association recommends at least 25 percent),[9] well sited on the latest information highways, open many hours a day and closed a minimal number of days a year. Most of all, they should have millions of books, thousands of periodicals, and myriad microforms and on-line reproductions when they can't have as many of the real McCoys as they would like. Rare book collections are not rare in great universities, nor are house publications—national journals—that publicize the collections and scholarship resulting from their use.

It is easy to compare and rank the budgets, total numbers of books, numbers of serials and periodicals, volumes added annually, and size of staff of our best university libraries, as the Association of Research Libraries does annually.[10] It is less easy to assess the quality, currency, breadth, and depth of the collections, the quality of staff service, student *use* of the collections (circulation figures per student give some notion), or expenditures relative to resources (which spending per student or per faculty member can address, as can the percentage of the budget spent on the library).

4. GRADUATE PROGRAMS. By definition, great universities must offer not only outstanding undergraduate education but graduate and professional programs of excellence. The best and biggest universities usually offer graduate programs in most of the fields and departments offered at the undergraduate level. These are evaluated and ranked periodically by expert committees of the National Research Council and, less reliably and much less thoroughly, by *U.S. News*.[11] Unless a university is doing its part to educate and train the next generation of scholar-teachers at least for top-notch institutions like itself, it will simply not attract and hold the best faculty and cannot be considered to belong to the first rank of universities.

5. RESOURCES. All the things mentioned thus far—the best faculties, students, libraries and labs, and graduate programs—cost a great deal of money. Great universities, public or private, have

ways of getting lots of it to mount and maintain their eminence. They have large endowments, healthy rates and levels of annual alumni giving, success in winning federal, foundation, and corporate support, and, if they are state institutions, continued access to generous public funding as the flagship universities of their systems. But again, their wealth must be measured not only in absolute terms, but per capita as endowment or academic expenditures *per student*. They must have either well-subsidized low costs or substantial scholarship funds to attract a diverse student body and enable them to attend.

Since 70 to 80 percent of a university budget goes for salaries, the best universities must have generous funds to attract and hold their excellent, ambitious, and mobile faculties, especially their "stars." And money must be available for many other things that spell the difference between above-average and excellent: building and grounds upkeep, improvement, and expansion; competitive staff and administrative salaries; the huge array of social services that any student population expects today; and the perquisites that are needed to hold excellent faculty, such as regular research leaves, secretarial assistance, the latest computers or lab equipment, travel grants, university housing or subsidies, parking, health care, reasonable teaching loads, and subsidized tuition for family members.

These five components seem to me to constitute the heart of any great university. Perhaps we should add two more for the sake of completeness before mentioning some desirable but not necessary characteristics.

6. UNIVERSITY PRESS. Because the advancement and transmission of knowledge are the primary functions of a university, a great institution will have its own university press to publish the latest and best scholarship of its own and other faculty members. If the quantity, quality, and accessibility of its books (and now

digitalized spin-offs) make it self-sustaining, so much the better. Even if the press loses money every year but publishes prize-winning and nationally recognized titles, the university will find its press subventions well spent, especially if its books are well designed and produced with craft and care.

7. ART MUSEUM. By the same token, the modern university must pay serious attention to the history and future of the visual arts. The best universities support art museums on campus, mostly to provide their students with firsthand learning opportunities with a representative collection of the world's artistic expressions, but also to house and display collections of exceptional range or depth donated by alumni or faculty members. Slides are no substitute for real art, and the best institutions will provide plenty of the latter, not only in the museums' permanent and traveling exhibits but in evocative sculpture thoughtfully placed around campus. A publication program enhances the use and reputation of its collections.

The best universities also have a number of other features which, together with their primary advantages, serve to maintain their position in the front rank of universities.

Alumni. One of the most important is successful and generous alumni whose loyalty and sense of obligation are based less on the university's athletic successes than on their own educational experiences as students. The alumni of major universities can be ranked by their service on school admission committees and other alumni groups and by the per capita rate and level of their annual giving to the university, even, perhaps, by their rate of nondefault on student loans (which according to *Money* magazine is supposed to measure their postgraduate success).

Student life. Alumni memories are less likely to be warm — and giving generous — if the quality of campus life is substandard. Although many universities around the world let their students fend for themselves, the best American universities have, since the early twentieth century, housed most of their students in residential colleges or dormitories. Good (or at least palatable and plentiful) food, personal safety, and social outlets add to student satisfaction and morale, which pay intellectual dividends.

Extracurriculum and athletics. Perhaps believing in the educational (not merely commercial) value of sound bodies as well as sound minds, the most competitive universities tend to support many competitive teams of intercollegiate athletes, along with a wide array of intramural sports and extracurricular activities for all students, particularly a daily newspaper, a campus radio station, and theatre. Their students, men and women, are used to winning in all their endeavors and carry their competitiveness beyond the classroom.

History. Most of our best universities were founded before the twentieth century; they have a patina of age that reinforces their rankings. Assuming that modern realities have kept pace with past glories, institutions that can claim founding in the colonial period or as the first schools of their type or in their respective states reap additional benefits in advertising and public relations. Heritage and longevity enhance institutional pride, which usually translates into ambition and resources for excellence.

Campus design. The older a university, the more eclectic and potentially jarring are its layers of architecture. Many great universities have the resources, taste, and foresight to impose a central vision on campus evolution and to bulldoze past mistakes, open vistas, plant greenery, and commission new buildings with a harmonizing eye. A campus and its architecture are the physical embodiments of a university's educational ideals, and a great university will tend to both.

Trustees. In legal charge of both buildings and goals are university trustees. In a great university they will be accomplished in the leadership of complex institutions of various kinds, diverse, visionary yet fiscally prudent, devoted to the sustained excellence of the whole institution, not just one or two favorite parts, and fiercely defensive of academic freedom, refusing to meddle with the day-to-day operations of the university, faculty primacy, or curricular design.

President. The trustees' most important job is to choose, support, and monitor the university's president and its chief administrative officers. The president of a great university particularly should have vision and experience in higher education and should be liberally educated, versed in the history of higher education, consultative, accessible (up to a point), and able and willing to articulate the university's distinctive goals and philosophy and to analyze higher education's needs and problems for a national as well as local audience.

University relations. The university must have regular and effective communication with its many constituencies in order to project its past and present excellence into the future. Key to this mission of gathering economic resources, morale, and general support for its ongoing philosophy and programs are an official newspaper, an active news or public relations office, and an alumni magazine that features more than alumni kudos, necrologies, and big-time sports. Homecomings and reunions should be occasions for continuing education and serious updating of alumni memories of university life as well as for tailgate picnics and renewed friendships.

Curriculum. Finally, although most American universities have similarly large and elective-rich curricula, a university could not be considered great if its undergraduates were not required, at a minimum, to take a number of general education or liberal arts courses, distributed widely across the three major divisions of disciplinary knowledge (sciences, social sciences, and humanities, in the traditional nomenclature), and to concentrate or major in one discipline or interdisciplinary area, both in some kind of coherent sequence or pattern. A fully elective curriculum, without strong advising or cogent distributional and major requirements, would serve its students as fortuitously as a supermarket serves its variously mature, disciplined, and educated customers.

Great universities, then, are the products of high aspirations and the human talent, will, and material resources to realize them. As many new universities in the twentieth century have discovered, often much to their chagrin, great ones are not easy to build and, once built, not easy to surpass or supplant. For while ambition is cheap, the best students and faculty, outstanding facilities, and deep endowments are anything but cheap and are correspondingly hard to come by. This explains why the list of top-ranked universities changes so seldom and so little. Success feeds on itself. Once universities attain distinction, as Clark Kerr noted, their reputations tend to sustain themselves and the institutional realities behind them.

Although the United States has nearly three-quarters of the world's great universities, they are in relatively short supply.[12] Not every motivated and talented high school graduate can attend one, nor can every ambitious and bright Ph.D. profess at one. But we can all profit from great universities by aspiring to and seriously working toward their qualities and features customized to fit our own and our institutions' best talents and realizable resources. Great universities tend to be strong across the board. Although the rest of our universities possess strengths in fewer areas, they are nonetheless capable of earning distinctive reputations and the affection of students, faculty, and alumni for making the most of them.

PLEASURES

CHAPTER SIX

Confessions of a Bibliolater

When I get a little money
I buy books; and if any is left,
I buy food and clothes.
Erasmus

SCHOLARS IN THE humanities at least, and perhaps in the social sciences as well, are attracted to the academic life for many reasons, but the one magnet that draws them all is books. If they did not love to read, own, fondle, and, yes, show off books, they probably would not have chosen a career in academe. A love of books per se might send a person into bookselling or librarianship, but a love of reading them, teaching them, and doing research in them is what makes a scholar. That's certainly what drew me initially to the professorial life.

Oddly enough, books were not a memorable part of my childhood. For someone who can now remember the call numbers of favorite books, I can't remember a single book that made an indelible impression on me until I was in junior high school. My home simply didn't have many books when I was growing up. Neither my father nor mother read books or bought them. I'm sure they bought a few dimestore "Golden Books" for my younger brother and me, but I don't recall ever being read to or their titles, characters, pictures, or plots. I didn't read *The Wind in the Willows* until I went to college. After my parents were divorced, my stepmother brought a few shelves of books to our new ménage, largely Reader's Digest condensations and mysteries. But these lightweights were interspersed with some contemporary novels and short stories and a few classics, mostly from the Literary Guild. I do remember being dragooned into reading Booth Tarkington's

Penrod to satisfy a Cub Scout badge requirement by my step-mother, who doubled as resident pedagogue and den mother, but nothing about the book itself. *Penrod* probably would have been more memorable if she had *forbidden* me to read it.

In junior high I discovered the public library and the self-absorbing genre of teenage adventures. When I happened upon it, the library occupied a long, high-ceilinged, ill-lit room in the village municipal building. The limp wooden floors creaked and smelled of linseed oil, a smell I still associate with libraries. A couple of round tables and a few hardbacked chairs were crammed into the front of the room, leaving just enough space for patrons to use the minuscule card catalogue, checkout desk, and periodical racks. The books, such as they were, were housed in three or four rows of tall shelves in the back half of the room. The uneven lighting and hushed quiet of that place made the process of culling the week's reading a special, if not yet sacred, enterprise.

Like many young boys without adult guidance, I gravitated to heroic stories of teenage woodsmen, hot-rodders, and basketball stars, several by Jim Kjelgaard, one of the few authors I recall. Since I was too young to drive even a conventional car and not (yet) interested in the opposite sex, I put most of my imaginative energy into reliving the stoic life of a preternaturally able guide in the Minnesota lake region, who caught giant muskies on irresis-tible handmade plugs, or in playing out the bounding on-court life of a junior Bob Cousy, whose manic desire to practice even in the snow impressed his coach and elders no end. Of course, nei-ther woodsman nor hoopster had much time for reading books except other imaginary "autobiographies."

Then in my junior year in high school I suddenly acquired faith in "serious" books and became a self-consciously hyphenated "scholar-athlete." An excellent English teacher and a small-town dream of attending a big-time university sent me to our sterile new red brick library, across the street from the old one, for "name" authors and "classic" titles. I even began to buy my own books in small doses; *Dr. Zhivago* was among the first. Somehow these lofty tomes failed to make much permanent impression on me, though they lent my college applications a tone of studied high-mindedness to complement the modest razzmatazz of my sports portfolio. To my new intellectual persona, the letter of acceptance from Yale seemed as much a ticket to the boundless recesses of a great library as a pass to the polished surfaces of a huge gymnasium.

At Yale books ceased to be the arcane totems and talismans of "The Intellectual Life" and became the familiar fundaments of my own. At first textbooks seemed challenge enough. For many years I kept my freshman *Introduction to Philosophy* in which I had diligently underlined, with ballpoint and ruler, practically the whole text because it was all so important and so novel. But in several courses the professors sensibly assigned real books—novels, criticism, histories—that did not insult even a greenhorn reader with double columns, inane pictures, and boldface subheadings every three inches. With ten courses a year, a student's library was bound to grow, if he resisted, as I largely did, the siren song of "buy-back" week at the college bookstore. When I sold texts I was usually trying to exorcise an unpleasant academic memory or to get enough funds to buy a hardback from the trade or scholarly sections. One of my most ambitious purchases was the three blue volumes of Werner Jaeger's *Paideia: The Ideals of Greek Culture*, which came in very handy as I was writing my second book on education in colonial New England.

Until the summer between my junior and senior years, most of my books were new. I did not discover the dusty pleasures of used book shops until I went to Oxford to attend a graduate summer school on seventeenth-century England. For a wide-eyed American Anglo-biblio-phile, Oxford was Paradise Found. Blackwell's, even before expansion, was truly awesome in its range of titles and ease of credit. Moreover, they didn't mind if you pulled up a seat or plopped down on the floor to read a book rather than buy it. Another shop on Broad Street was, to my eyes, even more tantalizing. Thornton's front window was jammed end-to-end with used books of every description, usually of a scholarly nature. It was a liberal education just to read the spines and to contemplate how their subjects might dovetail.

That summer in England I also decided that the academic life was not only appropriate for a budding bibliophile but possible for this one. Learned lectures by Christopher Hill on the English civil wars, Hugo Dyson on Shakespeare, and E. J. Dobson on language had something to do with it, but the Bodleian Library had more. Between preparing essays for tutorials, field trips to Great Houses, and lectures, I haunted the Oxford libraries in search of a senior honors thesis. I found it in the papers of John Locke, recently deposited by Paul Mellon, and in a copy of James Tyrrell's *Patriarcha Non Monarcha* (London, 1681), annotated and corrected in the author's hand. After summer school ended, I rented "digs" for a week and worked daily in the Bodleian to learn how to decipher seventeenth-century handwriting from Hans Aarsleff, a visiting Locke expert from Princeton, and to transcribe Tyrrell's notes. Working with that little octavo volume in its original calf, and learning not only that Locke and Tyrrell were close friends and Whig soulmates but that Tyrrell had written his book, which so closely resembled Locke's *Second Treatise of Government,* in the same house where Locke lived yet unbeknownst to his more famous friend, gave me my first taste of the pleasures of scholarship and a large appetite for more. To this day, I regret that I was never able to purchase my own copy of Tyrrell's book, which did so much to condemn my soul to everlasting bibliolatry.

My final year at Yale was a veritable holiday of bookish pleasures. It began in the Sterling Memorial Library with collateral research on the Tyrrell thesis. Sterling is Yale's cathedral of learning, the Notre Dame of New Haven. Built during the twenties with exquisite craftsmanship and generous funds, Sterling was indeed meant to inspire worship in its communicants. Its plan was very much that of a Gothic cathedral: the checkout desk served as the altar, framed by beautifully carved wooden grilles. The nave and transept featured vaulted ceilings several stories high, carved stonework, and Gothic-looking wrought-iron lamps suspended from the ceiling. The main reading room to the left of the altar was a baronial hall, filled with giant oak tables and high-backed leather arm chairs. To the right lay a periodical room and an enclosed archway leading past a grassy courtyard to the rare book room. Raised on the intellectual asperities of small-town Congregationalism, I devoutly paid homage to all these stations of Sterling's great architectural cross.

My second invitation to bibliolatry came with election to the somewhat effete Elizabethan Club, which occupied a diminutive white frame house in the midst of larger and uglier academic piles. In addition to afternoon tea, deep easy chairs, and current copies of *Punch*, the "Lizzie" (as it was affectionately known) offered a weekly ramble through its bank-size vault containing a small but exquisite rare book collection. Shakespeare first folios and quartos were much in evidence, but so were numerous other Tudor and Stuart rarities of cultural as well as dramatic interest. I remember being impressed not only by the good taste of the donors of these books but by their personal wealth and peculiar generosity. It seemed rather wonderful then, as it does still, that men—Yale was not yet co-ed—would donate rare and expensive books, the pride of any personal library, to a small literary society where they would be hardly ever used and seen only once a week on ceremonial occasions.

The third redaction of senior year bore the imprint of the Bibliophiles, an informal undergraduate group of bookworms who wished to learn more about the technical side of printing, binding, and bibliography. Our mentors were, respectively, the director and the doyenne of the rare book and manuscript collection,

Herman "Fritz" Liebert and Marjory Wynne, who gave us Ronald McKerrow's *Introduction to Bibliography for Literary Students* and an infallible recipe for leather binding preservative (half lanolin, half neat's-foot oil, which when blended on a too-hot stove could produce ghastly odors, particularly if the lanolin was rancid). Every month we were treated to some of the treasures of the Yale trove—medieval manuscripts, incunabula, even the Gutenberg Bible—and shown how to find the colophon in early books, how a book is printed in sheets, sewn in signatures, and bound in boards, and how to cite references to books without page numbers. One memorable afternoon we were invited to tea at the Lieberts'. No one failed to be impressed by Fritz's world-class collection of Samuel Johnson, but my eye and fancy were caught by a small collection of books in a downstairs bathroom. In a neat row over the "loo" and in a small wall of shelves in front of it, Fritz had thoughtfully assembled a miscellany of bathroom-related titles, such as *Ring of Bright Water*, the *New York City Plumbing Code*, and *The Agony and the Ecstasy*.

Inspired by great collections like the Lizzie's and the Lieberts', a few of the Bibliophiles entered the annual book-collecting contest, which offered a substantial prize for purchases of one's choice. Between Oxford and the Yale Coop I had begun a modest mélange of titles—I won't say collection—on seventeenth-century English politics, philosophy, and history. But it could not touch the range and novelty of the eventual winner: a collection of railroad timetables gathered by a train buff whose room was festooned with engineer's caps, lanterns, and zebra-striped crossing bars. Naturally, we sore losers felt morally superior to such childish enthusiasm and not a little disappointed in the august committee for giving way to its own.[1]

To judge by the statistics on national reading habits, graduation from college means for an astounding number of Americans a precipitous decline in their acquaintance with books. I was in little danger of becoming a statistical casualty because I signed on for my postcommencement summer with a rare book dealer, who occupied cramped quarters over one of my favorite men's stores. C. A. Stonehill & Co. was owned and operated by a father-and-son team of Robert Barrys. Bob Senior was a rotund, cigar-chewing man who looked as if he would be more at home flogging used cars than rare editions. But he was a consummate bookman and he showed his Princeton-educated son, Bob Junior, all the ropes. Together they successfully stalked the acquisitions librarians of the biggest and best libraries in the world. When I used to drop in during my senior year, they would gladly show me the latest treasures in their vault, most of which would end up in the likes of the Bodleian, Houghton, and Yale.

Before I became an employee, however, I was a customer, albeit very small potatoes indeed (so small that the Barrys laughingly forwent their usual commission). As commencement neared, with the prospect of congratulatory checks, I began to look through some of their book catalogues from other dealers. In an English catalogue I found an eight-page octavo pamphlet that rang a distinct bell: *The Recantation of Daniel Scargill, Publickly made before the University of Cambridge; In Great St. Maries, July 25, 1669*, published by the "Printers to the University" upon the event. I had recently seen a reference to it in a book on the opponents of Hobbes's *Leviathan*, but the author hadn't pursued it very far. As a quondam student of Stuart political thought, I had to have it. At the British equivalent of ten dollars, I could hardly go wrong. It was my first rare book and it cost gratifyingly little, but I hadn't reckoned with how to store such a fragile, thin item. So, in the bullish economy of graduation extravagance, I paid fifty dollars to have a New York bindery (one of whose best customers was the Yale rare book department) make me a handsome quarter-calf slipcase for my ten-dollar pamphlet. (This, by the way, proved to be excellent training for a later indulgence in cheap prints, which invariably required frames costing at least ten times as much as the print.)

I have never had any regrets over the expense of that slipcase because the pamphlet led to my first publication, a special, even sentimental moment in the life of every scholar. While the rest of Yale's seniors were becoming Old Blues at commencement, I flew to England with the combined Yale-Harvard track team to challenge Oxford-Cambridge. Ensconced at Cambridge, we were scheduled for practices twice a day. But I was so taken with the Scargill story that I played hooky in the mornings to ferret it out. On a borrowed bicycle with a borrowed research student's gown billowing in the breeze, I made my way to the archives of Corpus Christi College, from whose fellowship the twenty-two-year-old Scargill had been expelled for being "an *Hobbist* and an Atheist." There in the faculty records I traced the short, ill-fated career of the young don who dared to drink and gamble with his students at local pubs and to argue too zealously for the materialistic Hobbist position in the formal disputation "Schools." For which and other notorieties he was deprived of his degree as well as his fellowship and forced to make public recantation in the Church of St. Mary's, a stone's throw from Corpus.

The light but heady wine of English scholarship lost little of its flavor when I returned to Stonehill's for the summer. One of my jobs was to comb the latest dealers' catalogues, note the books published before 1700, and enter their prices, a code for the dealer, and the date beside the entries in the firm's interleaved *Short Title* and Wing catalogues. This enabled my bosses to buy and sell within sight of current market rates. My other job was to collate new acquisitions and to write catalogue descriptions in standard form à la McKerrow. Counting signatures and noting them in pencil on the back flyleaf was not particularly exciting, but the exact training in bibliographical description served me well when I began my doctoral dissertation in the fall.

My return to Cambridge as a married man was auspicious for at least two other reasons. The first was that, with the Barrys' blessing, I was allowed to claim professional discounts from European book dealers for being associated with Stonehill's, a name that opened many doors and cabinets in the next two years. The second was that, having been baptized in the faith at Oxford, I was soon consecrated in the unholy order of bibliolaters, whose principal vow is poverty. For her part, my innocent bride became a blessed martyr to the cause.

On second thought, she shouldn't have been so innocent, for during our academic-year courtship I had dropped several strong hints of books-to-come. Even my proposal was made by the book. In a copy of Sir Geoffrey Keynes's handsome blue *Bibliography of John Donne*, which I gave her sometime before Christmas, I had pasted my own commercial bookplate but with the owners printed in the conjugal plural. When she accepted as readily as had John's Anne, her wedding present was a journal of blank pages, gilt-edged and hand-bound in full green calf by Sangorski and Sutcliffe of London, one of the world's premier binderies. Her initials were gold-tooled on the raised spine and her married name before "Her Booke" on the front cover.

Armed with a couple of modest Yale fellowships and the license of a bona fide doctoral student, I resumed the hunt for bibliographical trophies in my spacious specialty—the history and culture of Tudor-Stuart England and early modern Europe. Cambridge had two main preserves—Heffer's and Bowes and Bowes—and several smaller poacher's delights. One of the most enjoyable fields was the weekly open-air market in the center of town, which always had at least one stall devoted to cheap books. With a trained eye and some practice, one could snag scholarly and even rare "sleepers" for a couple of shillings, walk across the square to Heffer's used book department, and resell them for a substantial profit, which could then be spent on the spot.

But because I was after bigger game, I had to range farther afield and to develop greater cunning in the chase. Realizing that

I was personally too apolitical to pursue Stuart political thought with any keenness, I had chosen for my dissertation the educational writings of John Locke. This entailed a critical edition of *Some Thoughts Concerning Education* (London, 1693), which went through a fifth enlarged edition in Locke's lifetime, with extensive annotations, a long introduction, appendices of other writings, a checklist of printings, and a collation of the five editions. It was the checklist and the collation that sent me plunging into the costly thickets of the rare book world. Of course, I could have used the editions of the *Education* in Cambridge and in the Bodleian, where I did most of my manuscript work. But then I would have missed the smells and thrills of the hunt—and a valuable lesson in my bibliographical education. This acquisitive appetite I rationalized, as I have done ever since, in good American fashion, as the road to efficiency. By having the books on my own shelves, I said, I could save countless hours in travel to and sitting in far-flung libraries. I could work at all hours, when libraries were closed. And I wouldn't have to take laborious notes; slips of paper or discrete penciled underlinings and marginalia would suffice. I could go on in this self-serving vein, but the cold truth was that I had been struck dumb by bibliolatry and was about to be ravished by its economic consequences, unless I found means to pay my own way. Wives, even devoted new wives, don't mind a little sacrifice for their husbands' pleasures, but they also like to eat and pay the rent.

My task, then, was to collect every edition of Locke's *Education* I could get my hands on, without going bankrupt. Fortunately, two godsends and an acquired skill made it possible to indulge my bibliographical fancy and to assemble the largest private collection of the *Education* in the world, the third largest collection after the Bodleian and the British Library. The first godsend was a listless market for Locke on *Education*; no one seemed to want it and the prices for all editions but the first were correspondingly low, usually less than fifteen dollars (in mid-sixties' pounds sterling). By using my Stonehill discount in the pricey shops of Pall Mall and turning up fugitive editions on market stalls and in antique shops, I managed to collect all three of the seventeenth-century editions and thirteen editions from the eighteenth century, including the first Dutch, the first Italian, and the best French edition, the latter a presentation copy from the translator to the woman with whom both he and Locke lived while the book was being translated.

The other godsend was Arnold Muirhead, a former schoolmaster and rare book dealer in St. Alban's, who resembled an aging Ichabod Crane. Arnold was a close friend and associate of the Barrys, who kindly put me in touch with him. Not long after we arrived in England and many times thereafter, my wife and I went to tea at the Muirheads' to sample not only Dorothy's famous scones and cold Scottish pancakes but Arnold's mouthwatering personal and vendible collections of seventeenth- and eighteenth-century books, many of them on education. In the course of those ambling, apparently aimless conversations that bookmen have along the shelves, Arnold taught me a great deal about the state of the bibliographical art and particularly how to recognize true quality at reasonable prices. I will never forget his crusty kindness in knocking down prices, extending credit, tolerating my sophomoric questions, and parting with some of his own Lockes for the sake of my specialized collection. It was he who found the association copy of the French edition and who secretly sold to my wife, at a fraction of its true worth, his own rare first edition of the *Education* as a first-anniversary present for me.

One of Arnold's economical suggestions was to buy good editions in poor condition and to learn enough bookbinding to restore them to full value. Always short of shillings, I followed his advice and enrolled in a local adult education class, taught, as it turned out, by two craftsmen from Grey's of Cambridge, a close rival to Sangorski and Sutcliffe for fine binding. During the course I managed to reback perhaps half a dozen rare books. Three were eighteenth-century *Education*s, which I still have; the others were resold at a happy markup to a London firm to purchase more Lockes.

These and similar tactics kept me in Lockeana, but by the second year in Cambridge I was becoming absorbed by Locke's relationship to Newton and the new science of the century. When I discovered that Locke had published anonymously one of the best and most comprehensive reviews of Newton's *Principia* in a French-language periodical in Holland, I felt I had clear warrant to expand my collections in an ambitious new direction. Brief research trips to Amsterdam and Paris provided the opportunity to track down these *New York Review of Books* and *Nation*s of the day as well as to begin an extensive collection of Newtonian popularizations for women, children, and other nonmathematical geniuses. If we had lived in the land of the IRS, all of these purchases, of course, would have been tax-deductible, for the irrelevant reason that I wrote three or four articles on or from the books at issue.

But rationalizations have their limits, and in the spring of 1965 I nearly exceeded mine. One afternoon I came whistling home to find my wife bent over the bathtub washing the week's clothes to save a few shillings from the laundromat for some necessity like food. Unfortunately, I was carrying the first volume of the sumptuous new edition of Newton's *Correspondence*, which did contain several references to Locke but which had also cost a king's ransom at Heffer's, who gladly put it on our tab. I assure you that the tears that fell into that tub did nothing to clean our clothes or whiten my reputation. On the spot, without *peine forte* or *dure*, I vowed to sell a book for every book I brought into the house, at least until our economic circumstances improved considerably.

It was hard to keep such a vow after visits to two of the finest personal collections in England. The single greatest library I have ever seen at close range belonged to Sir Geoffrey Keynes, M.D.

Through the good offices of a Yale college-mate who happened to be a Keynesian offshoot, I had a guided tour of his incomparable collections of John Donne, Sir Thomas Browne, William Harvey, Sir William Petty, John Evelyn, William Hazlitt, William Blake, Jane Austen, Rupert Brooke, and Siegfried Sassoon, which formed the heart of his definitive bibliographies of all these authors. I know I was too awestruck by the quality and quantity of Sir Geoffrey's books to ask even remotely sensible questions, and before I could recover my composure it was time to go.

Fortunately, I suffered from no such impediments in the second library because we were houseguests there on several occasions. As my interest in the history of science unfolded, we were befriended by Marie (Boas) and (A.) Rupert Hall, who invited us to their dashing new four-story townhouse overlooking the Thames. Until I saw their living room I had never seen rare books in such beautiful condition or displayed under spotlights to such glorious advantage. Well oiled and flawlessly bound, their collection of early modern science, particularly Boyle, Newton, and technology, fueled the engine of my own Newtonian collecting, which continued to putt along on much lower octane.

To my mind, those were halcyon days, just before the aggressive push of Texas, Illinois, and other big-money universities into the British market, when a lot of enthusiasm, a modicum of taste, and only a little money could still bring home bargains and "finds" to one's heart's content. For as soon as my dissertation was published in 1968, a small fry like me could no longer afford even late editions of Locke, if they could be found. Ironically, the scholarly attention I had given the *Education* and the boom mentality of other American buyers ensured that a collection like mine—some twenty-seven editions in six languages—could never be assembled again by an underendowed graduate student.

Today, my life with books is somewhat different. In fact, as soon as we returned to America, started our first jobs and a family, and bought a house, my consuming lust for rare books lost its keen edge, as thoroughly as if I had swallowed a handful of salt-peter. Don't get me wrong: I am still a card-carrying book nut. I still go to any lengths of self-rationalization to buy the scholarly books I desperately want but claim to need. I still regret with touching sincerity every book I've ever sold to lighten the bur-den of several academic moves. I remain convinced that book-filled walls are best for keeping out the cold. And I still spend as much time poring over used book catalogues as I do with my dog or yard. But I have completely sworn off rare books of any sort, only partly because ordinary trade books now cost more than the Lockes and Newtons I used to buy thirty years ago.

The main reason is not that real estate is a better investment than rare books—which is arguable—but that my own sons have turned into bibliolatrous clones, with appetites for books as big as their hunger for CDs. As I learned long ago in Cambridge from a not-so-innocent spouse, nothing puts a crimp in a bibliolater's style more than a close relative who loves to buy books as much as he does.

CHAPTER SEVEN

The Making of a Scholar–Athlete

Mens sana in corpore sano.
(A sound mind in a sound body.)
Juvenal

UNLIKE STUDENT-ATHLETES, who seem to sprout annually and effortlessly from the scholastic soil, scholar-athletes are a somewhat rarer hybrid. They are relatively scarce because the resources needed to succeed in one endeavor are demanded by the other as well. Moreover, scholars and athletes peak at different ages. Scholars, particularly in the humanities, mature slowly, not so much in technical skills as in canniness of judgment, sharpness of eye, and depth of understanding. Athletes, by contrast, realize their potential at relatively young ages, in most sports by their early to mid-twenties. So the range of ages when the two forms of mastery overlap is fairly narrow and dictated more by the athlete's body than by the scholar's mind.

The paucity of scholar-athletes is a function of the limitations of the twenty-four-hour day, human energy, and our educational institutions. Training to excel in a sport and learning to master a scholarly discipline both require copious quantities of time, effort, focus, and motivation. Needless to say, it is difficult to maximize the development of both sets of skills in tandem without some personal sacrifices and major assistance in the mundanities of existence. For good reason, the home of the scholar-athlete is the college or university, where the rest of adulthood's demands are put on hold and where vital services—food, shelter, laundry, library, and long hot showers—are provided.

Since most college upperclassmen in a major are only beginning to master a discipline, the best place to find the true scholar-athlete is in graduate school, where the neophyte must jump the dissertation hurdle to join the scholarly guild. But in American universities at least, postgraduate athletes are not eligible for college sports. Unless they can compete as members of amateur clubs or teams, they will have small opportunity to realize their athletic potential.

By the same token, the athlete who turns professional has unlimited scope for physical development but virtually no time, or incentive, to pursue a scholarly career. The extreme specialization, travel time, and sheer physical energy needed to hone one's athletic skills and to satisfy the team owner work against a balanced effort.

For these and similar reasons, it is difficult for most people to name many scholar-athletes. Perhaps most names are conjured up from our own collegiate heydays or from media coverage of some later stage of the person's career. Because I have long been a watcher of the species, I can call to mind Supreme Court Justice Byron "Whizzer" White, a football star at Colorado; Ham Richardson, a Tulane tennis star who led the American Davis Cup team in the late fifties; Pete Dawkins, West Point All-American in football; former Senator Bill Bradley, Princeton's All-American in basketball; Representative Tom McMillen, All-ACC basketball player from Maryland; and novelist John Edgar Wideman, All-Ivy roundballer from Penn.

All of these men are memorable as scholar-athletes because they won Rhodes Scholarships for study—and play—at Oxford, where they maintained and even burnished their dual identities for at least two years. While preparing to teach at West Point, Dawkins was glorified by the American press and scrutinized by the British as he competed with Yankee enthusiasm in rugby, hockey, cricket, and crew. Wideman, one of the two first black Rhodes, read English literature toward a teaching career at Wyoming and the University of Massachusetts–Amherst and made two of my winters miserable: I was assigned to guard him in several lopsided Oxford-Cambridge basketball games. And when in

December 1964 I read that the 6-foot 5-inch Bradley had been selected as a Rhodes and was postponing his professional debut, I was mightily moved to complete my doctoral research and head home so I would not have to guard *him* the following season.

In recent years, as my own athletic past creaks toward oblivion, I've often wondered where these hybrid highflyers come from. Are they born or made? What are some of the costs and benefits of a dual identity? Do the two poles of that persona only repel one another or do they also attract and reinforce each other? Do scholar-athletes ever lose their bona fides or do they continue to draw sustenance from their young reputations and self-images?

To answer these questions, I've done no research and conducted no polls. I've only read a couple of sports biographies, talked with a few friends who used to fit the category, and dredged my failing memory. Having chosen to cannibalize my own lean experience as a scholar-jock, I've had to proceed in the vain belief that my experience is, in its essentials, not wildly different from that of many others. In their relative mediocrity, my credentials as an ex-scholar-athlete may speak more credibly for the species as a whole than would those of the rare talents who command the attention of the Rhodes committees and the Fourth Estate.

As a scholar I was definitely a late bloomer. To judge by my freshman grades at Yale, I was destined for the groves of academe only as a picker or packer: my first-quarter average was a juicy 69 (a fact of great comfort to my college-bound sons). Only by dint of stark terror and overtime "grinding" did I eventually get the hang of it. After my junior year, a happy stint at the Oxford International Summer School and the discovery in the Bodleian of the author-annotated political treatise that would become the subject of my senior honors thesis seemed to confirm my nascent belief that I had been tapped by Clio for a scholarly life (though I had only the faintest notion of what that entailed).

So off I went to Trinity College, Cambridge, to garner a Ph.D.

(the D.Phil is Oxford's concession to American credentialism). While writing my dissertation on John Locke, I prematurely launched my hoped-for scholarly career by publishing three short articles, two of which were caesareaned from the dissertation; the other was the love child of a more innocent commencement-summer fling. By the time I left England with a first draft, my athletic career was also ready to enter a new phase; the hyphenated scholar-athlete was about to come unhinged.

The paperwork on the jock side of my vita is somewhat longer but no more breathtaking. There are no Olympic medals or world records on my walls. In a small upstate New York high school I was the captain of a winning basketball team; I even attended Bob Cousy's summer camp to sharpen my skills (and played the lousiest ball of my life for a solid week). In track I was only an average sprinter but the first person in our region to broad-jump (as it was then called) twenty feet.

At Yale I switched my allegiance wholly to track, set the indoor long-jump record at 24 feet $1^3/4$ inches (which my history advisee Calvin Hill, the future Dallas Cowboy star and father of basketball star Grant Hill, cruelly smashed a few years later—off the wrong foot!) and the outdoor triple-jump record at 47 feet $9^1/2$ (which lasted an even shorter time). In the process I won a few Heptagonal (Ivy League plus Army and Navy) titles but always went nowhere in the IC4As, the big northeastern regionals.

As a graduate student at Cambridge, I won two Blues in track ("athletics") and two half-Blues in basketball (a still-suspect American import). For the latter team, a global gallimaufry of rank amateurs, I was often the high scorer by default, except when we played Oxford; then I saw more of John Wideman's hand than the rim. Since two players from each team had to be, a young Egyptian and I were selected (somewhat anomalously) for the All-England Junior Team. In track, before chilblains had time to form, I set the Cambridge record in the long jump and won the British Universities title. At the annual "Varsity"

(Oxford-Cambridge) grudge match at White City Stadium in London, I won the long and triple jumps two years in a row.

The closest I ever came to celebrity—my fifteen minutes in the Warholian sun—came in the first year, 1964, when I inadvertently broke the forty-one-year-old long jump record held by Harold Abrahams, the former Olympic sprint champion who covered the meet for *The Times*. Unhappily, I did not attend the awards banquet and therefore missed receiving the medals from Abrahams himself because my wife was not permitted inside the exclusive men's club where the dinner was held. But I don't carry a grudge. On the contrary, whenever I hear the theme music from *Chariots of Fire*, the Emmy-winning film about Abrahams's track triumphs, I snap to attention and experience a frisson of remembered delight. My sons find it all embarrassing.

* * *

Their derision always reminds me that the genesis of a scholar-athlete usually lies buried in the piebald past of junior or early high school, when a *student*-athlete first becomes conscious of his somewhat unusual combination of talents and determines to cultivate them against all odds. At first, he (or she) is only a quick, well-coordinated kid who can outrun, outjump, or outthrow his friends and actually enjoys the challenge of homework, tests, and answering teachers' questions in class. But it begins to dawn on him—if it hadn't already in grade school—that his playmates and the bright lights in his scholastic circle constitute two largely different, often antagonistic, peer groups, whose pressures upon him only confirm the mixed messages he receives from parents and teachers, coaches and counselors.

If he attends a school of any size or social complexity, numerous peer groups and adult lobbies will pull him in different—and not necessarily predictable—directions. Adults will not always root for studies and peers for sports. The pressures may be just the opposite: coaches and parents toward sports, a brainy set of friends and a real or potential girlfriend toward books. The same may be true for college plans: mothers, counselors, "academic" teachers, and peers may encourage him to shoot for the distant Ivy League or Stanford, debt-conscious fathers, teammates, phys. ed. teachers, and other loyal alumni to head for Proximate State U. Although I was ranked fourth or fifth in my high school class of a hundred, I was virtually alone in wanting me to go to Yale. The guidance counselor particularly thought I was wasting my time and should concentrate my applications on acceptable state colleges. Obviously, she had given even less thought to my athletic ambitions or potential.

An all-around student-athlete who prefers or has the potential to excel in just one sport would often benefit from specializing. Yet "public" and coaches' pressure may make such a decision difficult. After making a thin-thighed freshman effort to become a place-kicker on the high school football team, I opted for summer and fall devotion to basketball practice and writing up the football games for local newspapers. In the spring of my junior year I went out for track, largely to take a short breather from my year-round addiction to the roundball game. I also wanted to avoid the stereotypical trilogy of football/basketball/baseball to which most of my friends subscribed. Had we had a tennis team at the time I might have chosen it over track. I was certainly being a conscious snob in eschewing football and baseball, the former because I thought it too crude and unimaginative a sport, the latter because it seemed too uneventful for most of the players and not much of a physical challenge. To my green mind, only basketball, tennis, and track qualified as a "thinking man's" sports.

If a student-athlete becomes truly outstanding in one sport or another, a new set of pressures will arise to affect his college selection. If he believes—or has been led to believe—that he could go "big time" in college and perhaps professionally, his choice of a college becomes supercharged with importance and perhaps a local or national media event. Signing a "letter of intent," so far, is a phenomenon reserved for high school athletes, not computer whizzes or National Merit finalists. But for those teenagers who are as good in the classroom as they are on the court, track, or field, as serious about their liberal education as they are about winning a spot on the varsity, the list of acceptable colleges will be considerably shortened by the quick elimination of gigantic "jock factories," with their snake-oil recruiters conspicuously silent about honors programs, fine arts majors, and foreign study.

The obverse of the coin is the special problems that the recruitment of serious student-athletes poses for most college coaches, who by and large do not think first or easily about the intellectual development of their recruits. What can they hold out to entice these complicated youngsters? Mandatory study halls, "academic coordinators," special tutors, early-warning systems to detect classroom trouble, preselected "gut" courses to ensure eligibility? All such crutches for marginal "scholarship" athletes would be more than mildly insulting to an "A" student who wanted to major in plasma physics, pre-med, or Russian studies.

And how much segregation and special privilege will a budding scholar-athlete accept? Will he want to live in a special athletic dorm with other jocks—Bear Bryant's "Alabama Hilton"—and eat at a training table where the food is always better and in greater abundance than the other students can get in the dining hall or cafeteria? If he is expected to work for part of his scholarship, will he settle for a cushy or bogus job sweeping the stadium steps or polishing the trophies in the Athletic Department, rather than learning new skills in the library, the Career Counseling Office, or as a professor's research assistant?

For the sake of an athletic scholarship, how many other trade-offs and compromises is the student-athlete willing to make in his pursuit of academic excellence? Will he avoid certain lab courses and seminars because they conflict with afternoon practices? Will he forgo weekend field trips in geology, botany, or art

history because of games or meets? Will he feel free to skip practices occasionally because he has an exam to prepare for or a paper to write? Will he carry a reduced course load during the season because of a heavy travel schedule? Will he, in sum, demand
to be treated like the serious student he is or allow himself to be
coddled as a member of an athletic elite whose privileges come
at the expense of his classmates?

How he resolves these important dilemmas may often be fore-
cast by how he decided a whole host of lesser issues during his
gestation as a student-athlete. Deciding to pass through the social
gauntlet of high school as a student-athlete, if I remember rightly,
entails four years of delicate balances and sometimes tough decisions. At a time when peers play the biggest role they will ever
play in one's life, fashioning a self-image that is tolerably true to
oneself is fraught with added angst when the image you seek is
double, not single.

One of the first concerns of the student-athlete engaged in
self-fashioning is fashion: what should he *look* like? What are the
sartorial semiotics of student-athleticism? In high school particularly, I looked a bit like a six-foot-two praying mantis, well-
coordinated perhaps, but all arms and legs. With tongues firmly
in their cheeks, my classmates voted me the senior male with the
"Handsomest Legs" (this was still in the dark ages of sexism, remember), mostly because I was virtually the only one to play two
sports in short pants. I was overexposed in another way: with
weekly newspaper coverage of our games and meets and the flash
flood quality of school gossip, I was too well known for my athletic activities. Report cards and college ambitions were much
more private. So I tried to correct the balance throughout high
school by playing down my sports persona and accentuating my
academic one. My goal was parity of presentation and, like most
teenagers, I went to great, self-conscious lengths to achieve it.

From the beginning of high school, I adopted a button-down
image over anything discernibly *sportif*. On the days when the

Varsity Club lettermen were to be photographed for the school yearbook, I had to borrow a white letter sweater from the graduated brother of a classmate; I refused to buy one, partly because I knew that it had a limited life span, but mostly because I didn't want to flaunt my athletic markings around school. For similar reasons, I never owned a high school or college letter jacket. Since demographically most jacket-wearers were football and baseball players, I tried to distance myself from their sports by not wearing one.

Naturally, I took keen pleasure in suddenly having to wear glasses for reading in my junior year of high school. I chose black-and-gray horn-rims to accentuate my studious mien, too naive to know that brown was the preferred color of true intellectuals. Since I couldn't wear them for any other public appearances without risking collisions with unseen or blurry objects, I made frequent trips to the public library. To be seen hard at "scholarly" work was, in the student-athlete's bifocal world, very heaven.

In the late fifties, haircuts could also be implicated in the definition of a student-athlete. Crew cuts and flattops were very popular with many boys, especially jocks. I had one or the other until my senior year, when I got down to the serious business of applying to colleges. After researching the question in a few "back-to-college" issues of *Esquire, Playboy,* and such, I decided that a little more hair with a part would cut a more scholarly figure. So I grew my flattop out over my postjunior summer and tried valiantly to subdue a pair of fiercely independent cowlicks, fore and aft.

Not much else had to change to fashion a scholarly image, for I was already wedded to the Ivy uniform of the day: khakis, loafers, and cordovans (*never* sneakers off the court), button-down Oxford shirts (preferably with lightly frayed collars), and crew-neck sweaters. At that age I wasn't sure that clothes *didn't* make the man, so I affected the look of what currently passed for scholarly.

Once at Yale I had no difficulty managing the image of an Ivy League "scholar" because everyone dressed pretty much the same. Since ties and coats were required at lunch and dinner in those pre-coeducational, early-sixties days, and since I lived on the third to fifth floors of my respective residences, I elected to dress "up" for the day to avoid having to run up to my room and down, and to show a certain amount of respect for the professors, who constituted one moiety of my role models. The tie-and-coat routine lost some of its natty cachet at basketball and track practices, however, when tweed and challis had to be hung in cramped and humid (or worse) lockers. Doing up a tie after a hot workout and shower was a daily test of the jock's resolve to pass as a junior egghead.

Even sports injuries could add a dashing note to one's campus wardrobe. But they were double-edged badges of honor. Fellow athletes regarded them knowingly as pieces of ill luck, with a "there-but-for-the-grace-of-God-go-I" wariness and finger-crossing. But a visible limp, a bulky wrap around a thigh or ankle, the camphorous smell of liniment or "atomic balm" (which sadistic trainers used to daub surreptitiously on bare buttocks before showers), or worse, crutches told your fellow scholars that you had another life where you walked—even ran—on "the wild side," lived dangerously or heroically for alma mater. But classmates were apt, as in most things, to be of two minds about them. While they might betray a trace-element of envy or quiet respect for your other life, they were as likely to be heavily ironic about your manifest clumsiness, lack of training, or participation in silly games for neckless wonders.

Looking the part of a student-athlete is usually a good deal easier than acting it, and involves fewer choices, some of them painful. For me, who liked and got along with all kinds of contemporaries, the social "necessity" of choosing close friends and associates—who to be (and be seen) with in school and in small-town society—was complicated by a kind of scholastic "class" system. It was fortunate, in our small school, that most of the best athletes were among the best students. This certainly made my social choices easier and eased my embryonic social conscience, which was increasingly sensitive to exclusiveness and its attendant pain for those left out. Yet I took some comfort from the fact that the criteria for inclusion were strictly meritocratic, and that the social boundaries around the group were fairly permeable. Most of the school day might be spent with the studious element, after-school hours with a mixed coterie of jocks at practices and goings-home.

For some of us, other choices were harder. In high school and even later, there were two supreme sacrifices that all athletes were expected to make: alcohol and sex. In the decalogue of most coaches, two commandments stood out: "Thou shalt not desecrate thy bodily temple with spirits" and "Thou shalt not spend thy vital forces the night before a game." In a mad frenzy of sacrilege, a few of my teammates occasionally shared a can of beer in a shaded grove, and they seem to have escaped both addiction and divine retribution. I was the odd man out: we had an open, full-sized bar and backbar in our paneled "rumpus room" in the basement, where I took my last drink—a face-twisting shot of 7-Crown—with a daredevil friend in the seventh grade. Growing up with a quiet but consistently alcoholic father, I had even more reason to follow the coaches' first commandment.

As for the affairs of Venus, I was a total tyro in high school and long after. At all-male Yale, I was so impecunious and starved for the mere company of the softer sex that I never bothered to determine whether my rare dates were drawn by my well-mounded muscles, my well-rounded mind, or just comparably acute loneliness. By the time I met my now-wife on a blind date at the beginning of my senior year, I no longer heard the second commandment ringing from the Athletic Office or believed in its sanctity.

The other love I found at Yale was history. By junior year,

when I took superb seminars on Tudor-Stuart England and the American Revolution, I had decided that reading and writing history were not only the best possible way to spend the future but a feasible way to make a living. Everything thereafter was aimed at getting to England to study the English background of American colonial history.

But I set my sights on an English graduate program also because I knew that I could continue to play serious sports for the university teams in a pure spirit of amateur competition. To pursue simultaneously the mastery of a discipline and of one or more sports at Oxford or Cambridge struck me as the best of all possible ways to launch a scholarly career.

* * *

Looking back on our time in Cambridge and all the scholarly-athletic preparation that led to it, I can now see a number of ways in which scholarship and sports mutually fed and reinforced each other, rather than pulled me in contrary directions. Many of those ways, I'm convinced by my desultory research, have contributed to the making of other scholar-athletes, however high they've flown.

One side of the equation is what the student and the scholar lent to the athlete. First, from "research" and reading, my high school jock persona received inspiration and then preparation. Like many teenage athletes but certainly not all, I stocked my imagination and stoked my ambition with fictional and biographical stories of great athletes, primarily basketball players. Then, as I reached certain levels of play on raw ability and dogged if unsystematic practice, I sought the advice of big-time coaches, stars, and other experts in "how-to" articles in sports magazines and books. I threw myself into research on the foul shot and fakes and later the broad jump as wholeheartedly as I did for a social studies or English paper.

Having one eye always cocked toward a scholarly future also

led me in part to choose sports that not only capitalized on my particular set of physical and mental attributes but came with coaches whose intellectual and moral qualities made them excellent teachers. In high school the varsity basketball coach had been my freshman math teacher rather than a stereotypical gym teacher. After a stint in the man-molding army, he put his military mien and his own canny sports skills to good use by teaching a dozen individualists to play a hard-nosed, disciplined style of winning basketball. At Yale, where I was "recruited" (in Ivy League fashion, without money) to play basketball, I quickly realized that neither the freshman coach nor most of my first-string teammates were unduly serious about the cultivation of intellect, on or off the court. I also saw that almost daily three-hour scrimmages, while good for the soul, were incompatible with my need to make up for a spotty preparation for college studies. So before the end of the first semester I resigned from the freshman squad to rescue my unstellar grades in calculus and economics.

When I survived midyear exams, I went out for track. My reasons were at least in part "scholarly": the track men I knew were a studious bunch, given to reading rather than roistering on bus trips, the total practice time for jumpers was only an hour-and-a-half if expedited, and the two coaches were both unusually learned—the field coach a Ph.D. in psychology, the head and running coach a magna cum laude from Holy Cross in classics and Thomistic philosophy. And I was perceptive enough to realize that in track I had plenty of room for improvement, whereas in basketball most of my potential had already been realized.

The scholar's third contribution to the athlete was the efficient management of time. I quickly learned the value of fewer and shorter practices. With lots of challenging course work always ahead and a twelve-hour-a-week scholarship job, I could not afford the luxury of three-hour practices, leisurely showers, and training table off the beaten path. I have no doubt that the daily discipline of time-budgeting off the track reinforced the evolution of efficient routines on it. As Frank Shorter, another Yale track-man and a pre-med student, testified, "I think my adherence to the study ethic helped my running because I learned how much I had to put in to get what I wanted and at what point diminishing returns set in."

Excellent coaching by my Yale mentors and the establishment of efficient training routines enabled me to participate in inter-collegiate sports at Cambridge at a level equal to the best I had attained as an undergraduate, all while I was married, practicing less under adverse conditions with no coach, and writing a doctoral dissertation. Both Frank Ryan, my field coach, and Bob Giegengack, the running coach, were masters of their sport and master teachers. Gieg became the Olympic track coach in Tokyo in 1964 and was an expert member of the Technical Committee of the International Amateur Athletic Federation, the worldwide governing body for track and field. Frank wrote books and articles and made training films on his events. (As a freshman I starred as the "before" to an Olympic champion's "after" sequence in the triple-jump movie.) They not only knew but generously taught their charges the physical, tactical, and physiological principles of the sport. They were canny enough to realize, as Frank Shorter put it, that "you just couldn't tell a Yale athlete to do something without explaining why to a certain degree. There aren't many sheep there." Like all master teachers, they held nothing back and taught to become dispensable.

What I learned from them became indispensable in Cambridge. The track was a good bike ride from the center of town and had no facilities for showering or changing. So you dressed for practice in "digs," pedaled out, practiced (often alone), and pedaled back to shower, or rather bathe. Since our one coach was primarily a running coach, the field men had to know how to train when they "came up" to university or they floundered a great deal.

The basketball facilities (to which I returned) were even more primitive. The so-called university gymnasium looked like a turn-of-the-century health club for bluestockings. The basketball court was so short that jump shots were easy from midcourt, and layups had to be terminated just inside the foul line to avoid smacking into the wall which arrived only inches after the backboard, an antique rectangular affair which no self-respecting high school in the States would have countenanced. Only the scheduled opportunity to play on regulation courts at American air bases, complete with fan-shaped Plexiglas backboards, kept the spoiled Americans on the team from taking up croquet or punting on the Cam.

The last legacy of scholarship to my erstwhile sports career, and perhaps the most valuable, was a saving dose of perspective: the conviction that while sports, especially team sports, were important parts of life and learning, they were not the alpha or the omega of becoming an adult. So upon finishing the first draft of my dissertation and coming home from Cambridge, I appeared in a regional AAU meet in my hometown and promptly put away my track spikes forever. With a postdoctoral fellowship and job-hunting ahead, I was, rather surprisingly, not even tempted to look back at the halcyon days of amateur athletics. I had no need to, because at twenty-three I knew that I had received as much benefit from sports as I was capable of absorbing and putting to good use. It was now time to throw my whole self into making a scholarly career.

* * *

Conversely, participation in athletics made several contributions to my scholarship. The first was that from basketball, one of the quintessential team sports, I learned something about the functional importance and aesthetic beauty of teamwork, the pulling together and subordination of self for the good of the whole. I also learned, sometimes painfully, that long-range success—the winning of a game at the end of forty minutes of play or a championship season—is the product of steady, patient, incremental, coordinated effort, not of technicolor bursts of individual heroics. From blending into a sports team, I instinctively knew the meaning, and was partial to the ethos, of the "community of scholars" when I made its acquaintance at Yale.

Intercollegiate track taught a slightly different lesson but one equally valuable for participation in the scholarly community. While track is a team sport, except for the relays the events are separate and individualized. One's contribution to the team is usually made in lone competition against a handful of opponents and teammates and the tape measure or stopwatch. The analogy to scholarship is rather exact. While scholars work for the cumulative, long-range good of their international community by advancing knowledge and understanding, they do so largely alone, teaching students and publishing books and articles under a single name. Only their acknowledgments pages reveal the magnitude of the help they have received from "teammates" and their purest purpose for "playing the game."

Another scholarly application I brought from athletics was that I at least realized the need, from facing a variety of superior opponents, to mask or sublimate my intense competitiveness. The object was threefold: to gain some psychological advantage over the opponent on the principle that a secret (or at least quiet) nemesis is harder to handle than an in-your-face known one, to focus my mental and physical energy upon the task rather than the person at hand, and, not least, to provide a quiet escape in the event of failure. Since scholarly opposition tends to be rather public, the first reason to mute one's competitiveness carries little cogency in the community of scholars. But the other two have a good deal of utility. If scholarship is to remain disinterested and focused on the communal search for truth, it must stay above personalities and personal animus (an ideal that scholars, no less than other competitive people, often honor in the breach). And in a world inhabited by legions of people blessed with sharper minds, more energy, more fertile imaginations, and swifter pens (or word processors) than ours, an acquired gift for rationalization, particularly of failure, is, as Ben Franklin knew, one of the thinking man's biggest assets.

In one important way competition in scholarship differs from athletic competition. The search for personal excellence in humanistic scholarship (as opposed to scientific research, perhaps) does not take the overtly competitive form of athletics. This is not to say that scholarship doesn't have its publicly competitive side, but the search for knowledge tends to be much more muted than the physical contests of sport. The major difference is that excellence in athletics is usually measured during the performance by objective standards—times run, distances jumped, strikeouts, birdies, aces—although a few sports, such as diving and gymnastics, are highly evaluative (and therefore subjective and political). Excellence in scholarship, on the other hand, is measured almost entirely by the subjective judgments of peers over much longer periods.

There are, to be sure, some public awards and rewards in scholarship, the publicity for which has the effect of cozening us into believing that they were made by objective judges applying objective standards. Anyone who has served on a selection panel or prize committee knows how fraudulent such an interpretation must be. But most media consumers, even scholars and teachers who should know better, are easily taken in by the superficial resemblance between a literary prize, an endowed chair, or a fellowship award and the outcome of a sports event. In athletics, particularly team sports, there are losers and winners at the end of each contest. But in humanistic scholarship, there are only occasional "winners" and no outright losers because the standard of measurement is suitably inexact and the goal is the same as the process, namely, to augment understanding and to increase knowledge through long-range, cooperative effort by the whole community of scholars. In scholarship, "how you play the game" is everything; "who wins" is meaningless in a communal sense except as public awards serve sporadically to inspire the toilers in the vineyard, all searching for the perfect vintage but knowing full well that the annual round of digging, nurturing, and pruning is and must be its own reward.

A career in sports also gave me a somewhat accelerated education in human nature through observing the behavior of people under pressure, handling success and failure on a regular basis, and having to motivate themselves day after day to train hard, suffer a certain amount of pain in the process, and neglect a whole raft of alternative ways to spend their time. I saw many well-muscled embodiments of that old cliché about quitters never winning and winners never quitting. Perseverance has as much value in scholarship as in sports. Frequently in our business, writing lots is the best revenge.

I also observed at Yale two master motivators at work. Frank Ryan, a psychologist, wasted none of his discipline in applying its principles to his student-charges who were not self-starters. His authority was not diminished by his Irish gift of gab and his imposing physique, which formerly threw the hammer and put the shot at championship distances. Bob Giegengack got more out of his runners than any coach I have ever seen, partly because it was well known that he always had. Not given to light banter or sophomoric nonsense (I remember being pulverized in an ethics debate in his car en route to a meet at Cornell), Gieg motivated his teams by the force of his knowledge of and the seriousness of his commitment to the sport. His mordant wit and withering sense of irony, accented with the peculiar lilt of Brooklyn, added to his authority, as did his ubiquitous whistle.

I got to study the human condition (in its largely collegiate manifestations) also by traveling with the team to a variety of cities, countries, and campuses. The best experiences came from being selected to compete with Harvard's best against our British counterparts, the combined Oxford-Cambridge select team. By virtue of scheduling (the meets were held every other year) and a bit of luck, I competed as a sophomore in the United States, as a senior in Great Britain, and again for Oxbridge as a second-year graduate student back in the States. In the first meet in 1961 I encountered a pungent piece of academic one-upmanship in the person of Adrian Metcalfe, a member of Magdalen College, Oxford, who at nineteen had run the year's fastest four hundred meters in the world. When Arizona State College, then one of America's premier track factories, tried to recruit him, he delivered a withering riposte. "I have written that I am at a university," he told the press, "which was founded when their ancestors were in the trees. I have no idea what they might suggest I should study. It's probably handwriting." Two years later, as an adopted limey, I roomed with sprinter Jeffrey Archer, who hadn't yet written any novels or served in Parliament but had served as England's president of Oxfam, the international relief organization, while still an undergraduate.

What I enjoyed most about the English teams was their intellectual seriousness, their maturity, and their earnest amateur spirit. Several members were active graduate students, as I was. Most were visibly older than their American counterparts and thought nothing of recovering from practice with a pipe and a pint of stout. Their one coach was relatively unobtrusive and certainly not interested in making nightly bed checks. The club spirit reigned and provided a refreshing contrast with the semiprofessional feel of many American college teams.

Athletics abetted my scholarship in another way: they made me, in spite of my early academic record, a plausible candidate for a Rhodes and other scholarships for study abroad. Unfortunately, I was too dull-witted or tongue-tied in the final interviews to win a Rhodes. But reaching the finals in a tough region apparently did me no harm when the Yale faculty awarded two fellowships for graduate study a couple of anxious months later. These took us to Cambridge for two years. Winning a Rhodes would have put a handsome cap on my dual career, but some disappointments work out for the best. As Pete Dawkins had discovered a couple of years before, only third-year Rhodes were allowed to marry. And, although I planned to write a dissertation on Locke, whose papers were in the Bodleian in Oxford, I wanted to work in Cambridge with Peter Laslett, the foreman of the "Locke factory," and to live in Cambridge's more bucolic precincts.

Perhaps the most important legacy I received from athletics was a basic reservoir of confidence which would continue to sustain me as I tried to gain my footing in the slippery new arena of scholarship. Having held my own against athletic rivals in two sports on two continents (however small the pieces), I was emboldened to try my hand at a different, more serious, kind of competition in the big league of international scholarship. That sustaining core of confidence came, I like to think, as much from knowing how to lose with some grace, from learning that losing and disappointment are not (in the long run) fatal and can even be salutary if they lead to regrouping and redoubling of effort, as from having triumphed now and again. Nonathletes are simply not inured to losing as publicly or as often as athletes are. The key role that confidence has played in my scholarly life has been to give me the kamikaze courage to commit myself to print, to stick my neck out before the judgment of peers and superiors, on a regular basis. Obviously, confidence can come from many sources—loving parents, good looks, success in school, love, or any number of endeavors, perhaps even a gentle gene on the double helix. But much of whatever confidence I have—and, I would bet, that of a substantial number of scholar-athletes as well—came from having competed strenuously and with some success in sports. Ironically, the strongest measure of that legacy may be this uncharacteristically familiar essay, which, while it took a quarter of a century to be written, never would have been without the excavation that it entailed of largely pleasant memories from my athletic attic.

CHAPTER EIGHT

Between Disciplines

Dealing with a world elsewhere comes
to much the same thing when elsewhere
is long ago as when it is far away.
Clifford Geertz

ETHNOHISTORIANS—the progeny of a common-law marriage of history and anthropology—are not born, ironically, but make themselves up as they go along. Although ethnohistory as an academic specialty was raised to journal and organizational status by the early fifties, I never learned about it until 1971, when I was thirty years old.[1] Only then did I begin my slow self-fashioning as an ethnohistorian, at some political risk to my academic career. Since I was among the first professionally trained historians to intrude themselves into the tight ethnohistorical circle dominated by anthropologists, my experience, I think, speaks for a larger cohort and illustrates some common advantages and pitfalls of trying to straddle two or more complex, constantly evolving, and somewhat jealous disciplines. Although mine is an American story, its lessons could have derived from and could be applied to academic situations around the world.

When students enter my classes today, they are introduced in the first hour to the concept of culture as the least common denominator of historical analysis and to ethnohistory as the most inclusively useful perspective upon the past. But when I was a jejune history major at Yale in the early sixties, the only notion of culture I was exposed to was "high" culture—the products of canonically great artists, writers, and thinkers, predominantly European. As an erstwhile student of philosophy, I gravitated to the brand of intellectual history taught by Franklin Baumer and Lewis P. Curtis, which was largely the genealogy of Big Ideas sired by equally Big (invariably male) Thinkers. The trick was to probe the connections between the mountain peaks and to ignore the ignoble valleys between and below that often generated, defined, and supported the cultural pinnacles. Predictably, my senior thesis was devoted to the political thought of James Tyrrell, a gentle-born friend and occasional housemate of John Locke, whose political philosophy bore a striking resemblance to Tyrrell's even though they were independently adumbrated in print. As I remember, I had no larger notions of history, society, or culture.

Going to Cambridge for doctoral work in 1963 began to change all that dramatically. I wanted to work on John Locke, but I was too apolitical, too impractical, and too secular-minded to choose his political, economic, or religious thought as a dissertation topic. His educational thinking was much more congenial to my own preoccupations, so I elected to write a critical, annotated edition of *Some Thoughts Concerning Education*, which had been published in 1693 and revised four times before Locke's death in 1704. Initially, Locke directed his advice toward the private tutoring of the male children of a gentleman friend. Only later did he generalize his thinking into book form, to some extent for all classes and both genders.

Introducing and annotating one man's thinking about the education of his society forced me to confront the inadequacies of my undergraduate notions of society and culture. Although Locke occupied a secure place in the Western canon of great thinkers, I quickly discovered that his educational ideas were as often the eccentric products of his experiences as a seventeenth-century physician, a confirmed bachelor, and a made gentleman as they were philosophically grounded in the *Essay Concerning Human Understanding*. I also learned that the formative influences on his educational thinking were not other great philosophers but a host of minor, largely French, writers on education whose books he owned, read, and excerpted in his journals.[2] This revelation (to me, at least) received support from the concurrent work of John Pocock and Quentin Skinner, who showed that several early modern political philosophers aimed their logic largely at small-time polemicists engaged in long-forgotten political or religious controversies.[3] So even in the rarefied realms of intellectual history, the broad contexts of popular thought were essential to an accurate understanding of elite thinking.

The democratization of my notion of culture received added impetus from the new work of my supervisor, Peter Laslett. I chose to attend Cambridge because of Laslett's reputation as a Locke scholar, but by the time I arrived he and a group of industrious colleagues were well launched on second careers as historical demographers.[4] Adapting the pioneering work of French demographers Louis Henry and Pierre Goubert to English conditions, Laslett and the "Cambridge Group" were in the process of revolutionizing our understanding of the social history of the early modern period through a painstaking collation and analysis of impersonal vital records. For the first time, the allegedly inarticulate "little people" of the past were heard from loud and clear and forced all historians to include them in their scenarios and interpretations of the past.

When I returned to teach at Yale in 1966, almost immediately I turned to a second book on the history of education. But this time I would deal with a whole society's—colonial New England's—attempts to educate its young, not only in schools and colleges but through the primary institutions of family, church, and apprenticeship. I was as interested in what Puritan parents and teachers practiced as in what they preached. I especially wanted to see what effect this pervasive educational process had on the young and as much as possible to imagine how they regarded it from their lilliputian or "waist-high" vantage point.

What I needed even more than imagination was a working concept of education more inclusive than that needed for treating one intellectual's pedagogical prescriptions.

I found such a concept in Bernard Bailyn's *Education in the Forming of American Society*, published in 1960. Bailyn proposed that education be seen as "the entire process by which a culture transmits itself across the generations."[5] In this sense, it was synonymous with the anthropologists' notion of *enculturation*, the communal process in which informal as well as formal agencies help to transform children into full members of a specific human society, sharing with other members a distinctive culture. To my mind, however, this idea of education, while enormously liberating, was *too* broad and too diffuse to help me focus on the complex relations between society and education. So I modified it slightly with suggestions from Werner Jaeger's three-volume *Paideia: The Ideals of Greek Culture* and Lawrence Cremin's compendious *American Education: The Colonial Experience, 1607-1783*.[6] Trying to unite the best of the anthropologists' universal and Jaeger's normative understanding of education, I approached the history of colonial New England with a definition of education as "the self-conscious pursuit of certain intellectual, social, and moral ideals (which makes it normative) by any society (from the family to the nation) that wishes to preserve and transmit its distinctive character to future generations (which makes it conservative)."[7] Such a notion allowed me to focus primarily on the socialization of New England's children, on the cultural ties that bound them to their society, and not on the many forces in their experience — ideas, social change, alternative lifestyles — that may have been individually liberating. In dwelling on the kinds of habits that New England society tried to teach its children, I was persuaded by the theoretical work of Philip Bagby and David Bidney that a society's habits — its regularities of behavior, feeling, and thought — were its culture.[8]

The School upon a Hill (1974) was a turning point in the evolution of my personal blending of history and anthropology. Much of the book's design looked back to older (though far from ancient) trends in anthropology. Although it was written during the educational upheavals of the late sixties and early seventies, it drew on a somewhat staid corner of the discipline known as educational anthropology and the far-from-fashionable works of George Spindler and George Kneller.[9] Its working concept of culture was rather generalized and took on the normative slant not only of Werner Jaeger but of Robert Redfield, whose stillwonderful book *The Little Community* (1960) emphasized that "the world of men is made up in first place of ideas and ideals." In the study of human cultures, he persuaded me, "the schemes of values of people are central and of most importance." However we conceive the little communities in which most humans have lived, "it is thinking that is the real and ultimate raw material; it is there that the events really happen."[10] Finally, my book's penultimate chapter on the unusual "adolescent" condition of Harvard and Yale college students took its inspiration from Arnold van Gennep's 1909 classic, *The Rites of Passage*, which had been translated into English in 1960.[11]

But the final chapter of the book pushed me toward a greater involvement in historical anthropology or, as I came to know it, ethnohistory. Part of the shift was the result of having my curiosity piqued and my conscience pricked by recent well-publicized protests by the American Indian or "Red Power" movement across the country—the capture of Alcatraz Island in California, the standoff with federal agents in Wounded Knee, South Dakota, the "Trail of Broken Treaties" caravan from the Midwest to Washington DC, and the takeover and trashing of the Bureau of Indian Affairs building. With apparent justice, my Yale colleague Jack Hexter worried (not to me but to a third party) that I was forgoing honest scholarship for the pop pursuit of a political fad.

The essential reason I sidled toward and eventually jumped feet first into ethnohistory, however, was an intellectual need to make sense of the English colonial experience in New England and later of the whole European experience in the Americas. Before I concluded *The School upon a Hill*, I learned not only that the English educated their young for lives in a new world but that the American natives also taught the newcomers, young and old alike, in three guises: as hospitable neighbors in a strange and often forbidding environment; as guerrilla warriors (both mortal enemies and supportive allies); and, most intriguing of all, as seductive models of a different way of life on the shadowy frontiers between cultures. Although I did not use the awkward word, I was much taken with the New England evidence I found for what anthropologist A. Irving Hallowell dubbed "transculturalization," the process by which the members of one culture undergo an unforced transition or conversion to the beliefs and mores of another.[12] Scores of English settlers—men, women, and children—were either captured by Indian war parties or ran away to native villages where they were adopted as full members of families and the tribe, often in the exact place of tribesmen or women who had died from European diseases or warfare. A few years later I expanded the story of these "White Indians" to all of British America, which version seems to have struck a popular chord by being reprinted twelve times to date.[13]

Hallowell notwithstanding, my initial foray into ethnohistory was theoretically innocent. Once I was alerted to the ubiquitous if largely invisible presence of Indians in American history, I simply plunged back into the English colonial documents (from which I had just emerged) in search of evidence of native influence on the colonists. I quickly saw with new eyes that the single longest index entry in virtually all official colonial records was devoted to "Indians." After I had worked my way through most of the New England records in order to write my concluding chapter, I realized that I had finally found a topic spacious, important, and neglected enough to hold my scholarly interest for a lifetime. The simultaneous discovery of New France prompted me to envision all of North America as the only defensible focus for colonial history because it took in all of the competing colonial powers—Spanish, French, English, Swedish, Dutch, and Russian—and all of the peoples who competed for the continent and cooperated for survival—Africans, Europeans, and native Americans.[14]

Discovering the vast array of traditional documentary sources for native history was exciting; finding a whole range of *non*traditional sources—archaeology, oral tradition, museum collections, cartography, geography, linguistics, pictorial art—was a revelation. Of course, the New Social History was making similar use of nonwritten materials to reconstruct the histories of other forgotten, allegedly inarticulate peoples, such as women, the laboring poor, and black slaves. But ethnohistorians, happily, were not seduced by the siren song of quantification and were less susceptible to social scientific hubris, which forced them to exercise their imaginations upon a wider and richer assortment of sources and methodologies.

For me, the challenge of ethnohistory was threefold: I needed to know just what it was, what it could do that other brands of history could not, and what place there was, if any, in its professional structure for trained historians. By 1980 I had satisfactory answers to each of these questions and had decided to cast my lot with the ethnohistorical tribe.

My initial help in becoming acquainted with the nature of ethnohistory came from a symposium on the concept in the journal *Ethnohistory* in 1961.[15] Most of the authors, anthropologists by training, seemed to agree that, although ethnohistory was not a discipline but a method or technique of analysis, it consisted largely of the ethnological study of small ethnic groups or tribes in the past through the use of written documents. Even more helpful—because less restrictive—were theoretical articles by William Sturtevant, Robert Carmack, Bruce Trigger, and especially William Fenton, the dean of Iroquois studies and one of the earliest and best practitioners of what in the early fifties used to be called "historical ethnology." [16]

But I have always been somewhat leery of theory, especially the self-defining kind. So I turned to ethnohistorical practice for a more candid view of the method's promise and problems. The practitioners I gravitated toward, understandably, worked on the same questions that interested me at the time, namely the formation and evolution of cultural frontiers in the greater Northeast and, to a lesser extent, the mutual acculturation of the colonial French and English and the Indians. Three books made a major impact on my thinking and did the most to convert me; each is a classic that has not been superseded or outmoded by changing fashion. Perhaps the first book-length ethnohistory I read was the 1969 second edition of Alfred G. Bailey's *The Conflict of European and Eastern Algonkian Cultures, 1504-1700*, originally published in 1937.[17] It demonstrated with uncommon literary flair (for a recent dissertation) and an abundance of arresting detail the mutuality of acculturation between the French Canadians and their Indian neighbors and partners. Equally impressive was Anthony Wallace's *The Death and Rebirth of the Seneca*, which I first read in 1971.[18] His story of the rise, fall, and revitalization of the Seneca Iroquois in the late colonial and early national period was crafted from deep documentary research and the cultural insight of a psychoanalytically trained ethnologist and fieldworker. Similar talents were applied to extensive fieldwork in the twenties and thirties among the Cree and Ojibwa peoples of Canada to make A. Irving Hallowell's collected essays *Culture and Experience* (1955) an invaluable and unforgettable guide to Northern Algonquian psychology, culture, and religion.[19]

Any scholar wishing to infiltrate another discipline quickly learns that even its best books cannot convey the distinctive tone, mores, and investigative procedures that make it intriguing or attractive in the first place. Only conferences and journal articles — those status reports on the state of the art — can do that. Knowing that I was unlikely to audit a graduate course on ethnohistory or to attend the vast strangeness of American Anthropological Association meetings, I joined instead the American Society for Ethnohistory, became an eager reader of its journal, and began to attend three smallish conferences where ethnohistory was spoken, its folklore communicated over drinks and dinner, and practitioners of any stripe welcomed—the Conference on Iroquois Research in upstate New York, the Algonquian Conference at various sites in Algonquian country, and the ASE annual meeting anywhere from Berkeley to Boston. There I had the initial discomfort and soon deep pleasure of meeting truly interdisciplinary scholars who not only knew the written sources for Indian history as well as or better than I did, but who commanded arsenals of different disciplinary weapons for attacking the problems of cultural change and continuity—and often arcane languages for talking about them. My education as an ethnohistorian really began as I listened to archaeologists, linguists, art historians, cultural ethnographers, historical geographers, museum curators, and native people themselves treating a common subject from their respective angles of vision and expertise, and often several at once. But to watch William Fenton talking or writing about his beloved Iroquois was to experience the rare pleasure of seeing the daunting ethnohistorical ideal realized in one person. No one melded the rigor of history and the many facets of anthropology more completely than this master of the field, the museum, and the archive.[20]

By 1977 I was ready to explain to myself and my fellow historians just what I thought ethnohistory was about and how its practice by historians differed in style, perhaps, but not in essential goals or methods from that of anthropologists. At the annual meeting of the ASE I defined ethnohistory as "the use of historical and ethnological methods and materials to gain knowledge of the nature and causes of change in a culture defined by ethnological concepts and categories."[21] Historical and anthropological practitioners could agree, I argued, that they both focus on the whole culture of an ethnic group or society as a developing

entity over time and space, that no cultural part is to be understood without reference to its place in the whole, and that each
culture, particularly those in contact on a frontier, must be understood in its own terms as these change over time. They could
also agree that, unlike the older anthropological penchant for
synchronic portraits of the "ethnographic present," which assumed that late-nineteenth- or twentieth-century Indian cultures
had not changed appreciably since 1491, the ethnohistorical emphasis should be on sociocultural change, as registered in a broad
array of sources including but extending beyond the written. Even
written documents had to be evaluated in the light of ethnological
concepts and sensitivities.

But theory, I advised, was to be applied lightly. As Fenton remarked, "a lot of what we call theory is a rationalization for kinds
of experimental or research situations."[22] Like most historians,
ethnohistorians are interested primarily in low-level, fact-specific
generalizations which can be cautiously compared with similar
hypotheses about other cultures in similar states of organization
and development. When their sources on a particular group run
dry, they turn less frequently to general ethnological theory—for
example, on band societies, peasants, Stone Age economics, or
ecological adaptations—than to descendant cultures of the earlier
group (on the assumption that major patterns of culture remain
stable over long periods) and to relative cultures in the same general culture area, preferably in the same period, which may be
expected to share cultural traits.

The theory I found most useful pertained to acculturation and
cultural change. With the intellectual luxury of two consecutive
years on fellowship in 1975–77, the latter at the Newberry Library
in Chicago, I began a three-volume ethnohistory of "The Cultural Origins of North America" as those origins could be found
in the frontier encounters of the French, English, and Indians,
and to a lesser extent, the Spanish, Swedish, and Dutch.[23] Anthropologists made the task of designing the series much easier

by having produced a sophisticated body of inductive theory on acculturation by 1953, to which they have since added fruitfully.[24] Whatever its nuances, that theory impressed upon me the need to search for evidence of the mutuality of acculturation among the frontier's constituent peoples, no matter how lopsided the eventual outcome in land, life, or liberty. This imperative has made me try to give equal space and attention to each of the frontier cultures, thereby restoring to the historian's page the rough parity they enjoyed throughout the colonial period.

But the most important conceptual conundrum I had to solve was a satisfactory working definition of culture, since that was my organizing perspective. After combing the anthropological literature, from Kroeber and Kluckhohn's 1952 survey of definitions through Victor Turner and Clifford Geertz, I decided that, for my purposes, culture was most usefully seen as "an idealized pattern of meanings, values, and norms differentially shared by the members of a society, which can be inferred from the non-instinctive behavior of the group and from the symbolic products of their actions, including material artifacts, language, and social institutions."[25]

It is obvious that such a definition acknowledges the active participation of the scholar/observer in discerning cultural patterns in the welter of past behavior. Yet it also assumes that such patterns can be read only in the symbolic actions of contemporaries and with their help. By contemporaries I mean not only the members of the society under study but their neighbors and enemies whose attitudes and actions help to define them by contrast or opposition. Ethnohistory, then, becomes a delicate process of triangulation, formed by lines of insight from the actors of one society, the actors of another, and the retrospective scholar who interrogates and then translates the imperfect documentary record of their interactions over time.

My operative notion of culture is somewhat more inclusive than the Geertzian model that has been much in fashion among historians for the past two decades. The reigning concept is semiotic: culture is an acted public document, a code of signification and meaning, "a multichannelled system of communication" in which actions are regarded as textual statements.[26] Such a metaphor for culture—and it is only one of many (Redfield found at least ten)—seems to me perfectly sensible and feasible but for my purposes unduly restrictive.[27] Because it entails microscopic attention to the particular contexts of meaning in which a manageably small set of actors played their roles—"thick description" in Geertz's famous phrase—it works less well for large, relatively complex societies, for two or more societies in contact, and for societies experiencing substantial change. A theatrical or discursive metaphor also makes it difficult for the historian to pay proper attention to the stubborn and sometimes cruel realities of politics, demography, and economics.[28] In short, the "textual tactics" virtually mandated by the semiotic metaphor—miniaturist, dramaturgical, "thick"—did not seem to lend themselves to the large- as well as small-scale cultural encounters I was attempting to paint on a demicontinental canvas.

If my experience in interdisciplinary brokerage has any portable lessons, the first might be that students should pick and choose freely among the methods, concepts, and findings of other disciplines in order to find assistance for their own particular inquiries and agendas. There are as many anthropologies, for example, as there are histories, and only some of the former will prove of any use to some of the latter. The one or two in high fashion may not be the most useful or fruitful. Moreover, the particular anthropology of service for one project need not serve the next.

The second lesson is that, in today's rapidly changing and expanding intellectual world, scholars should not be deterred by potential or imagined political consequences from forging interdisciplinary bridges, pontoon or high structural steel. The journeys across will more than compensate for the dangers actually faced.

CHAPTER NINE

Extracurriculum

To talk in publick, to think in solitude,
to read and hear, to inquire, and answer
inquiries, is the business of a scholar.
Samuel Johnson

O NE OF THE great inventions for the working world is the yellow post-it pad. Like other office workers, professors could hardly function without them. We write disposable notes to students and colleagues on them rather than deface clean correspondence or final drafts of theses and term papers. We mark book pages and articles we want to xerox with them and use them as nonskid bookmarks. We post emergency office-hour cancellations on our doors with them and leave tracks of our whereabouts for inquiring minds. But mostly we take phone or recorder messages on them.

In the past couple of years, my used 3 x 3s have tended to pile up next to my office phone at the college. When our department moved across campus two summers ago, I had the choice of throwing them all away in a clean sweep or filing them for later conning and sorting. As a record-conscious historian, I opted for preservation. For which I'm glad, because upon peeling them away one by one, I rediscovered an adhesive archive of outside invitations to spread my scholarly lore and pedagogical wings well beyond the classroom.

The majority of these offers I had accepted, not only because being asked was some small register of professional competence (or at least reputation, which is not the same thing), not even because a few promised remuneration, however small. I accepted because long before I became a public servant of the Common-wealth of Virginia (despite its appearance, history, and selectivity, William and Mary is a state university), I felt that college and university professors were obligated to share their studiously (if pleasurably) acquired knowledge and occasional wisdom with the larger society that had nurtured them, usually tolerated them, and always supported them, directly or indirectly. Some responses had taken no more than a phone call; others required only a short letter or a page or two of xerox. But most were more time-con-suming, so much so that they could legitimately be evaluated in annual merit reviews as significant "service," one of the three standard categories in which we are judged. But I have always chosen to regard such extracurricular activity instead as extended forms of "teaching" or as more or less traditional "scholarship." The application of professional knowledge to public problems and needs certainly can be seen as a service the professor renders his or her society. In the current climate of popular and legislative uncertainty over the appropriate roles of the university, anything that speaks to public service may serve to diffuse or defuse some of the prevailing anxiety.

But I would prefer that government officials and the public focus less on the *secondary* role of higher education—public ser-vice—and more on its *primary* roles of preserving, refining, and advancing knowledge through imaginative scholarship and trans-mitting that knowledge to future generations through infectious teaching. One way to do so is to regard professors' extracurricular outreach not as a separate and special category of service but simply as an extension of the skills, interest, and knowledge they bring daily to the students in their classes and to the readers of their scholarly publications. We would all be better served if the traditional bounds of teaching and scholarship were consensually enlarged to encompass these multifarious acts of application, in-terpretation, and diffusion.

When I went to graduate school in 1963 to become a professor,

I had no inkling whatever that a historian of early America might possess learning or skills that could elicit the interest or answer the needs of anyone but the students who elected his modest courses and the few but discerning readers of his books and articles. Had I remained a specialist in Tudor-Stuart and colonial education, as I began, I'm sure that my expectations would never have been disturbed. My only outing as an (admittedly junior) educational historian of one book was a one-day trip into New York to consult with several senior professors at the American Council of Learned Societies headquarters on the possibility of a cross-cultural history of education, a meeting that bore no fruit.

But when I discovered around 1969 — the same year — that I could not make sense of early America — nor of subsequent and contemporary America — without paying serious attention to its native inhabitants and began to publish in Indian (and ethno-) history, I suddenly, increasingly, and strangely found myself being asked to perform in a variety of extracurricular venues. Had I been free of my own historical blind spot and foreseen the insatiable growth of American interest in (and guilt over) its aboriginal peoples, I might have switched fields sooner to take advantage of the demand. But I was not and could not, because my own awakening coincided with the country's as the natives themselves, particularly savvy and aggressive leaders of the American Indian Movement (AIM), resorted to highly (tele)visible violence, protests, and takeovers to make their case before the court of public opinion when the judicial system failed to hear their ancient and growing grievances.

There probably would have been no demand for my services had I not established first an academic and then an extra-academic reputation in Indian history through publication. Professorial experts who do not publish what they have learned at such pains exercise largely local influence, seldom beyond their own institutions and communities. This brings them invitations to speak mostly before social clubs, service organizations, and self-improvement groups, all of whom require voluntary speakers on a weekly or monthly basis. There *is* a free lunch in America (usually chicken à la king), but it often carries a high hidden cost in preparation and underappreciation.

I had in fact published relatively little in my new, burgeoning field when I was asked to assume the most exciting, high-stakes, and nationally visible role I have ever played. In 1977 my first two books in Indian history were four years from publication, so the Native American Rights Fund (NARF) legal team for the Mashpee tribe chose me as their researcher and expert witness on the early period on the basis of only six articles—on such steamy topics as white captives, Christian missions, attitudes, atrocities, and acculturation in New England, and scalping.

Given my relative youth (thirty-five) and lack of relevant books, I might never have been asked had I not initiated contact with NARF. When I heard in the early spring that NARF was launching a federal case for its Mashpee clients (I was then an NEH Fellow at the Newberry Library and hobnobbed with the fellows of its Center for the History of the American Indian), I wrote to NARF to ask if they knew about the rich Mashpee material in the eighteenth-century manuscripts of the Reverend Gideon Hawley, which were housed in Boston's Congregational Library. I had just read through his corpus as part of my research for a book on colonial missions to the Indians and had, as I remember, no other motive in writing than to indirectly help an eastern Indian group obtain tardy justice. After an inquiry from NARF and a return résumé, I was hired as their principal historian for the trial scheduled for October in Boston's federal district court, Judge Walter J. Skinner presiding.

The first part of my job was research of a familiar kind, but the second embroiled me in an institution, behavior, thinking, and language totally foreign to my experience and not a little discomfiting. The Mashpees were suing for the return of eleven thousand acres of prime Cape Cod real estate, which had until the middle of the present century remained in native hands and under native control.

By the standards of American jurisprudence (or at least this particular judge's instructions), they were obligated to prove that they were an Indian "tribe" and had been continuously at least between 1790, when Congress passed the Indian Trade and Non-Intercourse Act to prevent the alienation of Indian land without federal approval, and 1976, when the suit was filed. I left the definition of "tribe" to the lawyers and anthropologists and concentrated on reconstructing Mashpee's cultural and political history from the earliest European records of it to 1870. In that year Massachusetts, without federal consent, declared the distinct "Indian District" of Mashpee a town no different from other towns in the commonwealth, its members for the first time required to pay taxes, capable of alienating property to non-Indians, and free to enjoy the alleged benefits of full citizenship.

To prepare for my testimony, I collated and outlined on 4 x 6 note paper the evidence NARF and I had collected in 1,747 pages of legal-sized xerox, by category ("Religion," "Politics," "Kinship") and chronology for ready reference. But I quickly learned that preparing for a public trial—a form of theatre—is little like outlining a narrative history, though both are carefully emplotted for plausibility and persuasion. In a trial the economic and political stakes are much higher than tenure or promotion, and the "reviewers" of one's work—opposing counsel—are seldom interested in accuracy or "truth," only in killing your credibility and winning.

To prevent the defense from succeeding, the three NARF lawyers—Tom Tureen, the legal brains behind the case, Barry Margolin, a young Harvard Law grad, and Larry Shubow, a crack Boston trial lawyer prone to accepting underdog cases—flew me once to Washington and twice to Boston for hard-nosed strategy and prep sessions. Playing the part of opposing counsel James

St. Clair, Nixon's Watergate attorney, and Allan Van Gestel, a high-profile Boston litigator, they went in search of my evidential jugular with ill-disguised glee, hoping to find it first.

What they did not prepare me for was the rough personal handling of cross-examiners and the courtroom tricks they use to hide the weaknesses in their case and to confuse the inexpert jury. One of the major problems with the defense's case was lack of probative evidence and sufficiently expert witnesses. Their documentary exhibits, beyond what NARF had collected, consisted of about thirty pages, none of them the least bit damaging. Their expert on New England's Indian history was currently a fellow at the Newberry Indian Center who had yet to publish anything on the subject and wasn't even working on New England but had published two competent books on Gandhi and India. Their anthropological expert for the modern period was a sociologist who had written a good book on modern Micmacs, a Canadian tribe, but who, because of her known employment by the defense, had to secure sociopolitical data from uncooperative Mashpees under subpoena rather than in the friendly field.

When I was called to the stand in the early days of the trial, I anticipated neither the extent of my personal investment in what I believed to be the historical truth and rightness of the Indians' case nor the pleasure I took from trying to stymie my cross-examiner's clever attempts to discredit me and to lure me into costly error. Since the great preponderance of historical evidence clearly supported our side, attorney Van Gestel had to circumvent or twist it by dragging red herrings before the jury box. For a very long day and a half, he tried to undo the two and a half days I had spent systematically putting the plaintiff's case into evidence. Through one line of questioning, he implied that my employment by NARF was somehow immoral as well as totally destructive of my scholarly objectivity. I assured him that I wouldn't have testified for the plaintiff had I not been satisfied, after studying all the evidence beforehand, that their case was historically correct. He then tried to insinuate that an NEH Fellowship (my second in a row) at the Newberry (to write a book on Indians) made me less qualified to testify as an expert than a fellow of the Indian Center (who had yet to publish anything in Indian history, at least the American kind). In another foray he asked me if I knew specifically what the land-granting policies were in several English towns surrounding Mashpee, which he named seriatim. I told him that I knew what there was to be known about land policies in Mashpee (where most land was held in common) and that the English were well known to have held most land in severalty; my expertise was in Indian policy, not land policy.

Early in his cross-examination, before I fully realized how the game was played, I nearly let my professional pride come unbridled. (The opposition scores big points when it exposes a witness's ego or anger.) One particular series of red herring questions sorely annoyed me because it was obvious (to me, at least, and I hoped to the jury) that this very highly paid attorney for the title surety companies—one of ten lawyers sitting at the defense table—had no interest whatever in historical verity but only in winning his case. So I replied, "If you can show me the relevance of those questions, I would be happy to answer them." When Judge Skinner gently but promptly reminded me that it was counsel's prerogative, not the witness's, to ask questions in a court of law, I realized that I was not engaged in a classroom debate or attending a session at the annual meeting of the American Historical Association and would have to play by different rules.

The best hand I had to play was a thorough knowledge of Mashpee's history to 1870. But that history was long, complex, and detailed and I had not committed every word of it to memory. Fortunately, expert witnesses, particularly historical ones, are not required to rely solely on their memories, as eyewitnesses are; they are allowed to consult notes and the documents that have been placed in evidence by either side. So when Van Gestel asked rapid-fire questions in hopes of tripping me into contradiction or damaging admissions, I slowly and deliberately resorted to my sheaf of notes for precise names, dates, and quotations—and noted with secret pleasure his facial register of frustration.

After four days in the hot seat and plenty of media coverage locally and nationally (in retrospect, a phone interview with National Public Radio's Scott Simon was my favorite), I returned half-eagerly to the quiet obscurity of my Northwestern classroom. The trial went on for a total of forty-one days. After confusing, conflicting, and often esoteric testimony from scads of scholars and Indian people, the twelve white jurors drew a nonsensical conclusion and found that the plaintiff had not proven its case.

Judge Skinner had been no help to the jury or to the Indians. He did not establish a definition of "tribe" for the jury's use until after the presentation of evidence, and his choice of definition was outdated, unhistorical, and transparently skewed against the plaintiff.

Then he instructed the jury to decide whether the Mashpees had constituted a tribe according to that definition on six specific dates (day, month, and year) in the political history of Massachusetts between 1790 and 1870. The jurors managed to recall compelling evidence of tribalness for only the middle two dates. This implied that the Mashpees—who were unarguably Indians in the seventeenth century and at the trial and admittedly had always lived in the same location—had somehow slipped out and in and out again of tribal being in a matter of just eighty years. I was, of course, disappointed that justice—as I saw it—was not done the Mashpees. Although the outcome confirmed my (probably elitist) lack of faith in the jury system in cases involving complex historical and intellectual questions, I did take pleasure in testing my scholarly mettle against some of the shrewdest minds in the legal profession and in communicating, however briefly, my interpretation of Mashpee's unique history to a sizable national audience. In that distinctly pre-postmodern courtroom, I also received a strong hint that the "truth" is a slippery trophy and that there is always more than one way to play the game. I remain convinced, however, that enforceable rules of fair play must be agreed upon and that raw power, rhetorical tricks, and sheer self-regard cannot decide the "winners."[1]

The audience an expert witness can reach in court and in the resulting media coverage is, while potentially national in scope, relatively small and evanescent compared to the number of "students" historical museums reach annually and often repeatedly. Newspaper readers and radio listeners usually receive very short, one-stop history lessons from those media, and the lessons are not even scripted or controlled by the historian. Museum exhibits, on the other hand, are sustained, multimedia narratives which, like giant, illustrated books, are capable of instructing (and entertaining) prodigious numbers of visitors of all ages and more than once. While the professor appearing in a news story has only a very few minutes or even sound bites to get his lesson across, the academic designer or guest curator of a museum exhibit can count on having his audiences' full attendance if not attention much longer, though not indefinitely and only briefly—less than half a minute on average—at any one case or segment.

The designer's challenge, therefore, is to prolong the visitors' engagement with the exhibit's story line by keeping it relatively, but not misleadingly, simple and by appealing to more than one of their senses. Although history museums, unlike books, are fueled by material artifacts from the past, those primary sources must be given resonant contexts and embedded in a coherent narrative of significant processes and events. Such a narrative will inevitably include words on panels and labels, but in a state-of-the-art museum it should also be imaginatively plotted and fashioned from visual images, sounds, and even smells and touchable surfaces. The sensory stimulation and reinforcement promoted by a skillful museum exhibit so efficiently and effectively conveys its intellectual message that even college professors are well advised to take a page or two from the museum book in teaching their more complex, often more abstract courses on the distant and foreign past.

In the 1980s I was invited to participate in the narrative and visual design of two history museums largely because my teaching and writing had already borrowed profitably from the museum world. In both books and classroom, I had learned to blend material artifacts and visual images (and in teaching, even historical tastes and aromas) into the familiar stream of words. I had also sought to make my narratives only as complicated and long as they needed to be for historical accuracy and to fashion a writing and cognitive style aimed at able college sophomores, yet accessible to younger audiences and challenging to older ones.

The first museum to take a flier on this interested but untested academic was the Rochester Museum and Science Center, which was building a 7-million-dollar, three-story addition to its handsome but crowded quarters in western New York. We were not exactly strangers. By the fall of 1984, when I was first approached, I had attended for many years the annual gatherings of the Conference on Iroquois Research with Charles Hayes, the research director, Betty Prisch, curator of anthropology, and other staffers. I had also just spent two days during the summer going through its unmatched series of Seneca Iroquois archaeological materials from c. 1540 to the Revolution (which I knew partially and at second hand from several excellent RMSC publications) and some of its ethnographic collections from the last two centuries.

As chance would have it, the museum was planning a 5,500-square-foot exhibit in the new wing called "At the Western Door: Seneca Indians, Europeans, and Americans in the Genessee Valley," to complement and update the older ethnographical exhibits on the second floor and to honor the *longue durée* of the region's native inhabitants. When Charlie Hayes asked me and several other museum and academic experts to critique a staff-generated outline and script, I readily accepted.

Three weeks later I sent back six pages of general comments and 142 specific suggestions; these included ideas for visuals and additional artifacts, which came from my daily habit of showing slides for at least half an hour in my lecture classes. I found the overall plot compelling but noted some imbalance of treatment, lack of audio presentations and especially printed quotations from primary sources, and the need for editing and rewriting to give a single, simpler voice to the lengthy, technically daunting labels and panels produced by several hands. A week later, Charlie called to ask if I would serve as the senior editor-writer to give that voice to the final script. According to Virginia Najmi, the renovation planning coordinator, my book *The European and the Indian* had been "an inspiration from the very early days of the project," partly because of its accessible style, partly because of its "confident approach to cross-cultural analysis"—one of those rare, unsolicited, and totally unexpected testimonials that warm the cockles of writers' hearts. But now I had to deliver in a terse new medium—artifact labels (40 words maximum), secondary panels (110 words), and exhibit and theme unit introductions (130 words)—for an unimaginably large, heterogeneous, and distractable audience of over four hundred thousand visitors a year.

The following March I was sent a new outline of the exhibit's core on contact between Senecas and Euro-Americans, which incorporated additional suggestions from outside reviewers and staff changes. After penciling comments on the manuscript, I urged the staff writers to eschew the venerable but illogical use of the singular denomination of plural tribes ("the Seneca were . . .") and to save space and face by calling the natives "Indians" (which most of their descendants prefer) rather than "Native Americans" (a government neologism).

Two months later, in May, museum officials held a crucial series of meetings with Seneca leaders to hear their reactions to the
latest script. Chief Corbett Sundown of the Tonawanda reserva-
tion spoke for the majority when he objected to the display of any
consecrated masks used formerly or currently in the False Face
religion. Fortunately for the exhibit planners, masks made for
commercial sale were acceptable; we could not imagine explaining the power and longevity of Seneca religion without them and
their Husk Face cousins. Other spokespersons suggested that, because many artifacts in the exhibit came from native graves, provenience labels should say simply "from Seneca sites" rather than
describe the artifacts as "grave goods" or "offerings for the dead."
Museum officials were delighted by the leaders' thoughtful spirit
of cooperation and their suggestions, and I, as editor and historical ombudsman, was especially grateful for their near-unanimous
dislike of "Native American."

The big job of shaping, shortening, and harmonizing the
contact-period script came in the summer, mercifully, after
classes ended. One important task, for which happily I was prepared by my own research in Iroquois history and culture, was
to incorporate appropriate quotations from contemporary historical writings into the secondary panels and on separate panels
for spotlighting. I had sold the museum planners on the use of
original quotations to spice up and authenticate the impersonal
paraphrase of exhibit prose by pointing to their effective employment in the 22,000-square-foot museum at Ste. Marie-among-
the-Hurons, the reconstructed seventeenth-century Jesuit mission near Midland, Ontario; after three visits and careful study of
its planning, I regarded it as the best historical museum in eastern
North America.

I quickly learned that, until the exhibit cases are constructed
and the labels and panels have to be laser-etched and silk-
screened on them, the "final script" is a misnomer. In September
and again in May of the following year (1986), I took the oppor-

tunity to make more revisions, applying a red pencil remorselessly to my own deathless prose after each period of salutary separation. For once your words are locked behind exhibit glass, they are as difficult to change as those locked in book type. Still, two years passed before the thirty-three-case show opened in May 1988. Later that summer I got my first look at our joint handiwork. Even spotting a heart-stopping typographical error in one of the panels could not spoil my enjoyment of and admiration for the exhibition, with its six audio-narrated tableaux of figures modeled after living Senecas, two thousand well-chosen objects in inventive settings, walk-in 1790s log cabin from Tonawanda, fifteen-minute audiovisual presentation on "Being Seneca" today, and ubiquitous panel descriptions for children and the blind.

My second museum stint also began in the fall of 1984, when I was invited with three archaeologists to help Jamestown Festival Park begin to plan a renovation of its two-gallery museum and the building of a new "Virginia Indian Gallery." The project was long overdue. The park had been built by the state in 1957 to commemorate the 350th anniversary of the English founding of Jamestown. The theme had been egregiously celebratory and ethnocentric. An Old World Pavilion featured campy tableaux of Elizabethan and Jacobean Englishmen arriving in America to save the "virgin land" from savagery and to spread the blessings of representative government and Christian religion. Indians had no role save as hostile impediments (like the environment) or as English-loving converts (such as Pocahontas). A New World Pavilion housed an eclectic array of pictures and artifacts to illustrate the contribution to American life made by Virginians, especially eight U.S. presidents. Traces of women (save a mannequin of Good Queen Bess), blacks, ordinary folks, and the downside of English imperialism were scant or nonexistent.

We met in a small conference room which I, a relatively recent transplant from the North, was shocked to learn had not long before served as the "Colored Women's" restroom. Still more problematic was that the new museum had virtually no collections to display, once we quickly decided to restrict its mandate to the seventeenth century. The Civil War cannonballs, presidential busts, and campaign buttons, even the nineteenth-century cypress dugout from North Carolina, were ruled ineligible by our strict new regime. This left us with only a few late-sixteenth-century de Bry engravings of Roanoke, a brooch of suspect Pocahontas provenience, and a small legacy of archaeological Indian artifacts from the National Park Service. Everything else would have to be bought, borrowed, or stolen.

At our second meeting in December, the staff presented a short and general theme outline for discussion, which maintained an ethnocentric focus on the English as the only historical movers and shakers. After years of teaching a lecture course on "The Invasion of North America," I countered with a detailed one-page outline for three integrated galleries (in both senses) with six to twelve subthemes for each. The English Gallery would describe who left the (other) Old World and why. The Powhatan Indian Gallery would describe the native peoples of Tidewater Virginia and how "Indian" culture evolved after migration from Asia. The Jamestown Gallery would narrate the evolution of seventeenth-century Virginia in peace and after war with the natives. Visitors would then exit the renamed Jamestown Settlement—including accurate reproductions of a Powhatan village, the early Jamestown fort, and the three ships that brought the first English—and head to eighteenth-century Williamsburg and Revolutionary Yorktown for a complete and concentrated colonial package.

By May, three new gallery advisory committees, including four Virginia Indian chiefs, had endorsed my proposed scenario, which Mike Puglisi, one of my doctoral students and a museum intern, had begun to flesh out. Unlike the Rochester script, which was largely outlined before I was brought on board, I had an opportunity to help fashion the Jamestown design from the start. I seized the initiative not only because I was the only historian on the committee at the time—and this was a history museum—but because I had suffered through too many faculty meetings without any clear direction or with an excess of political posturing and jockeying. I noticed that he who set the agenda controlled the meeting, and in academe that meant handing out a typewritten sheet so that everyone was literally on the same page. Knowledge of the outline and many of the details of Virginia's intercultural first century did the rest.

To induce the planners to reify the script as I envisioned it, I persuaded the trustees and leading staff members to visit Ste. Marie-among-the-Hurons during the summer of 1985. When they returned, one of the trustees, an influential member of the Virginia General Assembly, boasted in the press that Virginia "can outdo that with no trouble at all," which I considered a good (if windy) omen. When the state appropriated 5 million dollars for a 30,000-square-foot facility, I began to feel cautiously confident that we could build a true rival to Ste. Marie or even surpass it.

While curator Dan Hawkes imaginatively and resourcefully assembled period artifacts from around the world, partly with 690,000 dollars in private funds, Mike Puglisi researched and wrote three- to six-page "position papers" on the exhibit subthemes. The staff then prepared increasingly detailed theme outlines, which I was asked to critique and refine. Actual ground was broken in October 1987, and in late November the exhibit design firm sent instructions for writing texts that had a familiar ring. Panel copy, they said, should be seventy-five to one hundred words, object labels only fifty. "Use simple, direct words that a child would understand (text does not have to read like a first-grade primer; just be careful not to use words or phrases that only a Ph.D. candidate would understand.)" Whether this was an oblique warning to the professors on the advisory committee or one of their graduate students on the research staff I couldn't tell, but I took its general hint to heart. When I received the staff's rough draft of the text in March 1989, I faced more than one hundred hours of editing, cutting, and rewriting to prepare it for the designers. In the end, since I was teaching full time, I could manage only the Indian and Jamestown Gallery scripts; my colleague in Tudor-Stuart history, Dale Hoak, was persuaded to take on the English Gallery.

The museum opened in April 1990. Today, 450,000 visitors a year perambulate its colorful precincts. Few bother to read all of its texts and labels and most pause less than twenty seconds before any case or exhibit feature. But all are exposed to a carefully constructed historical narrative that can hardly fail — notwithstanding reader-response theorists — to insinuate itself into their individual consciousness or, at worst, their collective unconscious, and some of whose richly illustrated details will undoubtedly stick in their memories. Those who return for a refresher tour may, like re-readers of more conventional books, absorb even more of the anonymous lessons on its walls and in its cases.

Teaching by display is not an art I acquired suddenly in 1984 when major opportunities fell into my lap. I had worked my way up the museological ladder. My apprenticeship had come, inauspiciously enough, during the biweekly brown-bag colloquia that I organized for our graduate students. When they wanted to explore the ever-popular question of "publish or perish," I arranged on our super-long library table exhibits on "The History of a Conference," " . . . an Article," and " . . . a Book." By showing them the whole step-by-step sequence of scholarly production, from first note cards to final product, reviews, anthologizing, and even remaindering, I wanted to demystify the process, to render it more manageable and less threatening, and to suggest that the process itself is as important as the results.

One day I happened to mention these amateur displays to our rare books librarian. She had a short-term vacancy in her small museum and invited me to fill it with an exhibit we soon titled "The Nuts and Bolts of Scholarship: Publishing in Academe." So I mounted the histories of an article and a book with my own publishing artifacts, describing each phase with as much wit as I dared on neatly typed, postcard-sized placards. The number of students and faculty who visited my inaugural foray into museum pedagogy during its month-and-a-half run is, alas, lost to posterity. From personal comments I know that a few curious—or lost—souls managed to see it, appropriately deep in the bowels of the library.

A small amount of experience in one facet of museuming has a way of leading to invitations to acquire more in others. But even without experience, academic experts are often called upon to assist museums. In the Williamsburg area, college colonialists are invited regularly to give training sessions to museum interpreters and staff on subjects about which we are reputed to know something. In 1986 I addressed the folks at Jamestown on "European Attitudes toward Other Races." The previous year, on two separate occasions, I taught a seven-hour minicourse on "Education in Colonial Virginia" for the interpreters and docents at Colonial Williamsburg, complete with final exams and course evaluations. In 1988 I repeated that marathon experience (now happily truncated) with a slide- and artifact-packed course on "Indians of the Eastern Woodlands."

From teaching interpreters and writing labels it is a small step to consulting more generally. After getting my start in Rochester and Jamestown, I was in short order called in by the National Museum of History (Smithsonian), the McCord Museum of Canadian History in Montreal, the Hampton University Museum, and the Winthrop Rockefeller Museum of Archaeology at Carter's Grove (Colonial Williamsburg). My charges were variously to brainstorm a Columbus Quincentenary exhibit, to consult on renovations and expansion, to edit an exhibit catalogue, and to critique an exhibit script and rewrite two large introductory panels on Indian culture. All of these and similar tasks should be considered forms of pedagogical outreach and recognized as such by college administrators, legislators, and the public. They certainly *feel* like teaching.

My museum engagements also led to heavier and riskier involvement with national media, not only at home but in Canada. In the mid-seventies, well before the Mashpee trial, I had been asked to critique two prolix TV scripts on Indian history for Marlon Brando's Black Elk Productions, but the ambitious series never got off the ground. By the late eighties, however, I was being asked to serve as a "talking head" in front of the cameras, far more frequently than I was comfortable with. I do not have a rich, mellow speaking voice suitable for audio transmission, and, while I usually dress presentably (for a professor), my looks would never be mistaken for an anchorman's. I have also seen many an interviewee shoot himself in the foot or land in a peck of public trouble with the devious help of an interviewer bent on controversy. Understandably, I was not overly eager to hear or see myself thrust before millions in media over which I had minimal control.

Nonetheless, on more occasions than I like to remember, I succumbed to tempting opportunities to say my piece, to historicize, to broadcast to unimaginably large audiences some of the learning and lore I normally reserved for my relatively small classes. Radio was the friendliest medium because interviews, often by phone, are much like casual conversations and because I seldom heard the original broadcast and only later winced at the pitch of my voice upon playing a tape sent by the station. Distance also helped: three of my four radio stints were heard exclusively in Canada. In 1987 I talked about the history of scalping through a Canadian Broadcasting Corporation (CBC) station in Alberta. Four years later, many minutes of my bons mots on white images of Indians were heard across the frozen North on a prize-winning two-hour program originating in Winnipeg. Only in the week of Thanksgiving 1995 did faithful public radio listeners in Virginia get an hour-long earful of me and Helen Rountree, the leading authority on Virginia Indians, discussing Indian-white relations in colonial Virginia and New England and the "true" origins of the turkified holiday.

164

In my experience, television has been a much more frustrating and hugely inefficient operation for conveying scholarly knowledge or even opinion. All but one of my half-dozen tangles with it left me convinced that I could find far better ways to spend my time and to get my messages across, even if more traditional audiences were minuscule by comparison.

My first encounter turned out to be the least irksome and certainly had the best results. In October 1989, a crew from England's Granada TV descended upon Williamsburg to shoot some scenes for a major six-part series on "The Shape of the World," a social and cartographic history of imperialism funded by IBM. After lunch with two producers, I was invited to talk on camera about native relations in the colonial East and the difference between English and Indian attitudes toward the land and property. We met later in the afternoon at Carter's Grove, a beautiful eighteenth-century plantation house along the James River, for filming. Without too much delay in setting up equipment and waiting for a photogenic sunset over my right shoulder, we shot about forty-five minutes of my responses to a series of rehearsed questions.

When the program aired worldwide the following April, I was relieved to be seen in not too ponderous a pose (though I did tend to gesticulate as if I were in a classroom). In a one-hour program, I got to teach only a couple of minutes in toto, but those minutes were effectively contextualized and supported by the rest of the material and the learned cast. And the audience stretched appropriately around the globe, as friends' postcards from Hawaii and Australia testified.

Unhappily, the results of my other timid forays into televised teaching diminished steadily. The second one had the potential for considerable gains in public understanding of the proper design and value of museums, at least in Canada, but it was reduced to a typical exercise in prime-time bear-baiting. In October 1989, I spent a week at Carleton University in Ottawa as visiting senior scholar, giving six lectures and talks in five days—another common form of academic outreach. I was excited to be in the capital again also because the new Canadian Museum of Civilization had opened in June and was said to feature bold new designs, exhibits, and technology in its History Hall. But when I went to see it, I was totally disappointed.

The building itself is an architectural gem. Designed by Alberta Indian Douglas Cardinal, its natural curves, slopes, and layers blend beautifully into its site opposite Parliament on the Ottawa River. But partly because of its awesome size (creating fifty-foot ceilings on three hangarlike floors), partly because of its excessive cost for the basics (well over 300 million dollars), and largely because of Director George MacDonald's eccentric philosophy, the history exhibits were a major disaster. Canada's rich and largely rural past was reduced to a three-quarter-scale, outmoded "streetscape," beginning with a Viking landing site in 1000 A.D. and the cutaway of a Basque whaling ship from 1584 and proceeding through a tightly wound trail of all Euro-Canadian and mostly urban structures—houses, shops, fort, sawmill, shipyard—less than half of which were completed. The one indispensable ingredient of a history museum—authentic artifacts from the past—were in shamefully short supply, and replicas (often unlabeled as such) were everywhere, this in keeping with the director's McLuhanesque preference for Disneyland and Epcot Center as models and his view of the national museum's extraordinary collections as "patients in a geriatric hospital on life support." Worse yet, the exhibits that did appear to be complete provided virtually no labels, guides, or information to orient the visitor geographically, chronologically, or historically. In short, they neither educated nor entertained. A few character actors, some recorded sounds, and an occasional TV screen could not redeem the inert, expensive botch.

While I was having dinner with a dissident curator, a CBC reporter happened to call about the mounting criticism of the museum. My host put him onto me and the next day I was interviewed on the radio as a disinterested critic from the States. One thing led to another and the following February "The Fifth Estate," Canada's equivalent of "60 Minutes," invited themselves to Williamsburg to film my complaints about the Canadian Museum of Civilization. We set up in the historical Great Hall of the college's Wren Building. After fiddling interminably with light and sound equipment, we proceeded to shoot and record at least two hours of humorless anatomizing of the museum's flaws and philosophy; the transcript ran to twenty-five single-spaced pages. Then we spent another two hours relocating to another handsome campus building and shooting countless takes of the professor walking artlessly through a colonnade and out a gate, all for filler's sake.

You can't imagine my reaction upon viewing a tape of the show that was beamed to millions of Canadian homes in April. In a sixteen-minute segment, I appeared—mostly grim-lipped—four times, for a total of less than two minutes (if you count my courtyard ramble). None of my specific criticisms of the museum made it off the cutting room floor, only some general remarks about the indispensability of authentic objects and the director's "feel-good" philosophy of the past. Since the big networks assume that the privilege of public exposure is compensation enough, the cost of the six hours I spent to earn two minutes of air time would, in any sensible economy, lead to bankruptcy.

My next two television ventures, both happily offscreen, led to negative results and a real gain only in experience. As soon as I finished filming for "The Fifth Estate," I rushed over to my office to meet another TV crew whose overly complicated scripts I had been editing for several months. They had arrived to shoot a longish interview with a "scholarly authority" on the Powhatan Indians of Virginia. My cramped, cinderblock office proved unsuitable, so, as a last resort, we moved to my house. After endless settings-up, adjustments, and rearranging of furniture, we taped an hour or two of historical chatter before my unsuspecting wife arrived home to find a Hollywood lot in her living room. But all for naught: the show never made it past the "talking head" stage.

Neither did another series, better planned and potentially fascinating if more highbrow, on "The Creative Faculty." After I read several drafts of an intriguing pilot that featured Natalie Zemon Davis discussing "Women on the Margins" (her now-published book), WNET/Thirteen in New York was unable to secure funding and the project folded.

Not all of my TV fiascoes were unmitigated. Children and their parents the world over never got to see a "Sesame Street" special on Columbus, Indians, and a time-traveling minivan in 1992 because it, too, failed to find enough sponsors. But I had a wonderful two years helping to develop such a show with the talented staff at Children's Television Workshop in New York. Only a brief imbroglio with another advisor over an Afrocentric interpretation of pre-Columbian contacts marred our creative and fun-filled voyage in history miniaturizing. Although our work led nowhere visible, I treasure my autographed picture of Big Bird and a yellow tailfeather, which I keep on my office desk. It has broken more ice with shy students than I could have imagined, which in turn allows me to begin teaching the way most of us prefer, one on one.

To be fair and to promote my main point, I acknowledge that many professors have enjoyed far more success and endured less frustration in their television encounters than I have. Friends have thrived as consultants to and onscreen commentators in the Burns brothers' specials on the West, the Civil War, baseball, and Thomas Jefferson.[2] Others have worked on biographies for the Arts and Entertainment channel and provided learned and lucid introductions to historical films on the History Channel. Still other academics ply their wits and wisdom on a variety of talk shows, Sunday morning news panels, and the six o'clock news when scholarly experts are called for or thought necessary for intellectual ballast. I like to imagine that all of them found the time they expended and the inconvenience they endured worth the results in public influence and pedagogical outreach.

Another relatively large audience for a professor's extracurricular teaching is the readers of local and national newspapers, less when he (or she) is the news than when he is asked to comment on a burning or combustible issue. Talking to reporters is much like giving tutorials, and no matter how much time you spend with them, it is all too easy to get singed or scorched by the results. For historical stories, the time required to paint the big picture and to fill in some of the choice details can be considerable. (Few reporters deign to read your books or articles beforehand.) I've gotten many telephone neck cricks and consumed many office hours telling reporters some of my (published) "trade secrets." On subjects that are still safely immured in the past, I have usually not rued the results; the tutorials were long and apparently clear enough that my messages managed to get through. But when the subject is more contemporary or controversial, the public fallout from a rabble-rousing article, even if my contribution is small and evenhanded—can sometimes induce monastic oaths and often plain ones.

My opinions on the difference between Christianity and native religions (in an area paper), on the ethnohistory and racial mixture of Connecticut Indians (in a Danbury paper), and on the significance of the archaeological discoveries at Jamestown fort (in the *New York Times*) seemed to raise few eyebrows when they were published. But during the Columbus Quincentenary, everyone had an opinion about the admiral and his legacy and didn't hesitate to voice it. As an Indian historian but also chairman of the American Historical Association's Quincentenary Committee, I tried to bring some balance and historical sense to the debate but often found myself between a rock and a hardnose. When I was quoted at some length in *USA Today* under the inflammatory headline "Critics of Columbus 'are not historians,'"

I'm sure that many Indians and their advocates were not amused, just as many white readers of my critiques of hypocritical missionaries, shady traders, and xenophobic settlers are not. The same Indians probably also took umbrage at my remarks in a *Washington Post* feature on a native suit to force the Redskins football team to change its racist name. Although I thoroughly agreed with their goal, I disagreed with their historical arguments that "squaw" meant "vagina" in eastern native languages and that "redskin" originated in the early colonial business of paying bounties for enemy scalps.

The sharpest reaction I elicited from newspaper readers resulted from a short comment in an area paper when I agreed that it might not be a bad thing to change the name of v-j Day to something that put less direct onus on the Japanese, who are now our strong allies and biggest trading partner. (Why a colonial historian was solicited for an opinion on such an issue I cannot fathom, but on the telephone one is often seduced into chatting with reporters as if they were just curious people with no agendas.) When I was quoted (out of context) as saying that "There are no real victors in any world war"—referring, of course, to the huge losses of life, time, and property that all sides suffer, inventive readers rose like hornets, particularly ex-servicemen who populate the base-filled peninsula where we live. My favorite response was a misspelled, hand-printed letter from an alumnus who claimed to have removed William and Mary from his million-plus-dollar will as a reaction to my "muddy-minded machinations" and "prattle-headed notions." (Our president kindly assured me that no such bequest was on record and probably was never intended.) Happily (so far), course evaluations by students have not elicited such stinging endorsements.

Another class of supplicants who sometimes require the written equivalent of tutorials—and who, on occasion, can also dent an author's ego with their own productions—are students who write to request historical or biographical information. If a scholar reaches *un certain âge* and reputation, he (or she) may become the subject of historiographical or research seminar papers or even theses and dissertations. This fate requires him to respond to semiflattering inquiries from graduate students, undergraduates, and even high schoolers for full vitae (the *Directory of American Scholars* is woefully out of date and various biographical compilations are seldom adequate) and answers to sometimes quite personal questions about one's life and work. On the five or six occasions when I've been put on the spot, I've retaliated by asking for the final paper. Apparently, the courses are well taught because each student has eschewed panegyrics for hardheaded evaluation of their subject's work, sniffing out biases, blemishes, and omissions with disconcerting perspicacity.

More typically, outside requests seek historical information or bibliography, and a return phone call or short note suffices. But sometimes even the best-intentioned academic is at a loss how to respond. A charmingly stilted letter from a graduate student in Japan sought "any small information" about "Native American[s]" because, she said, she had read that William and Mary had been founded to educate Indians and hoped that we might "still keep documents and the like." Since her letter was addressed "to whom it may concern," I used the cloak of anonymity to hide my inability to honor her vague request. I was also forced to ignore another, addressed to my chairperson (a Latin Americanist) by a gung-ho seventh-grader from North Carolina. This young scholar was preparing an entry in the National History Day competition on "Pocahontas: Ambassador of Three Nations." In preparing her "display," she wanted to go beyond mere "historical facts in books" to solicit "expert theories, legends, facts, or opinions that historians believe to be true." To obtain this expert fare, she enclosed a daunting questionnaire containing forty-eight precocious questions, many of which called for article-length answers. Her envelope was dated October 25 and she needed replies by November 10 at the latest. Would that I had been able to respond with the omniscience and alacrity she required. I trust that the chiefs of three Virginia tribes to whom she also wrote were able to improve her previous third-place finish.

By far the greatest number of yellow post-its in my archive document requests to carry individual classes and even mini-courses from my own university to other locations and audiences or, what amounts to the same thing, to invite new audiences to our hallowed halls when the regular students weren't occupying the seats. Thus I have taught history of various complexities to Cub Scouts and Boy Scouts, middle schoolers and high schoolers, California schoolteachers and Connecticut do-gooders, Daughters of the American Revolution and Rotarians, Town and Gowners and Elderhosteliers, homecoming alumni and Yale Clubbers, International Housemates, Chinese scholars in America, and European scholars in Italy, NEH Seminarians and Mellon theoreticians. And like many academics, I have given conference papers in myriad venues (not all of them warm and wonderful) and guest lectures on campuses all over North America.

But the scariest class I have faced consists of the two-, three-, and four-year-olds at my wife's preschool. Every year just before Thanksgiving, I take my courage and a packbasket of props in my hands and attempt to tell the gibbering, wriggling rug-rats the action-packed story of "How the (carved wooden) False Face (mask) got its broken nose" (the Iroquois creation myth). After thirty years of teaching, it remains the sole occasion when my stomach is tied in anticipatory knots: no vaudevillian or Catskill comic ever faced a tougher crowd.

One final category of extracurricular teaching is easy to overlook. Because they are faceless and seemingly impersonal, scholarly publications often fail to be considered pedagogical *occasions* (as opposed to mere *instruments* of instruction). Yet the silent, private, engaged reading of books and articles is potentially an educational encounter of great power and efficiency: virtually all college courses rely on reading to supply even our best performances in the classroom. When professors cannot achieve their best during the fractured, quotidian day, they can send the student into the evening with the most thoughtful, thorough, and eloquent realizations of their and their colleagues' efforts to teach their subjects and values. The collegian's attention span being what it is, it is safe to say that more learning takes place over those black-and-white pages, in the synapses of the student brain, than in the most Socratic seminar or the best-delivered technicolor lecture.

Moreover, publications extend one's pedagogical reach geometrically. Although they are not and were not intended to be bestselling textbooks, which circulate in the tens and hundreds of thousands, five of my Indian books have modestly sold more than ten thousand copies apiece and are still plugging along. They have therefore already reached more students than I will ever teach in the classroom in a lifetime. And I'm reasonably confident that the quality of thought and expression in my chapters exceeds that in my outlined but largely ad-lib lectures.

Books and articles teach other professors as well as their students, who learn from them indirectly through lectures based on them or directly through assignments in them. They move freely across campuses, borders, and oceans, rendering the community of scholars and learners coterminous with the globe. At their best, they are our best teachers, capable of informing, absorbing, and inspiring the least studious and most scholarly. When legislators, editors, and other critics of higher education facilely call for more professorial time in the classroom, they should realize that modern college teaching takes myriad forms and occurs in many places, and that the quiet library can be the liveliest classroom on campus.

CHAPTER TEN

College Towns

A university is a strange country
and a privileged one.
George Whalley

R ETIRED ALUMNI know it, faculty families know it, and their lay inhabitants know it—college towns are unusually attractive and enlivening places to live. They are a special breed of urban animal, for historical reasons far more plentiful in the United States than elsewhere. Many, perhaps most, grew up beside their collegiate institutions, which were attracted to their sites by old-fashioned Chamber of Commerce-style boosterism in the eighteenth or nineteenth century. In the westering nation, communities recruited immigrants by proffering the prestige and economic prospects of a newspaper and a college. In turn, these "Athenses of the West" vied with one another to attract the most promising college by offering free land, tax exemptions, and lump sums. Literally hundreds of American communities began life as college towns, while in centralized Europe universities were concentrated in a few ancient cities.

Despite the nation's periodic spasms of anti-intellectualism, college-town fathers continued to regard their institutions as boons to the local economy and sources of communal pride. Students had to be fed, clothed, housed, and entertained—for a price, and the faculty comported themselves for the most part with unobjectionable middle-class dignity. Even when the colleges sublimated or left behind their denominational origins, and presidents, trustees, and faculty were no longer recruited from the clergy, their towns traded on their associations with men of learning and institutions of higher education.

College Towns

In the nineteenth century, many towns—perhaps 60 percent of them—lost their collegiate character when their frail institutions failed for lack of students or support. Today, while the United States boasts nearly thirty-seven hundred institutions of higher education, including two-year community colleges, many college towns have evolved into larger, more complicated communities whose dependence on their local colleges for economic viability and communal identity has diminished. Indeed, the tandem evolution of the postindustrial economy and of higher education has transformed some of the best examples of college towns into university towns, whose service economies no longer depend solely on student populations and whose general economies are based on much more than service.

What makes these towns special? Why are the best of them—Ann Arbor, Chapel Hill, Princeton—growing so fast with educated retirees, high-tech industrial parks, and yuppified commuters that their distinctive character is being endangered by the dilution?

The first two things you notice driving into a college town are the large-scale buildings of the campus and the generous variety of green spaces that separate and decorate them. Most college campuses are little "academical villages" (as Thomas Jefferson called his new creation in Charlottesville), self-contained and self-sufficient. Their buildings are larger and more monumental than even the commercial establishments of the town, thanks largely to the economy of scale necessary to accommodate hundreds or thousands of students away from the support systems of home. But generous benefactors with a taste for memorial grandeur, presidents seeking to leave their material mark, and architects who took their models from the Classical, Romanesque, or Gothic piles of Europe have also contributed to the noble elevations and weighty fabrics of campus buildings. Because most colleges were founded in the nineteenth century and have evolved considerably since then, they usually present a pleasing, if not always harmonious, variety of architectural styles and fashions—from gray-stoned "Collegiate Gothic" and red-bricked Georgian to the least inspired and inspiring flat planes and glass surfaces of boxlike "Modern." In a traditional mode, the no-longer-mandatory chapel (once capable of seating the whole student body) and the more contemporary gymnasium (often capable of doing the same) dominate the architectural scene, now that the original wooden administration building, "Old Main," has likely burned down.

Between, around, and up the college buildings stretch ample sweeps of greenery—broad lawns, old shade trees, shrubs and hedges, and, of course, quintessential ivy growing up the walls, until in recent years cost-conscious groundsmen noticed that its tenacious roots devoured brick and stone and required major repointing and repairs. (Even urban campuses present a green face to the world in hopes of attracting students—or their parents—who want the sophistication and culture of higher education but also the imagined health and purity of the countryside.) Long swaths of verdant playing fields nearby complete the image of the college as well-watered country club or English estate. Out of shame, emulation, or just good sense, the rest of the town tends to be equally protective of green space and foliage. The borough of Princeton is so jealous of its woods and wildlife that it prohibits any hunting within its precincts, even for biological balance. The runaway deer population, which lives off the citizens' gardens and dents many a nocturnal fender, is particularly grateful to the green peace they inhabit.

The most appealing college towns are small enough—towns rather than cities—to be suffused with, if not always dominated by, the college—its physical presence, its faculty, students, and staff, and its spirit and ethos. This is what creates their essential appeal. Collegiate architecture, often timelessly "classical" or reminiscent of the Middle Ages when the university was born, lends a strong note of stability and tradition to the town ringing contemporary changes on Main Street and in outlying malls. Because the college owns so much of the town's real estate, the administration can throw its weight behind slow growth, sensible zoning, and long-range planning. College towns tend to be livable communities, where quality-of-life-conscious faculty and spouses actively encourage racial integration, good public schooling, parks and recreation programs, recycling and other forms of ecological awareness. Some of these "liberal" causes contribute to inevitable town-gown tensions, but most carry the day because they make sound human sense for the whole community and its future.

College towns not only *are* livable, they *look* it because most of them are economically viable and are able to invest with the knowledge that they are likely to remain so. While the non-profit colleges don't pay property taxes, many make annual good-neighbor grants to their towns for municipal services, and all pump substantial sums into their communities' various coffers through the wages they pay their faculty and staff, the supplies and services they purchase locally, and the necessities and amenities of life their students buy off campus. The general level of prosperity is reflected in the town's streets, storefronts, and domestic appearance, which must appeal not only to the full-time campus inhabitants but to a large transient population of parents, alumni, trustees, sports fans, rival teams, prospective students and parents, and tourists. The last alone give Colonial or Early Federal college towns, such as Hanover, Williamsburg, and Princeton, historical and aesthetic reasons beyond college pride to put their best faces forward.

The relative prosperity and large youthful clienteles of college towns endow them with several advantages for producers and consumers alike. Unless the college is totally residential, which very few are, local homeowners and entrepreneurs can make a decent income renting rooms, apartments, and houses to students and young faculty, even though the former tend to raise

the overhead in noise, wear, and tear. By the same token, purveyors of new and used rugs, refrigerators, furniture, computers, and
bikes enjoy a ready and nearly captive market every autumn.
Students with cars rent garages, buy gas, need towing, jump-
starting, and repairs, and pay municipal fines for traffic violations,
mostly for parking in the wrong spots when they oversleep for
class. Those without wheels require cabs, limos, rental cars, buses,
trains, planes, and travel agencies to get them in and out of town
for vacations and assignations of various kinds. And the insatiable
appetite of the students for music, clothes, and food carries re-
sidual benefits for the rest of the population.

College towns attract upscale products and franchises—Ben
and Jerry's and Haagen Däs, Reebok and Nike, Benetton and
The Gap. Although fast food and pizza emporia invariably
abound, as they do in most towns, local families who are not
afraid of youthful exuberance gravitate to the student-oriented
eateries that festoon every good college town, mostly Asian, Italian, and mixed American with reasonable prices. The patronage
of well-traveled college palates fosters and allows the survival of
more varieties of international restaurants and food stores than
most towns can support. The best college towns also offer a selection of cafés and coffeehouses, where students and faculty can
stretch out a conversation or a liaison with a book and no one
hurries them along. Music stores carry the latest CDs in pop, rock,
rap, and country, but the college ear for classical ensures that they
also carry less-expensive tapes in that mode for the unhip faculty
who haven't graduated to ultra sound. The major presence of a
music school or department creates an additional market for sheet
music and instruments, as an art or architecture program does for
art supplies.

Ever since I set my college-bound sights on Yale in the late
fifties, I've regarded college towns as dependable oases of "Ivy
League" style in the shifting sands of sartorial fashion. Today as
thirty years ago, I dress for the classroom in a uniform as stock

178

and traditional as that of a Catholic parochial or English public school: khakis, tweed sportcoat (with elbow patches as it matures), button-down Oxford cloth shirt, and silk foulard or rep tie. When I was in high school, the closest source of these articles, which I had carefully researched in the "Going Back to College" issues of *Esquire* and the early tame *Playboy*, was Cornell's Ithaca, by car a good two and a half to three hours over hill and dale. Soon I learned to take advantage of the summer sales at J. Press in New Haven and Paul Stuart, Brooks Brothers, and Rogers Peet in New York. Today, I'm likely to order my mufti from a Land's End or L.L. Bean catalogue or to fetch it from the local Brooks Brothers outlet. But I still enjoy most the sales at "traditional" clothiers in the college towns and cities we visit on our summer drive to Maine. My collegiate sons and students, on the other hand, are just as happy to purchase their unplanned wardrobes from unisex Gaps, Banana Republics, and (when they can be found in our increasingly peaceful world) army and navy surplus stores. Happily, college towns cater to both generations and are still able to profit from both.

College and high school students are the most visible beneficiaries of college-town prosperity—they scoop the ice cream, peddle the pizzas and CDs, and model the clothes. But the well, sometimes highly, educated spouses of the college faculty—male and female—and the increasingly educated spouses of the rest of the town's employees may also have an easier time applying their talents than they would in most American towns of a similar size. If they are not employed by the college as support staff or administrators (which many are), they often teach school, tutor, run libraries, museums, or foundations, do freelance editing or desktop publishing, give music, dance, or art lessons, or write newsletters for professional groups or columns for the local newspaper. In our almost mandatory two-salary economy, spouses with regular and fulfilling jobs contribute immeasurably to the quality of life as well as the standard of living of college towns.

As a growing proportion of the American population attends four-year colleges and universities, the places where they decide to live after graduation will also be expected to provide some or all of the cultural advantages of the college towns they have come to know. For beyond the classroom, most college graduates have been exposed to a rich array of intellectual and cultural resources normally found in such profusion only in larger, less convenient, and more expensive cities. One of the major reasons for the recent return of retired alumni to their alma mater towns is their desire to remain intellectually active. The proliferation of Elderhostel and continuing education programs in attractive college towns, both in the summer and during the academic year, testifies to an unsatisfied hunger among a growing and increasingly savvy segment of the population, a hunger that college towns are uniquely capable of feeding.

The college, of course, is the major source of cultural sustenance, not to mention sheer entertainment in various guises. Visiting and local lecturers cast their pearly wisdom before public audiences almost daily; if they show slides, so much the better. Poets and novelists come to read their latest creations, sometimes in several-days-long writers' festivals. I will never forget the sonorous renderings of the ancient Robert Frost at Yale in 1961 and the electrifying, poetizing, convocation speech of Maya Angelou at William and Mary some thirty years later, nor will the numerous townspeople who helped fill the vastness of Woolsey and William and Mary Halls. Less-famous and somewhat less-spellbinding authorities periodically dispense their knowledge of and enthusiasm for everything from cold fusion and hot music to Victorian divorce rates and the sex lives of dung beetles. When historical anniversaries roll around, you can be sure that the college will commemorate them with experts (usually academic) whose latest books may be purchased in the lobby or at the college bookstore. None of this is bad. The college lecture circuit is the academic author's equivalent of five-minute spots on "The Today

Show" or "David Letterman," except that college hawking lasts the standard fifty minutes of classroom lectures and is, to all appearances, less brazenly mercenary. If the lecturer manages to pique the audience's interest in pursuing the subject further, surely a pittance of university press royalties will not damage his scholarly integrity, even if he is asked to sign the books like some rock star or Nobel prizewinner. It's as close to soul-warping hubris as most lecturers are likely to come.

If college towners have heard enough lectures as undergraduates to last a lifetime, they can always opt for listening to local or imported musical performances. All colleges have accomplished and budding musicians on their faculties and in their student bodies, and most have music departments that regularly showcase their talents. Toward the end of the academic year, the campus newspaper is filled with announcements of upperclassmen and -women giving recitals. College choirs, glee clubs, chamber groups, bands, and orchestras perform at least once a year; holiday concerts abound. If the college alone can't satisfy the town's appetite for good music, many colleges and most universities offer concert series of guest performers. At William and Mary the concert series is always sold out within two or three days of being announced, with good reason. For a modest sum, subscribers are treated to moving Verdi and Puccini by the New York City Opera Company, virtuoso Mozart by the Hungarian String Quartet, and subtle renditions of Beethoven and Bartók by Ruth Laredo. Colleges such as Oberlin with first-class music schools, of course, can offer even more variety and depth in their musical menus.

The dramatic and plastic arts also flourish in college towns. Universities with graduate drama schools offer first-rate theatre for less-than-Broadway prices, but even modest-sized colleges provide outlets for neophyte actors and actresses. Some student productions reach the level of true art; most never make it because even "the willing suspension of disbelief" cannot enable audiences to accept that college-age bodies and voices belong to middle-aged or elderly characters, but the theatrical experience endures. College grounds often sport outdoor sculptures of variable quality, student and professional. I remember the artistic stir caused at Yale by Claes Oldenburg's giant vertical lipstick mounted on an army tank-bed ("Make Love, Not War"?) in the broad granite courtyard near the president's office. At several colleges, among them Princeton and William and Mary, are cleverly placed, startlingly lifelike bronze sculptures by J. Seward Johnson, Jr. of students reading or eating lunch, perhaps for the benefit of college tours when the real things are absent.

Another stop on those backward-guided excursions is the college art museum, maintained less for blockbuster show than as a tangible course in the history of art. Collections, therefore, tend to be broad and selective rather than deep or rich. Few college or university museums enjoy the world-class status of Yale's Mellon Center for British Art, Indiana's African collection, or Colby's Winslow Homers, the gifts of major collectors and philanthropists. But many host specialized traveling shows or mount special theme exhibits of their own and borrowed objects, which are always open and usually free to the community. Countless schoolchildren have learned to appreciate art and art museums in their local college galleries, which stands them in good stead when they move or retire to their former college towns or visit the Big City.

Even after the video revolution and the advent of myriad movie channels, connoisseurs of film continue to be fed by college film festivals and series and by small arts theatres that seem to survive, if no longer thrive, in college towns. Outside cities of some size, only college towns offer their denizens regular exposure to foreign-language and experimental films. The serious classroom study of film as an art form and the video-expanded tastes of the young create appreciable audiences for large-screen showings, which are shared with noncollege aficionados. In the sixties my wife and I were first exposed to the heavily symbolic cogitations of Bergman and Fellini in New Haven's little Lincoln Theatre, tucked away between a residential neighborhood and an interstate. Today, when the mood strikes, we resort to the arty (and subsidized) Williamsburg Theatre downtown to see Australian, Japanese, and Brazilian flicks which the other ten shopping-center cinemas in town eschew for Hollywood or, at best, British fare.

Fortunately, college towns are not unremittingly highbrow; they provide a large measure of sheer entertainment that noncollege towns simply do not. Student high jinks occur at any time, but sports events can be anticipated. Division I-A teams obviously provide the most proficient and most expensive entertainment of the kind, short of professional clubs (which, sadly, some of them virtually are). But some of the most watchable and enjoyable sports are played by truly amateur athletes—male and female—at colleges of all sizes and at small universities, where fans have some chance of knowing all the players, not just the highly publicized and highly subsidized stars. The lower-division lack of perfection and size promotes a more razzle-dazzle, open style of play that leads to surprises and plenty of scoring. And you can always get a seat in a college stadium or gymnasium, even when a ticket costs a fraction of what Big Ten or PAC-10 fans have to pay. Ivy League marching bands, among others, are notoriously unafraid to milk sacred cows while blowing on their horns, a witty (if ribald) way to spend a halftime. And what child within us doesn't love the onfield or courtside antics of a floppy, oversized mascot impersonating a Brown bear or a Princeton tiger?

Equally diverting are the rites surrounding college games and events. Old-fashioned pep rallies with towering bonfires still illuminate autumn night skies in many college towns. Homecoming parades are nearly universal. When undergraduates unleash their imaginations, they can create floats and routines that stick in the memory—and sometimes the craw—of the least nostalgic alum. My favorite entry in William and Mary's homecoming parade is "The Kappa Sigma Lawnmower Drill Team," which annually puts a fleet of silent Toros through militarily-precise maneuvers down Duke of Gloucester Street. The Redcoats who lost the town in 1781 would be proud.

Student escapades, such as T.P.ing the local police station or reassembling a VW Beetle on the chapel roof, can erupt in any college town, depending on the exam schedule, the weather, and serendipity. For my money, the good citizens of Princeton enjoy—or perhaps endure—the jolliest and freest collegiate spectacles. One is the June reunion "P-rade," in which the reuning classes "march" through town and campus in every conceivable costume of black and orange, accompanied by a circus-like montage of caged tigers, donkeys, elephants, stilt-walkers, hand-walkers, marching and Dixieland bands, unicyclists, antique cars, and antiquer alums. All of which is pretty tame compared to the "Nude Olympics," in which male and female sophomores drop their clothes and streak through the town and a restaurant or two at midnight on the occasion of the first snow. After the local constabulary resorted to video cameras, the athletes counterattacked with ski masks and camouflage for telltale birthmarks. The arrest rate dropped precipitously, much to the delight of late-night townspeople, who can never be persuaded to press charges. Some college-town entertainment is just too good to miss.

Despite the fun and high spirits, college towns are serious places where the production and transmission of knowledge are the major industries; sometimes education is the only game in town. Since universities were founded in the twelfth century and especially since Gutenberg, teaching and learning have proceeded primarily through the written word. As knowledge makers and users, colleges and universities are still overwhelmingly dependent on print. However useful the latest electronic technologies become, machines will always transmit *words* that need to be read and interpreted by human beings. Moreover, the printed book is still, and is likely to remain, the most versatile, user-friendly, and durable technology for the conveyance of thought. If Marshall McLuhan and other students of media revolutions are right, new information technology does not render previous technologies obsolete but simply overlaps them and adapts itself to their best features. The invention of television did not obliterate audiences for radio, nor will computers and the Internet drive readers from their books. Books we shall always have with us, thank goodness, and college towns are a major source of them. For die-hard readers and bibliolaters like me, that's their primary attraction.

In college towns, books can be found in three venues, each with its own assets and liabilities. The largest repository by far is the college library. Today, a decent college or small university library can harbor half a million to two million books and five thousand to thirty thousand periodicals. Readers eager for the hottest titles in pulp fiction or experimental poetry may have to resort to the public library or one of the bemalled chain outlets, but those looking for serious or durable titles in most fields will find them in the college stacks, along with international newspapers and journals in every conceivable subject. For the community patron who walks in from the street, however, the new college library has erected a couple of daunting, though not insuperable, barriers.

One is the high cost of books, replacements, repairs, security, and staff shelving and search time, which most colleges and virtually all universities have reluctantly decided must be shared by all users of the library, not just the tuition-paying students. Libraries that once were open and free to the public—everyone from little old genealogists in tennis shoes to gum-chewing high school students in search of term-paper topics and dates—now routinely charge substantial fees for borrowing privileges and access to the stacks. The more numerous the potential borrowers, the higher the fee. When I was a postdoctoral fellow at Harvard in 1965–66, a library card would have set me back $500 (since my fellowship was only $3500, I chose to use the much smaller but free library at my wife's Wellesley); today the tab for certified "scholarly" access to more than 13 million volumes is $750. In the early eighties, when some 20 percent of its library's users were not members of the university, Princeton decided to levy a $200 fee for access to her 5 million books; today the public pays $128 to visit the books in the stacks and $329 to take them out. In the face of much less demand, William and Mary, a small state university, charges only $50 to join the Friends of the Library, which allows the member to pick and choose among its million-plus tomes. Similarly, in remotest New Hampshire, private Dartmouth charges only $100 for access to its 2 million volumes.

Once the reader gets past the electronic security gates of the library, he or she will encounter not the familiar and friendly card catalogue of yore but a bank of video monitors, keyboards, and "mice," something akin to the control deck of the Starship *Enterprise*. These machines allow—or prevent—access to the nirvana of print in the stacks. The problem is finding the "open sesame" formula to unlock the books' call numbers, locations, and availability status (one item the card catalogue did not provide). For first-time users, computer jargon can be intimidating and baffling, even when simple directions appear on the screen or on a printed card nearby. (This assumes, of course, that the whole system isn't "down" for one esoteric reason or another.) But friendly students or a reference librarian will soon calm their nerves and have them on their way to computerized catalogue competence and the targeted shelves.

The second source of books is retail bookstores, including the college's own. The difference between the new-book stores in college towns and in other towns is the academic character of the titles they carry. Every retailer stocks, at least briefly, the books that appear on "Oprah" and the *Times* bestseller list; since those are virtually all that discount chain stores carry, academic bookstores don't waste much space on them, knowing they can't compete in price. This leaves the serious book market to college-town stores and, increasingly, to mega-serious chain stores such as Border's, Wordsworth, and Barnes and Noble. In both types of stores, the staff knows the stock (which competence can no longer be taken for granted), the scholarly stock is large if not awesome, and ordering is fast and efficient because of the computer and UPS.

As a certified book nut who must bear with a college library that cannot buy every book published or catalogue it yesterday, I am a severe critic of bookstores and probably not a typical customer. Only in the best college towns (or university neighborhoods of cities) can I find most of the titles I want when I want them. In fact, I no longer darken the doors—or pull-down grates—of outlet stores because they are invariably frustrating. Stores that stock more remainders, nonbooks, tapes, and literary T-shirts than real books are high on my list of "Things Wrong with America."

Yet even the best academic bookstores have two drawbacks, at least to my aging faculty mind. First, they sell only new books, which to a scholarly book collector is a major (though not fatal) flaw. Scholars, particularly in the humanities, like old books, used books, more than the latest (and expensive) emanations from the academic brain. And historians prefer primary sources to all others, the documents left by generations past, most of which go out of print with sad regularity. Such books simply are not found in retail bookstores, no matter how large.

The second drawback is that a growing majority of even cloth-bound books are no longer Smyth-sewn for durability and ease of opening but are glued in a horribly misleading "perfect binding." This means that after very little handling, thirty- and forty-dollar books begin to fall apart at the seams, all because the publishing industry seeks to save fifty cents to a dollar and a little time on binding. When Detroit acted like that in the fifties, Japanese automakers left our false economies and "planned obsolescence" in the dust. I am waiting for some commercial David to topple the greedy Goliaths of Gotham with a little thread and an aggressive "truth-in-advertising" campaign.

Finally, there are used bookshops, to me the ultimate bonus of a good college town. People who are content to read only new or library books find it difficult to understand why, for other readers, nosing through used bookshops is one of life's sovereign pleasures. What's so great about them? They're usually dusty and cramped, with piles of books in the aisles and on the windowsills. By definition, the stock has all been handled by former owners and, by custom, its arrangement on the shelves displays a cunning logic accessible to few. Prices range from the sublime to the ridiculous. And the proprietor of so many words is either taciturn to the point of rudeness or profligate with his (less frequently her) own. These may sound like drawbacks, but they are merely challenges to the serious book collector. For he is on a lifelong quest, a search for bibliographical truffles wherever they can be found. Ambience, cleanliness, and chatter mean nothing; the condition of the book (pristine is not expected), its rarity (the harder to find, the better), its price (reasonable, if not a bargain), even its provenience (former discerning owners) are all that matter. If time is short, a certain degree of organization and verbal guidance is appreciated; if it is not, an extra frisson comes from discovering for oneself a book where it doesn't belong, agreeably underpriced, or sporting a bookplate with special resonance.

But not all used bookstores are alike and they are quickly distinguished: there are used trashy and middlebrow books for a pittance; there are exquisitely priced rare books in beautiful or original bindings; and there are reasonably priced second-hand or review-copy books of an academic sort. Only the last interest most faculty, and most of the best haunts of such titles are found around colleges and universities. The richest hunting grounds for scholarly books I have found in my North American travels are in Berkeley, Ann Arbor, Cambridge, and (because I also write and teach early Canadian history) Toronto. Each town or city around the university offers three or four scholarly bookshops of tantalizing range and depth. Williamsburg, alas, has none, but in earlier locations—New Haven and Evanston—we were well and truly challenged in purse and pocket. Every summer, for old time's sake, we stop at Whitlock's Book Barn, a converted barn and chicken house on a still-working farm in the hills outside New Haven. When I was an undergraduate, the two Whitlock brothers, men of few words and fewer smiles, also ran a decent shop on the university's main drag, two doors down from a first-rate scholar's den; both are now gone to the country and Yalies suffer from the second-hand drought.

In many college towns there is one final source of used scholarly books: college library or alumnae book sales. College libraries regularly receive book donations from alumni, retiring faculty, and local citizens in search of a charitable deduction. Most of the books are already on the shelves, so the library must clear space and raise a little money at least annually by selling the residue. For book lovers these are great challenges and treats because the books are usually arranged on tables and shelves higgledy-piggledy but priced uniformly low—so much for paperbacks (no matter how large or sumptuous), a little more for cloth. Alumnae groups also hold large sales to benefit their colleges. The two most ambitious we ever attended were both organized by the capable women of Bryn Mawr. One was a several-day affair in a jumbo circus tent near Evanston; a marginally smaller one was held in a New Haven church hall. Both were well arranged by subject, and items were individually priced, always in the buyer's favor. The major challenge in all these happy venues is to avoid being trampled and maimed by voracious book dealers and under-nourished graduate students, both of whom give nothing away to pro halfbacks in the stiff-arm department.

People are drawn to college towns not only because of their

physical attractions, economic well-being, and cultural resources, but because of the bookish and brainy people who live there, particularly the college faculty who in large measure give the place its essential character. But this is a tricky business because the professorial species today no longer fits the pipe-smoking Dr. Chips stereotype of the late forties and fifties, when today's youngest retirees were in college, but is considerably more varied in gender, race, class, and attitude, though probably not much more in behavior.

Professors are still an intelligent, literate, well-traveled, articulate, opinionated, self-confident lot whose schooling and scholarship have made them authorities on one or more subjects and sometimes (they think) the world in general. Maybe not individually but collectively they represent cultural sophistication and intellectualism, qualities presumably held in esteem by alumni and others who choose to move to college towns. At least initially, every transplant expects the level of conversation, the values, and the general tone of the town to be higher than in the non-college towns they came from. They expect the local newspaper to be editorially more thoughtful and grammatical, town council meetings to rise above mere politics, the public schools to be guided by enlightened pedagogical principle rather than benighted pencil-pushing principals.

Sometimes, perhaps often, they find what they are looking for. Professors who correct myriad blue books and term papers are likely to keep the local editor's feet to the fire over the niceties of style, logic, and political right-mindedness. Aroused faculty members who enter the political fray are able on occasion to appeal to history or higher principle with disarming articulateness. And professional higher educators are often capable of offering sound counsel to, and setting broader policy than, school administrators trapped in education-school dogma and quotidian bureaucracy. Certainly faculty families care about education and community standards more than most, and many invest themselves in the battle for both.

But even the most dreamy newcomers soon discover that having a passel of professors for neighbors is not always what it was cracked up to be. Let's face it: eggheads are an odd lot. No longer exclusively the WASP male of yesteryear, the don next door could easily wear a skirt, turban, yarmulke, or motorcycle jacket, inhabit black, brown, or saffron skin, and live with a same-sex partner. Then there are his or her work habits. Who else in town jogs or plays tennis during business hours, "works," that is, teaches, six or eight hours a week, burns the midnight oil at a desk night after night, and wastes ridiculously long vacations immured in the college library, a dusty archive, or an airless lab?

We don't like to admit this, but professors can be not only odd, they can be flawed. For all their IQs, learning, and savoir faire — or perhaps *because* of them — they also have a professional tendency to smugness, arrogance, and priggishness. This is the down side of college-town existence. If you are not a member of the doctored elite but only a businesswoman or househusband, it is possible to find yourself being regarded down a long professorial nose. In a college town, the faculty are in their element and their circle typically is not very wide.

And yet, for all the faculty's faults and foibles, college towns have a seductive ambience. Professors don't have to be conventional and hale-fellows-well-met (though many are) to be acceptable, even admirable, neighbors or to serve as powerful models of studied high-mindedness, commitment, and learning for the rest of the community. It should be enough that their lives and works give others, young and old alike, the inspiration to seek their best selves in the realms of mind and spirit and the courage to risk intellectual adventure.

But the faculty are not alone responsible for defining the character of their towns, nor are they the most visible movers and shakers. Academical villages are appealing also because they are infused with the colorful imaginations, high energy, and openness to change of an eternally youthful cohort. The presence of graduates and undergraduates ensures that the normally aging town is constantly rejuvenated, or at least persuaded that idealism, spirit, and growth are not and should not be monopolies of the young.

By example as well as precept, colleges and universities teach us the possibility of a better life, a life of real community and worthy pursuits beyond matter and money, and college towns benefit uniquely and directly from that high example. Even when their inhabitants fail to live a pure text, they honor the life of the mind that thrives in their midst and appreciate that the heart of the community beats to an academic rhythm. Every September, when the students reappear, the town is glad to renew its identity with the college because that institution speaks to and for many of its highest and freest aspirations.

CHAPTER ELEVEN

Academic Vacations

Academics are not the most
entertaining traveling companions,
not in the long run anyway.
Henrik Ibsen

A FEW YEARS AGO our then nineteen-year-old younger son declared that he would rather stay home with the demanding dog than accompany my wife and me on a vacation, including a wedding, in coastal Maine. The marriage of the daughter of dear friends — whose three very handsome younger sisters remained eligible — was enticing, he admitted, but as for spending a dozen days with us en route and in a converted artist's studio on Mount Desert Island, he could not bring himself to it. "You're too boring," he said, "and not a lot of fun to hang out with. Thanks but no thanks."

We were immediately stung by the harsh injustice of his indictment, so much so that my usually imperturbable wife threw a symbolic pen at her cheeky chick. But during the next twenty-four hours we pondered his low opinion of our vacational vapidity. After much soul-searching, we both concluded that out of the mouth of our babe had come hard truth: we *are* boring vacationers and not much fun for teenagers in search of summertime adventure. For we are an academic family, and academic vacations — ours, at least — tend to differ markedly from those taken by normal American families.

We know something about normal families; we rub shoulders with them daily in our hometown, Williamsburg, Virginia, home also of Colonial Williamsburg, Jamestown Settlement, Busch Gardens, Water Country USA, and The Pottery. From what we have seen, the average family works hard fifty weeks a year, saves a small bundle, and spends it happily on a two-week binge of manic activity, entertainment, and occasional edification. While some folks are content to restore their batteries in a quiet lakeside cottage or a visit with relatives, many American families head for the more exciting and costly venues of Disneyland or Disney World, Yellowstone or Jellystone Park, the Grand Canyon, New York, Washington, or San Francisco, dude ranches, Santa Land, zoos, and beach resorts, preferably with long streets or attached malls of shopping opportunity. If the kids are still young and biddable, the parents may opt for a soupçon of pedagogy en route—the Smithsonian, the Alamo, Epcot Center, Plymouth Rock, Fort Ticonderoga, Gettysburg, Mesa Verde. Whatever the goal, most of the family savings go to purchase the exotic freedom of standardized lodging, dining out, and spirited shopping.

We also know about normal vacations from having shared a few with my younger brother, a physician in California, and his family of three winsome females. Every second or third summer they flew east to spend one or two weeks with us in some winning vacation spot on the east coast. Before the cousins went off to college, we did Williamsburg (twice), Cape Cod (twice), and Mount Desert Island. In the selective memory of our younger son, the only "real" (that is, fun) vacations we have ever had were when his western relatives galloped in to rescue him from academic tedium. For them, money was no obstacle and time was to be actively consumed in entertaining pursuits. So we rode death-defying roller coasters and played video games, bowled and miniature-golfed ourselves silly, shopped till we dropped, and ate everywhere and did everything possible in our allotted time. Only when it rained badly (as it did once for a whole week on Cape Cod) were we allowed to read—and then only fiction, no "serious stuff."

What our son doesn't fully appreciate—and may never unless

he too becomes a professor—is that academic families are not "normal" because they labor under a special set of dispensations. Of course, if one spouse holds down a normal nine-to-five job with standard vacations, even an academic family will closely resemble its normal counterpart with one or two working parents. But ours has always operated on an academic calendar because my wife is a preschool director and teacher whose schedule follows that of the public schools. Our summers are relatively free from official duties, and so we have always had three-month paid vacations ("paid" because we elect to have our nine- or ten-month salaries spread out across the year).

What in early June looks like an endless expanse of Tom Sawyer sunshine ahead, custom-made for youthful freedom, has for most academic families a built-in set of hedges, constraints, and limitations. None of these is so serious that it prevents us from taking normal vacations, but together they conspire against it.

First, although a nine-month work year looks less than onerous to the lay eye, most academics need a healthy stretch of rest and recuperation from what they sometimes call "life in the trenches." Dog-tired dog soldiers they are not, but they do need to recover from the fatigue to body and especially soul caused by the extra-classroom parts of their jobs, such as reading and correcting myriad papers and exams of jejune concept and eccentric spelling, writing letters of recommendation to countless professional schools, government agencies, and corporate employers, holding innumerable conferences with students to discuss the previous two activities, advising student organizations, ordering books for courses and library, drawing up syllabi and reading lists, updating curricula vitae for annual merit reviews, playing campus politics, and sitting through regular and irregular committee and faculty meetings, particularly those terrible time-eaters in which future colleagues, temporary replacements, or graduate students are winnowed from literally hundreds of deserving and often desperate applicants.

While academic salaries are decent on a national scale, they are seldom equal to those of professionals of comparable education, experience, and family expectations. Thus many academics choose, or are forced, to teach one or both semesters of summer school to make ends meet or at least heave into sight of each other. The major problem with these courses is that they are compressed into four or five weeks of longer-than-usual daily classes and they yield proportionately much less pay than does the same course during the academic year. There is also little time for the kinds of thoughtful absorption, rumination, and cross-pollination that usually result from the more leisurely pace of a regular semester. So, with one exception in my professorial youth, I have avoided teaching in the summer in order to give myself over to research and writing, the biggest and most characteristic limitation on academic vacations.

Before graciously assuming the major burden for thwarting an academic child's summer expectations, however, let me suggest that other members sometimes contribute marginally to the family deviation from normalcy. For better or worse, the school year from September to June brims with duties, appointments, and good intentions for most households, not just academic ones. Mothers, fathers, and children are forever putting off chores and projects large and small until the longer, freer days of summer. So when school lets out, the family begins to feel the collective crunch to do that which they ought to have done during the previous nine months—make new curtains for the living room, paint the porch and garage, learn to play the acoustic guitar. Inevitably, vacation plans have to be launched around the flotsam and jetsam of conscience.

Even the kids are not exempt from responsibility for lousing up perfectly good summers. When they are young, the adamantine routine of swimming lessons, soccer practice, piano lessons, baseball practice, tennis lessons, day camp, reading contests at the public library, tutoring, and visits to grandparents cut deeply into familial flexibility. And as they edge into their teens, the siren songs of camp, sports, summer jobs, and true love woo the young away from family vacations of any kind, normal or academic.

Nevertheless, it is the family academic who must shoulder most of the blame for fashioning abnormal summer vacations, at least in our house. It was largely my scholarly monomania, self-induced poverty, and determined didacticism that drove our vacations away from the American norm. Abetted by a companionable and sympathetic spouse, we sought for the most part to take vacations that would take little time and resources away from, and enhance in direct and indirect ways, the professor's ongoing research, writing, and (by extension) teaching. The single-mindedness of this approach was mitigated only slightly by an equal insistence on maintaining close ties with parents, friends, and former neighbors created by our frequent academic moves. In other words, we purposely confused and suffused our vacations with our vocation, thereby leaving one nineteen-year-old with the uneasy feeling that he had missed something quintessentially American along the way.

He was not entirely wrong. But with the myopic memory of youth, he failed to remember the occasions when he and his brother were half their current size and we acted almost normal on our summer outings. His parents at least can distinctly recall hauling two tiny towheads around the stalagmites of Howe Caverns in upstate New York, giant human organs in Chicago's Museum of Science and Industry, the denimed cowpokes of an all-Indian rodeo in Scottsdale, Arizona (where the elder ethnologist kept asking, "Where are the Indians?"), coniferous campsites from Wisconsin to Gaspé, the differently odoriferous Bronx Zoo, and the decks of the Thimble Island tour boats off Stony Creek, Connecticut. Indeed, some of the boys' most durable memories are of floating in inner tubes down the Cullasaja River in front of their grandparents' summer house in the mountains of North Carolina and playing in the smooth-rock pools and falls below — the residue of vacations as American as apple pie.

But then there were the rest. Two of our earliest excursions were near-disasters, which only mother and mother of invention rescued. When the boys were aged two and five, "we" decided that it would be fun and educational to see French Canada — fun for the kids, educational for us. (In truth, I had recently discovered the history of New France and was looking to include it in a new course on colonial North America after some personal exploration of its physical remains.) So with typical assistant-professor parsimony, we loaded the camping equipment in the vw wagon and headed for the Gaspé peninsula and Quebec City, hoping that our college French would help us navigate the linguistic shoals that lay just across the St. Lawrence.

Despite an endless two-lane road that seemed to be under construction every few miles, we had a good (though occasionally drizzly) time careering around the well-wooded and -watered Gaspé. We arrived in Quebec City on a warm Sunday morning and, ignorant of the urban geography, parked well down one of the steep streets leading from the Lower Town by the river to the Upper Town and our cartographic destination. With the younger voyageur in a stroller and the older in hand, we set off uphill for the historical sites that had drawn me to the place after reading William Eccles on *The Canadian Frontier* and Morris Bishop's *Champlain*. With the laser focus of the young scholar, I was headed for the *Ancien ville* to commune with the spirits of Mère Marie de l'Incarnation and Bishop Laval at the Ursuline convent and the Jesuit seminary they had built in the seventeenth century.

Unfortunately, I had not yet read Willa Cather's *Shadows on the Rock* with its vivid descriptions of the city's precipitous angles and inclines. Having reached a somewhat level square near the Plains of Abraham, my tired, hot, and hungry troops, unlike

Wolfe's, mutinied at the mention of a longish march to yet another objective. I was so frustrated that my (adult-sized) battle
plan had been snafued that I was ready to leave them all where
they stood, *au milieu de la rue.*

In my eagerness to play the historian, I had forgotten that we
had all awakened early that morning to a blazing sun irradiat-
ing our red-and-brown nylon tent, emerging awestruck to see a
huge tanker ship gliding soundlessly by our campsite on the Île
d'Orléans. I had also conveniently forgotten the discombobula-
tion (terror?) I had caused at least some of my passengers when
en route to town I somehow had driven us onto an unfinished
four-lane highway (around signs that I must have missed or
mistranslated) and proceeded, fortunately very slowly—in the
eerie absence of any other traffic—to the edge of the pavement,
which mysteriously ended, *sans* sign or barricade, at the top of a
long forty-five-degree dirt drop to nowhere. One would think
that such a chastening experience would have tempered the driving ego of the would-be French scholar, but it did not. Only a
sensibly rebellious family could do that and none too soon, before I made a costly, perhaps irremediable *faux pas* of selfish
scholasticism.

Fortunately, calmer heads (at least a female one) prevailed and
we settled for a bite to eat and a relaxing carriage ride around the
famous battlefield, with hardly a *bon mot* of historical commen-
tary from the still-wounded "tour director" (as my family likes
to call me, with ill-disguised irony). Alas, because of our travel
schedule and other impediments, we never reached the Ancien
ville, and much later I had to visit the convent and its rich museum and archives vicariously through the eyes of a graduate student, to whom I suggested a thesis topic on English converts to
Catholicism in the French regime.

As balm to my aching academic ego, my wife bought me a
Native-made Christmas ornament, which instantly became my
favorite. Every year, when I hang the petite Inuit woman in wool

parka and leather mukluks on the tree, she reminds me of just how easy it is for the myopic pursuit of academic pleasures to endanger other joys far more important.

Didacticism is a besetting sin of many *patres familias*, but especially the professorial kind. As a historian of colonial North America and its Indian inhabitants, I wanted my sons from an early age to have a firsthand notion of what living in the woods was like, when natives and newcomers both had to worry daily about getting food, water, shelter, light, and warmth for themselves and their families. So my ever-game wife and I took them camping every summer, often to avoid budget-busting motels on our various travels, but also simply for the adventure of it.

That would have been within the bounds of normalcy but, in addition to my need to deliver impromptu and no doubt otiose history lessons about Cartier and Champlain, Squanto and Metacomet to my captive campers, I felt compelled to initiate them in venerable family rites of woodcraft (less than one generation old). While my father had grown up on a small farm (where I lived briefly after my parents' divorce) in upstate New York, he was no outdoorsman and liked his creature comforts too much to voluntarily spend the night in a tent. I, on the other hand, was a Boy and Explorer Scout largely so I could go camping with frequency. At eleven, I was willingly sent for eight weeks to the Adirondack Woodcraft Camp near Old Forge, New York, where we rode horses, acquired riflery and boating skills, and capped the summer with a memorable week-long canoe trip through the Chain Lakes. After that, I spent at least two weeks every summer at Scout camp. And I was one of the few in our troop who completed two annual cycles of weekend camping once each month. We even tackled Mt. Marcy, the highest peak in the Adirondacks, during the spring vacation of my high school freshman year when the snow was still several feet deep in places, covered by a hard crust. Weighing only 125 or so and toting an unfashionable but light and well-equipped packbasket, I earned the jealous hazing of my older and beefier colleagues because I skittered along the crust while they sank to the groin with nearly every painful step. I was, in short, an experienced outdoorsman by the time my sons were born—"The Adirondack Boy Scout" as my wife dubbed me—overweeningly proud of my skills and determined to pass them on to my progeny.

Late one summer, after a lean, mostly stay-at-home summer of book writing in semi-urban Bronxville, New York, we decided to take a quick weekend outing in the Adirondacks, home of my native spirit and camping hubris. As we drove up the thruway in the sultry sunshine, the radio program was interrupted with news flashes about an approaching storm front with tornadic potential. Maternal caution suggested that another weekend might be preferable, but the Ancient Camper would not be deterred by a little unlikely inclemency. By the time we reached a secluded campsite in the state park, the sky had darkened and light rain had begun to fall. "Nothing to worry about," I assured everyone from the wisdom of my long outdoor experience. "It'll blow over quickly." But as soon as we erected the tent and a fly over the dining area, the downpour was a deluge, the wind had kicked up, and the temperature had plummeted about thirty degrees.

We looked at one another for about three seconds and chorused, "How about a motel?" Leaving the nylon to its own fate, we scrambled into our German-made ark, the canoe still lashed to the top, cranked up the heater, and made a beeline for the nearest "Vacancy" sign. An evening of restaurant food, hot showers, and color TV not only restored our damp spirits but gave me new respect for the benefits of modernity, however unhistorical they seemed at the time.

The next day we woke to a clear sky, retrieved our wet gear, and put the canoe in a nearby lake for a consolation paddle and some youthful fishing. From then on, increasingly as the boys got worldlier and parental bodies softer, motel camping appealed more and more. We continued to take to the tent—with friends in Wisconsin, en route to grandparents in Florida—but camping was never the same after "The 'Tornado' of '76." Still, our didactic outings must have had some effect, for our older son is an outdoorsman of the first order, as proud of his camping, boating, fishing, and story-telling skills as the Adirondack Boy Scout ever was.

Even more academic vacations furnished a number of unadvertised adventures for the kids, despite the predictable tedium of traveling with a camera-toting pedagogue bent on historical immersion. The longest trip we ever took as a family was in 1981 to Fortress Louisbourg on the tip of Cape Breton in the Canadian Maritimes. It's not hard to find: you just turn right at Boston and drive halfway to England, stopping when the road peters out. Louisbourg is the partially reconstructed site of the eighteenth-century town, fort, and harbor whose fleets protected French Canada from English invasion during the last two intercolonial (mislabeled "French and Indian") wars. In the hands of Parks Canada, it is one of the best living history museums in North America, featuring bilingual character interpreters who, like their counterparts at Plimoth Plantation, pretend to know nothing of the world beyond their historical time (1745), the town's heyday just before a motley collection of New England militia surprised it from behind and captured it. I had long wanted to visit it, and after talking with one of my graduate students who had loved working there the previous summer, I was resolved to go, *en famille*. A summer research grant from the college made it possible.

We had beautiful July weather until we reached Bangor, where we reuned with old graduate friends from the English Cambridge. As soon as we set out for Louisbourg via New Brunswick and Nova Scotia, drizzle set in and lasted until we returned to the States. This altered our budget-minded camping plans to include motel tenting while still cooking on a Coleman stove from our own larder. At Louisbourg we were treated to two nights in the guest house by John Fortier, the park director and a former

William and Mary graduate student in history. The rain also forced us to cancel our proposed dogleg to Port Royal on the north shore of Nova Scotia to see the reconstructed Champlain *habitation* of 1605. It certainly clouded our fruitless daily search for a Moosehead beer T-shirt, our elder son's passionate souvenir request (for the animal portrait, we were assured, not the liquid). Naturally, we found one as soon as we returned to our tourist home in Virginia.

But the drizzle could not dampen the professor's zest for discovery nor his family's search for a partial antidote to it. We all lucked out when we detoured to the Pictou Micmac Museum, a grandiose name for a farmer's concrete-block collection of assorted junk plus the remains of a rich eighteenth-century Indian burial, which had been professionally excavated ten feet away in his backyard. The farm and burial were located on a beautiful sloping site overlooking the Pictou inlet, just the right place for a Micmac village and canoe beach. The collection included several birchbark grave liners and containers preserved by the oxidizing salts in numerous French copper pots, several bearskin wrappers for the kettles, red ochre paint, arrowheads, and a variety of personal possessions traditionally buried with natives to accompany their souls to an anthropomorphic Land of the Dead. The boys, ten and thirteen, had their eyes opened by several native skeletons, adults and children. Their titian-haired mother caught her breath over a scalp of discernibly red hair, apparently a war trophy lifted from the head of a French- or, more likely, Englishwoman.

But it was Louisbourg that made the 3,700-mile round-trip worthwhile. We saw it in a fine, cold mist, much as the poor Massachusetts militia must have. The costumed "population" was in short supply, but strategically placed theme buildings (with welcome fireplaces) and an excellent guidebook oriented us around the colonial town. Our older son, a rising high school freshman enrolled in his first foreign language course, was daunted by the liquid and rapid French he heard spoken by interpreters and visitors (though French comic books about Astrix, the likeable Gaul menace, acquired later in Montreal reduced his anxiety). The younger, with a future actor's ear and gift for mimicry, found it all inviting. At lunchtime we feasted on a freshly baked loaf of "soldier's bread," more than enough for a family of four unwilling to pay cabaret prices but cause for filial comment.

Somewhat more puzzling to my clan was my eager purchase in a local market of a dried codfish, the flake-drying of which the weather prevented us from seeing at the working harbor. I explained that I needed it for my classes to illustrate my favorite (and now infamous) lecture on the sixteenth-century Newfoundland cod fisheries. But they cut me off with blechs of disgust when I told them that I made my 9:30 classes eat freshly baked salt cod, cod liver oil, and aptly named hardtack (or ship's biscuits) to give them an authentic taste of early American history. I got my revenge when they had to endure the prop's salty essence all the way home. It could have been far worse: a dried cod can never match in lasting odoriferousness the raw beaver cods I brought home from a fur trading post in Winnipeg.

Fortunately, we had a nocturnal adventure that added a dash of excitement to the boys' academically induced ennui. On the second and last day of our stay, I went off to the park's archives to talk with the research staff and to cadge copies of a number of their excellent reports on the social history of old Louisbourg. The rest of the family holed up in the guest house, located eerily far in the woods outside the mostly francophone village. By the time I returned, they were edgy, bored, and hungry. A propane supper brought some relief, but as we lay in our beds after an early turn-in, we were startled by a small fleet of jeeps and pickups that rendezvoused behind our house, for what nefarious purpose we could only imagine and magnify. Without a telephone, we were certain that we were going to be murdered in our beds, buried unseen and unlamented in the wilderness only to be dug up by wild beasts and devoured by birds of prey. Had we thought of it, we doubtless could have defended ourselves with the lethal slab of salt cod or scared the intruders off by reading to them from the research reports. Alas, they eventually left of their own accord and scholarship was safe for another day.

Another academic excursion three years later tested the patience of only one son because the elder escaped to a high school journalism program at Northwestern, where I had taught briefly and which he soon attended. Thanks to an NEH Travel-to-Collections grant, I was able to make a thorough study of the ethnological and archaeological collections of several museums in Canada and the United States toward a book on the confluence of French, English, and Indian cultures in colonial North America. This involved packing the abbreviated family in the miniwagon, driving 3,200 miles, staying mostly with academic friends, and trying to entertain one captive thirteen-year-old, who was convinced from long experience that his life would be miserable for at least the duration of the trip if not forever, given his relation to a paternal pedant. In fact, with the aid of a durable cassette player and headphones, he proved to be a very companionable traveler, not least, perhaps, because he got the whole backseat to himself.

Our itinerary took us first to Montreal and the McCord Museum, where I expected to view a new exhibit on Hochelaga, the Iroquoian town that Jacques Cartier visited in 1535 and was partially discovered under the McGill University campus in the last century. But on the Tuesday we arrived, the museum was closed to the public. Fortunately, the exhibit's guest curator, Bruce Trigger of McGill's anthropology department, slipped us in for a guided tour. Try as we might, our teenager was not particularly moved by the historical resonance of charred pots and effigy pipe bowls.

Ottawa, the next stop, was more acceptable to the nonprofessors in the tour. They enjoyed the freedom and possibilities of the city and a hotel, while I buried myself in the ethnological collections of the National Museum of Civilization's warehouses in distant Bell's Corners. Riding the hotel elevators provided a frisson of anxiety after we heard that a male guest had recently been decapitated by one that had stopped between floors. As he tried to hold the door open for his wife to exit, the car lurched into motion, shooting his head into the car at the feet of his horrified spouse.

The Royal Ontario Museum in Toronto and the reconstructed Jesuit mission and museum at Ste. Marie-among-the-Hurons in Midland each had something for everyone, even something to rival the headless husband. While I took notes on the French trade goods in the ROM's collections, particularly the wares lost from fur brigade canoes that failed to run northern river rapids and found lately by underwater archaeologists, mother and son viewed a blockbuster exhibit on medieval arms and armor, whose imaginative possibilities were not lost on the younger reader. At Ste. Marie, which we were revisiting, the pictures and associated artifacts related to the horrific torture deaths of five missionaries at the hands of the invading Iroquois in 1649 provided a vivid parallel to *l'affaire de la tête*.

The final stop on what our son had good-naturedly but more than once labeled "the endless ride from hell" was the Rochester Museum and Science Center in western New York. Staying with old Yale friends and their two playful children made our two days there more than endurable for my flagging crew. As a bonus, they introduced us to the best pizza—all white—we have ever eaten. For the day and a half I needed to work through the museum's incomparable Seneca artifacts, the whole company was at peace, if seat- and suitcase-weary. But just to test their mettle, in every likely town or city we entered on the way home I asked with exaggerated eagerness, "Do you think they have a museum we could visit?" A teenager's equally exaggerated anguish from the backseat was my Pavlovian reward.

Academic vacations, of course, also occur at other times of

the year, most of them too short except to play catch-up with desk work or to attend a professional conference. But during spring vacation in 1986 I was invited to teach a one-week lecture-seminar on the colonial history of Anglo-America to about fifty European professors and graduate students in Sestri Levante on the Italian Riviera. As fate would have it, I was on an NEH fellowship for the semester, which allowed me to travel with my family for an additional week without missing any of my own classes. Equally fortunate for us, our then fifteen-year-old had planned to accompany his high school French Club to Paris during the same break but chose to cast his lot with familiar tour guides, a decision he soon had cause to regret.

After the usual exhausting all-night flight, we landed on Easter Sunday at Milan's Malpensa Airport and were immediately spooked by the concentration of Uzi-bearing soldiers and German shepherd guard dogs, there to foil the terrorists who were then bombing their way through Europe. In halting guidebook Italian, I managed to get us to our *pensione* in Florence (where William and Mary's Florence Program stayed every summer), one block from the gentle Arno. After small recovery, we headed out on foot for as many historic and artistic treasures as we could reach in the Renaissance city. In four days we visited the crowded Uffizi, the Bargello, Santa Croce and San Lorenzo, the Palazzo Vecchio, the Duomo, the Laurentian Library (of course), and assorted churches, museums, trattorias, and gelato shops in between. The youngest traveler palpably enjoyed the Bobili Gardens overlooking the city (especially the fat, naked man riding the turtle) and the shops on the Ponte Vecchio (where he bought a silk tie as a gutsy down payment on adulthood). His least favorites were the pensione's continental breakfasts (watery *cioccolàta* and no-sugar cereal), interminable walking, and my amateur history lessons. Like most visitors, even he was struck dumb by the awesome size and perfection of Michelangelo's David. But by the end of our stay, he said, he had seen enough *putti* to last a lifetime.

To prove his point, he refused to enter a single church in Siena, our last stop before returning to Milan. In fact, he arrived sick with a fever, went to bed, and did not venture out in the cold rain that greeted us for twenty-four hours. When he did, my feeble Italian ordered us the world's worst pizza in a tourist trap on the majestic Piazza del Campo; its main features were super-hairy anchovies (which none of us wanted in the first place), lack of tomatoes, and cardboard crust. This linguistic gaff he joyfully added to a host of others in his notebook, which he kept either for posterity or, more likely, blackmail in his tell-all *bildungsroman*. To add insult to injury, after I left him and his mother in Milan so they could return to the States while I went to "work" in a four-star hotel on the sensual Bay of Silence, their plane was delayed and they were stuck in a cramped, smoky waiting room for five hours. We find it providentially ironic that this hapless child is now fluent in Italian and even taught drill sections in it in college.

Despite their variety, our academic vacations have been marked by two constants: bookshops and shoptalk. Twenty years ago, when we made one of our first pilgrimages to Maine, I bought twenty-four fat and homely volumes of the *Collections of the Maine Historical Society* in scenic Castine, which the kids had to share limited space with all the way home. Nowadays, we leave our empty nest every summer without a single book, knowing full well that by the time we stop in Princeton, New Haven, Providence, Cambridge, Wells and Portland, and finally The Big Chicken Barn in Ellsworth, we will have a whole trunk of reading matter, far more than we could read even in two leisurely weeks on a Maine island.

As our kids can testify, the other certainty in our summer peregrinations is abundant shoptalk with our largely academic hosts and friends. This began to make sense and to become moderately tolerable when the boys went off to college and began to read—or to take courses from—some of our "household names."

The elder actually majored in history at Northwestern and the younger in American Studies at William and Mary, both (I always assumed) in spite of my calling, not because of it.

But maybe I'm being too hard on myself, and some of our abnormal, academic vacations worked upon their hardy teenage souls in mysterious ways. Only time will tell—and where and how they take their own children on vacation in the years ahead. I know one deprived child who will shepherd his progeny to Disneyworld and Epcot Center, which in his youth we had to pass at least twice for lack of time and funds. I wonder if he would allow a couple of old and odd fogies to tag along. For all the pleasures of academe, there are some that come from other groves.

CONCLUSION

Professors, Critics, and Higher Education

Why do most Americans look up
to education and look
down upon educated people?
Sydney J. Harris

W

HEN CRITICS of American higher education assign
blame for its major and minor problems, whom do
they invariably finger? Not boards of trustees, who
have the final say in and are legally responsible for everything their
institutions do. Not the administrations, whose luxuriant growth
and high salaries account for a lion's share of the newsworthy cost
hikes in the last three decades.[1] Not the students, whose spotty
preparation, myopic vocationalism, and voracious demand for extracurricular services also inflate the debit columns. Not the state
legislatures, whose steady but underpublicized reduction of support has forced public universities to raise tuition and fees and to
reduce financial aid — nor the voters who prompted them to spend
more on prisons than higher education, a feat they have now accomplished nationwide.[2] And not the parents, who often sell college to their teenagers as the route to social prestige, a good time,
or a good job. The only constituency that seems to be responsible
for the alleged "crisis" in higher education is the faculty.

But is the indictment fair? Is it helpful? Can it ever help us
solve our higher educational problems? Or does it merely divert
our attention from the real problems by scapegoating one easily
targeted group? I would argue that, first, there is no "crisis" in
American higher education except an artificial one manufactured
by variously motivated media and ideologues (crises sell books,
magazines, and air time better than things as they pretty well are),

and, second, most of our higher educational problems are either much less serious than they are alleged to be or they cannot be attributed solely to or solved by the professoriate.

Without a doubt, the nation's faculties are responsible for creating—and finding solutions to—several educational problems (though seldom without pressure from or complicity with other constituencies, within and without academe), and these we will certainly address. But the majority of newsmaking "flaws" and "scandals" in our colleges and universities, although they are blamed on the professoriate, are usually blown way out of proportion or grievously misunderstood, often deliberately, by critics who fail to recognize that higher education is much changed from their own (imagined) collegiate heydays and who mistake a few selective institutions for the whole national scope and variety of higher education. This leads to distorted views both of the distinctive nature, strengths, and limitations of our nearly thirty-seven hundred institutions and of the best solutions to their true problems.

As Odysseus warned, we should beware anyone bearing quick fixes and brandishing the word *crisis*. The English word derives from the Greek *krisis*, meaning "decision," and since the early seventeenth century has meant figuratively "a turning point . . . a state of affairs in which a decisive change for better or worse is imminent" (*Oxford English Dictionary*). The key word here is imminent; the outcome of this turning point lies in the future and it may turn out for worse *or better*. Therefore, the people best qualified to deal in crises are either soothsayers, who can read the ambiguous bones of the present to predict the denouements of current crises, or historians, who, with 20/20 hindsight and some imagination, trade in past ones. To judge by the spate of "crisis"-ridden critiques, alarms, and punditry in the last ten or fifteen years, American higher education is either doomed or has already fallen into moral decay and intellectual ruin.

As a historian of higher education, I find the latest reports of higher education's imminent or recent demise comfortably familiar; there have been many others since 1636, all equally exaggerated. And I dispute most of the daring diagnoses of the diseases that allegedly are killing or have already killed it. A major reason for the critics' misdiagnoses is their failure to understand or appreciate the peculiar nature of American higher education on the eve of the twenty-first century.

Today more than 60 percent of our high school graduates attend some kind of higher, postsecondary institution, whether a short-term trade school, a two-year community college, or a four-year college or university. This makes our system of higher education not only the largest and most accessible on the planet but the most diverse. There is something for literally everyone, from quick and easy diploma mills to hard and costly Ivy League universities. One result of such a system is that we, as a nation, feel the constant tension between providing generous *access* to higher education and the student population's differential *ability* to benefit from it. So we have sensibly operated with the implicit if not explicit understanding that relatively higher or simply further education is not necessarily the highest education possible for all. Our system accommodates both, 80 percent of all students in public institutions.[3]

But most critics proceed as if only the intellectual elite—the best known, highly selective, socially prestigious, mostly private colleges and their high-flying faculty and students—are and should be the touchstone for their assessments of "American higher education." This, of course, distorts the complex reality of higher education in our democracy and constantly highlights a very small, by definition atypical percentage of our colleges and universities for attention or obloquy. These stereotypical images created for public consumption are also extremely negative and invariably based on isolated incidents at this college or statements at that university raised to grand and prophetic generalizations about *The Fall of the American University*, *The Moral Collapse of the University*, or *The University in Ruins*.[4]

Conclusion

Yet the critics are not totally wrong to focus on our elite institutions. After all, they reason, if our best colleges are committing all sorts of folly and failing to live up to their—or the critics' notions of their—potential, we can safely assume that the rest of our academic institutions are not performing well either. In a system as diverse as ours, their assumption may be *factually* unwarranted, which it is, but they are not crazy to make it. Perhaps an equally reasonable explanation for their negativity is the "mission drift" that many of our colleges and particularly universities have experienced—or allowed—since World War II.

Mission drift occurs when an institution with relatively few clear and distinct goals and functions acquires others that it believes will attract more students, funds, or prestige in a competitive environment. When a traditional liberal arts college adds courses, majors, faculty, and internships of a directly vocational character, or a local community college decides to trump the liberal arts college by becoming not only a four-year institution but a "university" by adding a master's program or two, higher education suffers mission drift. Public universities are the most prone to this kind of slippage because they tend to equate growth with improvement, are responsive to the practical needs of their state's citizens, and have such mixed and ambitious missions to begin with that a few more mandates appear not to cause dilution or overcrowding. The end result is what Clark Kerr aptly dubbed "multiversities."[5]

Like the beleaguered American high school, our colleges and universities are expected to be all things to all people, to serve a large, mixed bag of social, economic, and intellectual needs in one place. Many of the problems critics see in higher education are the result of our failure to divide academic labor along sensibly focused, specialized lines and to make those distinctive institutions stick to their lasts. "The single most serious problem of our universities," argues Hanna Holborn Gray, former president of the University of Chicago, "is their failure to adhere steadily to their own purposes. . . . [They] need to return to the criterion that measures what they can do well, that other institutions cannot do."[6] Her Yale counterpart and contemporary, Bart Giamatti, agreed. "No university is strong," he said, "if it is unsure of its purpose and nature, and is unwilling or unable to make vital that nature and purpose for others beyond it."[7] Mature institutions do not have to remain eternally wedded to their founding charters and goals, but they should not drift very far in pursuit of younger, sexier models lest they sap their vital energies and squander their academic inheritance.

What, then, are the major problems in higher education, those perceived by critics and others that tend to get overlooked for (I would argue) more sensational though less important subjects? And how many can be laid at the feet of, or disposed of by, the professoriate alone? Here is a selective list of my nominees by way of illustration:

— Intercollegiate athletic programs that exploit academically marginal or unqualified participants, maintain little empires (alumni-funded) outside the control or oversight of the faculty and administration, undermine academic purposes and standards, fail to treat both sexes equitably, and run large deficits (virtually all do) that eat into funds for academics, intramural sports, and recreation for all students.[8]
— Sororities and fraternities that allow illegal hazing, the perpetuation of false values in superficial and hurried "rushes," undemocratic "blackballing" of candidates, the cliquish narrowing of social experiences and friendships, and the undermining of academic and moral values.
— Excessive, thoughtless, and often dangerous student sexual behavior and consumption of alcohol and drugs.[9]
— Weak or uneven student preparation for college-level work, resulting in costly remedial courses (30 percent of all freshmen now take them) or the "dumbing down" of regular courses to an unchallengingly low least common denominator.[10]
— Lopsided, largely class-based, access to higher education and even more skewed graduate rates, in which the children of par-

ents in the top economic quartile enroll and graduate in numbers far exceeding those from the bottom quartile.[11]

— Declining state and federal support for higher education and basic research, resulting in tuition hikes, reduced financial aid, and many public universities that are only "state-assisted" (less than half of their operating revenue comes from the state) rather than "state-supported."[12]

— College costs rising at rates above inflation, driven by the proliferation of administrative and student services, compliance with federal regulations to help the disadvantaged, improvements in student/faculty ratios, new technology installations and updates in dormitories, classrooms, and offices, accelerated increases in the cost of library books and periodical subscriptions, high start-up costs of science laboratories for new faculty and renovation of older facilities, new dormitories and classrooms to cope with enrollment pressures, and competitive salaries for highly educated, specialized professionals, including some increases to restore faculty wages deferred since 1971–72.[13]

— Steadily rising enrollments, despite rising costs and demographical fluctuations, resulting in larger classes, overcrowded classes and dormitories, more off-campus living, higher student/faculty ratios, less personal contact with professors, greater use of graduate teaching assistants and part-time faculty, and lengthened time to degree when required courses are unavailable.

— Excessive student and parental vocationalism, which compromises if not eliminates the essential offerings and values of liberal education while proliferating costly specializations of limited intellectual or philosophical import.

— Racial and ethnic tensions and loss of a sense of campus "community" (for lack of a better word), resulting from increased student and faculty diversity, fear and intolerance, self-segregation, double academic and judicial standards, misplaced altruism (admitting students to academically inappropriate institutions), admission quotas rather than equal opportunities, and long legacies of discrimination.[14]

We could undoubtedly add more trouble spots, but these seem to me the most serious for the institutions I and many Americans regard as the most benign, idealistic, and liberating in our society. None of these problems, significantly, was created by the action or inaction of the faculty, and only one or two can be solved (partially) or ameliorated by the faculty. Some simply arise from the facts of our new academic life, the product, in turn, of long-overdue changes in our society, economy, and culture. This is not an abrogation of professorial responsibility, a cowardly buck-passing (as some critics are bound to see it), but a simple description of the societal, student, familial, or administrative origins of these particular problems.

In addition to my list, compiled largely with an insider's eye, critics have drawn up a list of academic travesties and foibles that are almost exclusively attributable to the professoriate. I would preface their docket with one more venial but consequential sin—grade inflation. This problem originated largely in the most selective colleges—Harvard, Yale, Princeton, and Duke have addressed it recently—but the professorial rationalizations for it spread quickly in all directions. The trend toward giving all A's and B's and skimping on "Gentlemen's C's" began during the Vietnam War when college grades to some extent kept students from being drafted and perhaps dying in the jungles of Southeast Asia. Then, when some schools, particularly selective ones, continued their inflationary ways, allegedly because the secondary preparation of their students had steadily improved, other schools, even those unblessed with brilliant freshmen, felt obliged to up their antes to prevent their students from being outranked and underrated in graduate and professional schools and job competitions. We are now faced with a situation in some, perhaps many, colleges where grade point averages are almost meaningless, distinctions between students are almost impossible for outsiders to make, and a majority of seniors graduate with honors. Some of the inflation may be due to the professorial pressure to score well on student course evaluations for salary's sake, on the (statistically mistaken) assumption that easy graders are more popular with (undiscerning) students. Whatever the rationale, if professors are not willing to apply more realistic and harder-nosed standards, the administration or parents must force the issue to ensure institutional and intellectual integrity and the inherent value of a college degree.[15]

But grade inflation is small potatoes compared to other faculty enormities. On the critics' scales, the professoriate has been weighed and found woefully wanting on five scores: politics, curriculum, tenure, research, and teaching. Let's examine each charge briefly and assess their seriousness—from an insider's informed, admittedly upbeat but I hope not Pollyannaish perspective.

POLITICS. According to the 1995-96 Astin survey of thirty-four thousand representative faculty members, fewer than 5 percent describe their political orientation (with the usual imprecision of labels) as "far left"; another 38 percent are "liberal," while only four-tenths of a percent occupy the "far right" and 20 percent the "conservative" slot. More than a third (38 percent) stand in "the middle of the road." These ratios are virtually the same as those reported in 1989-90, save that the conservatives have picked up a couple of percentage points from the moderates.[16] If professors are intellectuals, and intellectuals are "people who think otherwise," representing a critical, countervailing force to social orthodoxy and conventional wisdom, it is understandable that the professoriate would lean a little to the left of center, given the generally conservative leaning of the (graying) national population in the eighties and nineties.

Despite their healthy numbers in both academe and the electorate, conservatives have long felt suspicious of and threatened by those to their left, especially since the student unrest of the sixties and the intellectual and curricular changes of the seventies and eighties. In general and by definition, conservatives do not like change, and higher education has experienced a great deal of it in the past thirty years: feminism and women's studies, affirmative action and the racial, ethnic, and gender diversification of student populations and faculties, multiculturalism and adjustments of the Western "canon," deconstruction and postmodernism, gay rights and campaigns against sexual harassment and acquaintance rape, greater curricular attention to race, class, and gender, and the implementation of speech codes to prevent censorship and intimidation.

In opposition to many of these changes, conservative intellectuals—aided and abetted, often unwittingly, by liberals who were bothered by some of the changes and by media that report anything that makes noise—concocted a mythology of "political correctness" in the late eighties and early nineties. Through endless recycling of a small number of ham-handed behaviors and stupid statements by reform-minded students, faculty, and administrators, most at marquee colleges and universities, through "exaggeration, deceptive omissions of key facts, and occasional outright invention," they persuaded large numbers of Americans (including two presidential speechwriters) that "leftist totalitarians had taken control of universities and were intimidating professors, censoring conservatives, politicizing curricula, and imposing a new 'McCarthyism of the Left' on higher education." In this inventive rewriting of recent history, conservatives, particularly white male ones, were the true victims, of the "feminazis," "thought police," "tenured radicals," and "PC totalitarians" prowling the nation's campuses.[17]

The promulgation of the PC myth was a brilliant stroke of public relations and political maneuvering. If it was not exactly the product of a conservative conspiracy, it was a carefully orchestrated, well-financed campaign of exaggerated misinformation for ideological and political purposes. Four well-heeled conservative foundations subsidized the writing of the five major books that laid the foundation for and consolidated the PC myth in the public imagination. Those and similar foundations also funded several notorious conservative student newspapers and underwrote a number of conservative policy centers, or "think tanks," which gave generous fellowships or sinecures to several leading PC antagonists. In addition, a devious organization called Accuracy in Academia was founded in 1985 to ferret out alleged leftist conspiracies in the nation's classrooms, mostly by planting student spies who reported anything—in or out of context—that smacked of "radicalism" (intellectual, cultural, economic, or political) to a whistle-blowing house organ. Nothing the "tenured radicals" did or could do (without swift and certain student or administrative reaction) came close to these kinds of conservative tactics in spreading a chill over classroom discussion and academic freedom.[18]

The conservatives' campaign to reify "political correctness" was a stunning success largely because people would never declare themselves politically correct, "so it was virtually impossible to counter the conservative attacks when a culture of sound bites defied the kind of analysis needed to refute the presumption that political correctness existed." Calling someone "PC" was "an unanswerable form of ridicule," a substitute for argument about the ideas at issue.[19] In short, it effectively silenced dissent and assaulted civil liberties, the very things conservatives claimed to be losing at the hands of the (radical) professoriate.

Fortunately, the myth of political correctness has been exposed and unraveled by John K. Wilson and others and rendered moot by the passage of time, as its newsworthiness declined from stale repetition and campus behavior failed to produce enough fuel to feed the flames.[20] But it certainly had its day. In 1994, "political correctness" was mentioned in nearly seven thousand media articles, mostly because journalists, who tend to know very little about what goes on in higher education, accepted uncritically the conservatives' versions of the facts and motives. Today, in academe itself, PC is virtually a dead issue, although, as a "rhetorical virus," it seems to have resilience in the public vocabulary of clichés and slogans; "like 'Willie Horton,' PC is easy to pronounce and remember."[21] Unfortunately, the PC mythologizing coincided with growing public uneasiness over higher education, particularly its costs, which helped conservative legislators on both state and federal levels slash funding for higher education.

CURRICULUM. Many of the most publicized changes in higher education in the past three decades have been curricular. Critics inside and outside academe have wrung their hands over a variety of course appearances, adjustments, and alleged "disappearings" (the dirty work of "leftist" faculty hit squads). Beginning in the sixties, black, ethnic, and women's studies made their debuts in course catalogues, followed in the seventies and eighties by feminist, gender, sexuality, and peace studies and an assortment of offerings often labeled "multiculturalism." A major thrust of most of these curricular irruptions was to acknowledge the historical importance and cultural contributions of groups, doers, and thinkers beyond the limited cast or "canon" of Western white males featured in prevailing texts and syllabi, particularly in English and history departments. This, in turn, led to recognition of the roles and achievements of the female half of the human population, an emphasis on pluralism and conflict rather than commonality and consensus in national histories, a diminution of the centrality and value of "Western Civilization," a globalization of the curriculum in general, a questioning of the canonical criteria of "greatness," an enlarged list of books worth reading, and a rise in cross- and interdisciplinary studies.[22]

Simultaneously, an influx of "postmodernist" theory, predominantly the esoteric and neologistic work of French and German philosophers and literary critics, threatened the humanities and (to a lesser extent) the social sciences by overturning or seriously challenging virtually all of their traditional ("modernist") assumptions and intellectual procedures.[23] To many intellectual conservatives and liberals alike, the proliferation of aggressive, often overtly political special-interest studies within the academy and the invasion of difficult, special-audience theories from abroad together posed a major threat to the status quo and induced no little angst in the halls of ivy.

The short-term costs and consequences of these changes were not all small or illusory. The curricular contests generated as much heat as light, and humor, sweet reason, and a sense of perspective were often casualties. "Politics," front-loaded as well as consequential, was heavy in the air as ideological postures were struck and group identities essentialized. "Victims" replaced "winners" as history's posterpeople, and critical understanding too often gave way to factional cheerleading and esteem-pumping. Perhaps the biggest casualty was—and still is—the loss of faculty enthusiasm for the traditional philosophy of liberal education. As disciplines have become more specialized and hotly contested, many faculty have grown battle-weary or -wary and have lost faith in "the ideal of an integrated undergraduate education."[24] This is a long-standing problem in American higher education, as old as the battle between the ancient classics and the newer sciences and literatures before the Civil War and the triumph of the elective system in the early twentieth century. But it is exacerbated by the dramatic increase in students who are no longer exclusively interested in a liberal arts education (as most were in 1900 when only 4 percent of the college-age population attended college) and have a varied set of vocational and certificational goals, short funds, and less time.

As a whole, the American college population is increasingly "female, public, part-time, local, adult, and in debt."[25] Fifty-five

percent are women, 80 percent attend public institutions, 80 percent attend college in their own states, 58 percent are twenty-
two years or older, and 40 percent receive financial aid. Only
25 percent major in any of the liberal arts; business alone attracts
as many, followed closely by health services and elementary
education.[26]

Equally germane, a quarter of all undergraduates are members
of minorities, many of whom are first-generation students who
bring to college legacies of discrimination and poverty as well as
curiosity and a desire to better themselves.[27] They and all their
classmates are in need of at least the fundaments of a liberal education, one of whose aims is to "break down the certainties and
provincial vision with which we are [all] born," to liberate us from
"the contingencies of [our] backgrounds." The challenge is to invite our students into membership of "a much larger intellectual
community" without destroying or denigrating the cultural identity and heritage they bring to college.[28] The nation's faculties
could do a better job of both, and the solid curricular changes of
the recent past make at least the second task much easier to
accomplish.

Partly because most critics have tarred the curricular contests
with the PC brush ("the Barbarians are at the Western gates") but
mostly because the contestants on both sides have eschewed the
long view, higher education watchers are unaware that the recent
imbroglios are not only not serious, in the sense of constituting a
pedagogical "crisis," they are the historical and desirable norm for
colleges and universities. To understand why, we need to look
briefly at the nature of curricula and the history of curriculum-
making in America, now well into its fourth century.

The eminent philosopher Alfred North Whitehead once remarked that "there is only one subject-matter for education, and
that is Life in all its manifestations."[29] As a practical guide for
curriculum-makers, however, that wise dictum leaves something

to be desired because, as an equally wise Yale dean has said, "no educational program can contain the whole of wisdom" (much less a host of other desirable acquirements).[30] So faculties must be selective in building curricula for their respective institutions. Probably because most professors are doctors of philosophy who approach their respective subjects philosophically, they tend to regard a curriculum as "an index of *intellectual* values, separate from though influenced by social values." Overall, most would agree with Clark Kerr that a curriculum is "nothing less than a statement a college makes about what, out of the totality of man's constantly growing knowledge and experience, is considered useful, appropriate, or relevant to the lives of educated men and women at a certain point in time." To frame the issue more historically, the curriculum is "one of those places where we have told ourselves who we are" but also, because it embodies our ideals for the emerging generation, who we would like to become.[31]

A curriculum, therefore, as "a locus and transmitter of values," is "a remarkably vital organism," containing within itself and its intellectual and social environments myriad "seeds of change." Academics, particularly reformers, love to say that changing a curriculum is harder than moving a graveyard. But, in fact, curricula are in constant motion, responding—sometimes tardily, often quickly, and always willy-nilly—to the changes being rung in the non-ivory society that sends the colleges their students and into which their students will graduate. Although curricula tend to be conservative in structure and pedagogical style, their contents—individual courses and syllabi—are much more responsive to shifting intellectual and cultural currents as well as to the larger social milieux of their students, trustees, and donors. So essentially flexible and responsive are college curricula that historian Frederick Rudolph has suggested that, rather than resort to the lifeless and disembodied entries in course catalogues, we should consult "society itself" as a more reliable source of "curricular illumination."[32] In his inaugural speech as president of Harvard in 1869, Charles W. Eliot suggested why that would be a reasonable approach, particularly in America. "The University," he said, speaking generically, "must accommodate itself promptly to significant changes in the character of the people for whom it exists. The institutions of higher education in any nation are always a faithful mirror in which are sharply reflected the national history and character. In this mobile nation, the action and reaction between the University and society at large are more sensitive and rapid than in stiffer communities."[33]

What we have witnessed in the late twentieth century—which comes as no surprise to anyone familiar with higher education in the late eighteenth or the nineteenth century—is that the larger and more diverse the student population has become, the more rapid, complex, and conflicted have been the pressures and demands on the curriculum for change. In the wake of such changes as the expansion and globalization of the economy, the GI Bill, the civil rights movement, the women's movement, Vietnam, and new patterns of immigration, the student population has grown steadily to more than 14 million polychromatic, variously motivated seekers.[34] Understandably, their curricular needs and demands are far greater and different than those of the tiny number of sons (not daughters) of professional and upper-class white families who attended the handful of colleges in colonial America. Thus it is the accelerated broadening and reshaping of the nation's curricula that have alarmed many conservatives and even liberals in the past thirty years.

Not only is curricular change normal, it is normally conflicted because we—faculties, students, and "society"—invariably harbor different versions of our collective past, visions of our future, and expectations of the new generation of college graduates. These are all serious matters, but often they are super-seriously regarded by the contestants. Frequently, curricular contests achieve apocalyptic billing, such as "battles" and "wars"—Armageddon—between "Ancients and Moderns," "The Two Cultures," or (more lightly) "Loose Canons," the fighting of which is spurred by the perceived "sacrality of reading lists."[35] But all reading lists—the essence of so-called "canons"—are socially constructed, provisional, and usually much newer than those who fight so vigorously over them realize.

Moreover, curricula change not cataclysmically, by faculty putsch or outside imposition, but gradually, by accretion and small attrition. Older offerings tend to remain and new ones are simply added, resulting in our current supermarket curricula. Contrary to recent alarms, Shakespeare and the history of Western civilization have *not* been dropped from the nation's curricula, prescribed or elective—they have just had to share space with newer books and courses of value and relevance to the students we are now educating and the pluralistic society we now seek to study and serve.[36] While colleges and universities maintain their time-tested requirements for core or general education courses, course distributions, and majors and minors, as the great majority still do, we will have little cause for curricular alarm.

We should have even less cause if we absorb three other home truths about curricula. First, the latest round of curricular debates has been focused largely on the humanities, mostly English and history, and general requirements in them. During the nineteenth century most of the action involved the sciences, and in the first half of the twentieth the social sciences were at issue. Even postmodernism's mighty challenges have scarcely touched the "modernist" priorities and protocols of the sciences.

Second, innovations in scholarship do not necessarily or readily make their way into the curriculum. In the humanities, introductory courses, lower-level surveys, and general education courses all tend to resist scholarly fashion and especially "theory."

And third, a curriculum is in many ways, as Rudolph reminds us, whatever students make of it. Despite the best-laid plans of parents and faculty, students manipulate the formal curriculum to suit themselves, or they skirt it by creating an extracurriculum that speaks more directly to their needs, values, and goals. Nor does the extracurriculum always subvert the faculty-made one; sometimes, as with the literary and debating societies of the nineteenth century, it complements it and inspires salutary and overdue change.[37]

Recent alarms over the curriculum, then, are largely unwarranted. As historian Lawrence Levine assures us, "the process the university is in now is a process it has always been in, which is change in response to the outside world." Modern colleges and universities "are performing precisely the functions institutions of higher education should perform: to stretch the boundaries of our understanding; to teach the young to value our intellectual heritage not by rote but through comprehension and examination; to continually and perpetually subject the 'wisdom' of our society to thorough and thoughtful scrutiny while making the 'wisdom' of other societies and other cultures accessible and subject to comparable scrutiny; to refuse to simplify our culture beyond recognition by limiting our focus to only one segment of American society and instead to open up the *entire* society to thoughtful examination."[38]

TENURE. Virtually no critics believe that college faculties can do their proper jobs without academic freedom. All would agree with the 1940 statement of the American Association of University Professors (AAUP) where it declares that "institutions of higher education are conducted for the common good, . . . not to further the interest of either the individual teacher or the institution as a whole," and "the common good depends upon the free search for truth and its free exposition" in publication and classroom.[39] But many critics do resist drawing a necessary connection, as the AAUP did in its founding principles in 1915 and has ever since, between academic freedom and tenure. Instead, they denounce tenure as a major source of academic ills — everything from harboring intellectual "deadwood" and shameless shirkers to wreaking unspeakable psychic damage upon young faculty during probation, comparable to "ancient rites of human sacrifice." Tenure's putative guarantee of lifetime employment is seen by many critics not only as "the ultimate protection from accountability" but as providing "security unheard of in any other profession."[40] When administrators and legislators are also seeking ways to trim costs by reducing faculties or abolishing whole programs or departments, the current hue and cry against tenure obliges the professoriate to explain and defend the practice with special clarity and care.

First, we need to be very clear about just who or what the professoriate needs academic freedom from. In the first half of this century, from the founding of the AAUP through the McCarthy era, the forces that threatened academic freedom were largely outside the university: benefactors, lay and clerical trustees, powerful parents of students, religious, political, and "patriotic" groups, corporations, media, and legislators. Though they are now less brazen, such parties still attempt to influence what scholars and teachers say about them and their ideas or interests; more than a few have tried to have offending professors fired or otherwise muzzled. If professors "speak truth to power," as they must if they are to serve the public good, they are with some regularity bound to disturb or offend those in power—and therefore to require the protection of tenure from their righteous anger or retribution.

Threats to and infringements of academic freedom also emanate from within the academy. Administrators and chairpersons, subtle or high-handed, seeking to rid themselves of pesky or redundant professors, aggrieved and litigious students, faculty "stars" or crusaders seeking to remake a department in their own image, and the ubiquitous, ever-changing factions and majorities in departmental democracies can all apply pressure to individual professors that compromises the latter's ability to teach, research, and publish with maximal concern for the truth as they in good conscience see it. A certain measure of job security shields them from the most damaging of those pressures, and society at large is the ultimate beneficiary.

Although the threats to academic freedom are real and omnipresent, many critics are no longer convinced that tenure is the only or even the best way to protect it. Whenever American businesses restructure and "downsize" (that is, fire people), as they did in the eighties and early nineties, critics find it somehow unfair—as if misery should be uniformly shared—that colleges and universities should offer "unheard of" security in the form of "lifetime" employment "guarantees" to *their* "employees." But colleges and universities are not businesses like other businesses and they should never be regarded as such. They are nonprofit service organizations whose students are not ordinary customers (nor always right), whose major employees—faculty—are highly trained professionals who also largely manage the operation, and whose product cannot be counted, weighed, or depreciated.

Moreover, the critics' characterizations of tenure require serious qualification. First, the economic security offered by academic tenure is not unique: the armed forces, the judicial bench, medical practices, legal partnerships, orchestras, and unions all offer similar long-term employment to their members. Second, academic employment is hardly protected for a lifetime. An academic life actually begins pretty far along, after four years of college and an average of seven years of graduate school, and tenure begins at least seven years later yet, which puts the newly tenured associate professor in his or her mid- to late thirties. If the uncapping of mandatory retirement does not unduly raise the average age of faculty retirees, the typical "lifetime" of a tenured professor is and will remain about twenty-five to thirty years, scarcely enough time to earn the proverbial retirement watch.

Not only is the term of academic employment shorter than one might imagine, it is not guaranteed in the sense of being irrevocable. In 1940 the AAUP's Statement of Principles underscored the notion that academic freedom carried with it "duties correlative with rights" and that a teacher's full freedom in research and publication was always conditional upon "the adequate performance of his other academic duties," primarily teaching. Knowing that even professorial talent was unevenly distributed, the expectation was for "adequate," not necessarily superior, performance. But professors could be terminated for "adequate cause" related to their academic duties.[41] In 1973 a Commission on Academic Tenure in Higher Education specified that "'adequate cause' in faculty dismissal proceedings should be restricted to (a) demonstrated incompetence or dishonesty in teaching or research, (b) substantial and manifest neglect of duty, and (c) personal conduct which substantially impairs the individual's fulfillment of his institutional responsibilities," such as gross moral or legal turpitude.[42]

Designedly, the Commission's list of terminable offenses, to which many institutions subscribe, does not include the critics' favorite: becoming "deadwood" (as if the university were a forest or lumberyard). No critic has ever marshaled any data—much less a precise definition—to support his allegation of insupportable amounts of faculty "deadwood" protected from pruning by tenure, because none exist. Although one disgruntled sociologist at a large state university estimates that 30 percent of the faculties he has known were dead or "rotten" wood, a Harvard dean puts the figure closer to 2 percent and two AAUP lawyers opt for a more realistic 5 percent.[43]

In thirty years of teaching at four different colleges and universities, I have known only two or three colleagues whose lack of performance warranted dismissal, and even they performed "adequately" in the classroom much more often than not. Neither was formally charged or proceeded against because they were close to retirement, which lends credence to the critics' charge that it is nearly impossible to fire a tenured professor; the expense in time and emotions of conducting fair and thorough dismissal proceedings against a colleague persuade most faculty members to look the other way until the culprit's retirement, or to gladly allow administrators to give him (or her) incentives to leave "voluntarily," by either making his life miserable (salary cuts, more or worse teaching assignments, downgrading his office location) or buying him out (paid leave, a severance package, reassignment to a non-teaching position, or early retirement).

But even without a draconian threat of dismissal, tenure does not offer professors anything like "the ultimate protection from accountability" bemoaned by critics. Faculty members believe they are constantly and heavily accountable, less to outside authorities—critics, media, even legislators—who have inconstant and imperfect understandings of the university's and the professoriate's proper roles and duties, than to the high standards of their own profession. As historian Thomas Haskell has emphasized, "the heart and soul of academic freedom lies not in free speech [per se] but in professional autonomy and collegial self-governance."[44] Like the other three gown-wearing professions (medicine, law, and divinity), the collegiate guild of scholar-teachers is a meritocratic monopoly of experts who self-regulate the production and practice of its members and function disinterestedly in the public interest. Society needs and sanctions autonomous professions because "professionalism is a way of using smart people productively without giving them too much social power."[45] Occasionally, professions need to be reminded of their central missions and public responsibilities, but then they are best left to their own judgment and sense of duty to correct course lest their morale, motivation, and disinterestedness suffer.

Academic accountability begins during long graduate school apprenticeships and rigorous six-year "tournaments" of pre-tenure probation, not unlike medical internships and residencies and the arduous run-up to law firm partnerships. Critics who lament the pressures that young faculty endure to earn tenure cannot then turn around and completely leave out the pre-tenure trial in their indictments of faculty unaccountability. Indeed, as soon as academics begin their scholarly and writing careers, they experience "perpetual exposure to criticism" in the form of dissertation directors, degree committees, book and journal editors, manuscript and book reviewers, conference organizers, commentators, and audiences, and opinionated readers of all sorts.[46] In their college homes, annual merit evaluations by chairpersons, departmental personnel committees, and deans determine salaries and promotions; students evaluate teaching at the end of each course, whose scores and comments weigh in the annual merit ratings; and increasingly, faculty are evaluated every five or six years in post-tenure reviews, which in many institutions can trigger dismissal proceedings if unsatisfactory performance, usually over three years, is not rectified after warnings, counseling, and a similar period of probation.[47] In some universities, mine included, even "permanent" endowed chairholders are thoroughly reviewed every five or six years to ensure against titular torpor or the deadwood disease. The accountability afforded by these external appraisals actually pales in comparison with the fierce self-criticism generated in the vast majority of professors as they measure themselves against the achievements of their fellow members of the ancient, worldwide community of scholars and the unreachable perfectionism of their guild standards. Far from being "unaccountable," most professors feel excessively scrutinized by the professional colleagues who count most, as well as by noisy critics and bandwagon media outside.

If "quality control" and adherence to high professional standards are the critics' chief concerns about tenure, the self-regulating model and mechanisms of the current system should be more than enough to allay them. Yet many budget-conscious administrators and legislators would like to curtail if not abolish tenure to obtain greater control over institutional costs and greater flexibility in program design, allocation, and elimination, regardless of its effect on educational quality. A brief examination of other salient arguments for tenure will provide ample evidence of tenure's ability to speak to, if not solve alone, each of these three problems.

I would argue that the current situation in academe is sufficiently flexible to satisfy even the most managerial administrator, with two exceptions. There is no doubt that tenure hamstrings administrators looking to quickly upgrade the quality of specific departments or the institution as a whole, or to staff large introductory courses annually with variable numbers of younger faculty, all of whom cannot be tenured. But under the AAUP's tenure guidelines, colleges have always been able to eliminate programs for good cause—with the understanding that the affected tenured faculty would be retrained or reassigned to other departments or programs rather than summarily fired. This proviso protects the academic freedom of the faculty while recognizing institutional needs for efficiency and economy.[48]

Moreover, the current profile of faculty status reveals not only plenty of institutional flexibility but an alarming trend away from the quality of teaching and scholarship fostered by the tenure system. Only slightly more than half of America's full-time faculty members are tenured, and perhaps as many as 40 percent of all faculty work only part-time, often for disgraceful wages and no benefits, not even a campus office. America's students are not served best by an unstable "migrant labor" force without any real stake in our institutions or any major and continuous responsibilities to them.[49] Nor do these hardworking, well-qualified professionals deserve to be permanently relegated to second-class citizenship in our amply endowed republic of letters; the loss to society from their underuse and abuse is incalculable.

The arguments against tenure focused on personnel management simply cannot compete with the economic arguments in favor of its retention and larger social benefits. First, the future promise of tenure increases the supply of faculty recruits, thereby lowering the institutional (and social) cost of hiring them. When asked to rank their reasons for choosing an academic career, professors of all ranks cite "intellectual challenge" and "intellectual freedom" as their top two.[50] The first without the second would not be sufficient to attract the same pool of talent.

Second, the relative economic security of tenure also lowers academic salaries from the competitively higher salaries of comparably educated professionals in government and industry. In 1987 the median salary of a Ph.D. in government was 10 percent higher than that of his academic counterpart, and in the private sector, 24 percent higher. Today, the private/academic differential is 38 percent and growing, as academic salaries struggle to keep up with even modest inflation. If colleges and universities dropped the tenure system for short-term contracts and necessarily competitive salaries, the American price tag for higher education would skyrocket. As it is now, professors pay for tenure out of their own pockets, and not with loose change.[51]

A third benefit of tenure is that it allows professors to undertake risky, long-term projects in both teaching and research, especially expensive scientific experiments but also all phases of social science research and humanistic scholarship. A measure of economic security not only encourages teachers to focus more of their time and attention on the classroom, such as in the building of bold, new courses and programs, but it allows scholars to forgo quickly produced, "safe" publications designed to enhance their marketability in favor of longer, adventurous books that reflect more brightly on their home sponsors.

Fourth, tenure enables older faculty members to select young faculty who are brighter and more productive than they are, thereby maintaining the professional meritocracy and preventing the department's and the institution's gradual loss of quality through fear and jealousy.[52]

Fifth, although the pre-tenure tournaments are tough on and often trying for the combatants, they constitute an efficient sorting process in which those un- or underqualified for tenure either withdraw themselves from competition or are forced to withdraw by "up-or-out" policies of promotion. They also promote abnormally high productivity for at least six years, which dips only slightly (about one article a year) immediately after the award of tenure but then returns after promotion to full professor (again one article a year).[53]

And finally, as Princeton economist Fritz Machlup argued more than thirty years ago, "all the disadvantages of a strict tenure system, whether they are borne by the institutions, by the individual teachers, or by the entire academic profession, are outweighed by one important advantage, accruing chiefly to society at large," namely the "social benefits of academic freedom" in the form of scientific and technological advances, which contribute visibly to the gross national product, and of social and cultural improvements from intellectual, moral, and aesthetic discoveries and refinements, which do not appear on balance sheets. In our increasingly knowledge-based culture and economy, highly educated professional faculties are and will remain essential to our national tasks of educating new generations and of transmuting endless bytes of random information into socially usable knowledge and even wisdom. Without full academic freedom to criticize, teach, and search for the truth, fully guaranteed only by tenure, the professoriate cannot fulfill those tasks for the public as it can and should.[54]

RESEARCH. Almost as often as tenure, and for far longer, academic "research" (including scholarship) has been caught in the critics' crosshairs and subject to cheap shots or overcharged salvos of opprobrium. An insider opines (that's the only word for it) that "the vast majority of the so-called research turned out in the modern university"—which we can safely assume the author has not read or even sampled—"is essentially worthless." Because it is largely the product of "scholarship at gunpoint" (the "publish-or-perish" imperative), "it is busywork on a vast, almost incomprehensible scale. It is dispiriting; it depresses the whole scholarly enterprise." A muckraking journalist, reaching for (spurious) specificity, asserts that "at best, only one academic in ten" makes any contribution to the "enlargement of human knowledge." And a former professor-turned-conservative-gadfly, equally omniscient, takes the indictment one step farther: academic research and writing are not just depressing, they constitute "the greatest intellectual fraud of the twentieth century." Depending on which critic you read, either "much" or "most" of the professoriate's published research is unreadable, esoteric, jargon-ridden, trifling, unoriginal, pompous, pedestrian, pretentious, unimportant, irrelevant, inconsequential, or some deadly combination thereof.[55]

And how did the critics learn this "dirty secret of the academic intellectuals?" Not, as we might assume, through superhuman acquaintance with, if not competence in, the myriad specialized disciplines, subdisciplines, and interdisciplines of the modern university, but through sheer audacity and reading the titles, not the contents, of a few academic conference papers and journal articles—the tactic whose anti-intellectualism once won popularity for Senator William Proxmire's "Golden Fleece Awards."[56] Short, specialized papers aimed exclusively at audiences of fellow specialists are, in any field of endeavor, an easy target for titular ridicule or ideological outrage (as in the curriculum "wars"). But while making for good polemics, such tactics make bad policy.

Once the critics have asserted—not demonstrated or proven—that today's research and scholarship is so much mendacious humbug, they draw two corollaries and two conclusions. The first corollary is that the "overproduction" of routine or bad scholarship "tends to conceal really important work by its sheer volume," if indeed it does not drive it completely out. The second corollary is that this "tsunami" of scholarly scribbling is not the product of

235

deeply personal inspiration, passion, or curiosity but the forced bloom of "those who cannot afford not to publish," of scholastic "careerism" in which "volume rather than insight is what counts, and conformity rather than originality is what is rewarded."[57]

The critics' conclusions are as unwarranted as they are unrealistic. The first need, they say, is to stop higher educators from demanding that "*everyone* produce published research." Too many faculty members are being dragooned into doing something they neither want nor are qualified to do, and such a system simply "wastes time and valuable resources" that could much better be put into serious and satisfying teaching. In the "zero-sum" academic world, energy devoted to (second- or third-rate) research is that much energy taken away from the classroom. The second conclusion is that if the research drive cannot be suppressed, "it is certainly reasonable to do all that is possible to discourage anything but the best." If, in fact, only 10 percent of academic research is valuable, surely it behooves the powers-that-be to dam(n) "the terrible flood of mediocre monographs-for-the-sake-of-being-promoted" and to reduce the number of journals to "some manageable, rational number." One critic, a professor's son, rationally suggests that "three-fourths," the "vast majority" anyway, of learned journals "could disappear tomorrow without the slightest diminution in the world's collective knowledge." One can only hope that this paragon of chutzpah would chair the committee called to draw up the periodical hit list.[58]

Perhaps the best way to respond to the critics' scattershot indictment is to return concentrated fire from high ground. To begin, as I have argued in chapter 3, the "publish-or-perish" imperative should not, and does not, apply to "everyone" in American higher education. Only colleges and universities that encourage research by providing reasonable teaching loads, research leaves, adequate facilities (particularly libraries and labs), summer, travel, and publication subvention grants, and merit pay systems have any business expecting their faculties to pursue research as part of their official job descriptions. And, in fact, many professors neither publish nor perish. A 1987-88 study of some eighty-three hundred full- and part-time faculty at 424 representative institutions found that while professors at four-year colleges had published an average of twenty-five items in their careers, the range at different kinds of institutions was wide. Consistent with institutionally appropriate mandates, faculty at research universities had thirty-eight publications, while those at comprehensive universities and liberal arts colleges claimed only twelve and eight, respectively. Even these figures are somewhat deceiving. A pronounced productivity fault line runs between one group consisting of all the research-oriented doctoral universities and about three dozen of the most selective liberal arts colleges (such as Amherst, Williams, and Oberlin) and another group consisting of the rest of our two- and four-year institutions with more exclusively teaching emphases.[59]

The Astin survey of 1995-96 points to a similar division of labor in the nation's faculty ranks. Two-thirds of all faculty at four-year institutions say their primary interest leans toward or is heavily in teaching; only a third give research primacy. During the academic year, nearly half of all faculty devote only four hours or less a week to research and scholarly writing; only 21 percent spend more than thirteen hours. Accordingly, nearly half of the professors had published four or fewer articles (the preferred mode of academic publication) to date; only a third had published eleven or more. More than half had never published a book, and only 8 percent had written five or more.[60]

Of course, all these figures can cut both ways, and the critics are very good at either ignoring the available data altogether (because they, unlike anecdotes, would sap the power of their doomsday generalizations) or using them very selectively to score debater's points. They cannot have it both ways. They cannot, on one hand, charge the nation's professors with "overproduction" and, on the other, assail them as slackers who do the minimum.

If we keep in mind the immense diversity of our higher educational institutions and their specific strengths, limitations, and missions, we will avoid simplistic and overblown characterizations that only kick up dust and solve nothing.

Secondly, whether the professoriate publishes little or a lot of research, it is largely impossible to separate the "best" from the rest *before* publication. A great deal of preselection does occur when manuscripts are peer-reviewed for potential publishers and periodicals. But once manuscripts are accepted, edited, and published, there is no reasonable or fair way to distinguish excellence from mediocrity or worse except through the current standard process of slow, patient, exacting assessment by "communities of the competent," largely but not exclusively academic.[61] This scrutiny also prevents the less good from swamping or drowning the superior because all scholarly disciplines recognize a hierarchy of periodicals and publishers, concentrate their attention on the best ones, and rely on a large company of expert reviewers, citation indices, select bibliographies, and collegial gossip to help them assign worth to the published corpus and, annually, award prizes. Busy teachers don't have time to waste pursuing low-grade scholarship, and they have both the noses and the tools (including the Internet) to home in on the best most of the time.

Another reason not to prejudge and dismiss published research, no matter how convoluted its argument or ungainly its prose, is that it may prove valuable in the future, either to a single researcher or to posterity at large. The histories of ideas, science, and technology are replete with discoveries that were too far ahead of their times to gain immediate credence and recognition. Had they been consigned precipitously to the dustbin or the flames, we would all be the poorer.

Even if, by definition, all scholars cannot produce the best work on an absolute scale, they can and should be encouraged, even prodded, to produce the best of which *they* are capable. Even if they do not possess the intellectual or literary skills to place an

238

article in one of the leading journals, they probably have the talent to make the cut of a more modest, more local, or more specialized journal where their contributions will garner at least a few readers interested in their subject or treatment. The most important thing about scholarship is less the number or even quality of results than the habitual process of critical engagement with the advanced ideas and materials of one's discipline. This is doubly true when the investigation leads to a dead end or a negative conclusion, for negative results often are heuristically as valuable as positive ones.

Nor do we need to fret unduly about the motivations of those who research and publish. Academe has its share of fast-tracking entrepreneurs who try to outhustle their imagined competitors by publishing every emanation of their minds. Our colleges and universities also harbor a number of professors who, for one reason or another, need reminding that taking a research-oriented Ph.D. entails obligations in kind to the scholarly community and need prompting to fulfill them with a combination of carrots and sticks. But in my experience, the first group, happily, is a very small anomaly and the second is perhaps larger than it should be but still unproblematically human.

It would be ideal if every scholar pursued his or her research from the purest of motives (sheer curiosity being the best) and with semidivine inspiration and deep passion. But it would be unrealistic to expect it, professors being as varied as the next professionals, and work, no matter how rewarding, being what it is. Thus the need for tenure tournaments, annual merit evaluations, post-tenure reviews, decanal pep talks, and perhaps my own "Twenty-five Reasons to Publish" (chapter 3). Most productive people, writers in particular, know that the daily application of seat to chair and sustained effort are much more fruitful than awaiting the elusive and often tardy Muse. If the undemonized "publish-or-perish" policy of our most ambitious and capable colleges and universities "encourages a recalcitrant scholar to share his [or her] discoveries with others, or to engage in research when he [or she] would not otherwise have done so, then that policy indeed serves a useful function."[62] As long as we reward quality and not mere quantity, and do not expect all faculty members to fulfill their academic responsibilities with exactly the same style and rhythm, the academic meritocracy will remain vital, efficient, and fair.

The final shibboleths we need to exorcise are that academic work is a zero-sum proposition and that the faculty compulsion for research has caused a scandalous "flight from teaching." As we have seen in chapter 1, academics rarely confine themselves to a forty-hour workweek (except perhaps in the summer).[63] On average they work about fifty-three hours a week, but those who mainly teach in two-year community colleges, for example, put in "only" forty-seven hours while those who both teach and pursue research in research universities commit an extra ten hours a week to their arguably more complex, demanding, and engrossing jobs. Of course, even within those various types of institutions, individual professors work longer and shorter hours than the average. Overall, those who do the most research, publish the most, and teach graduate students as well as undergraduates work the longest hours during the academic year and especially in the summer.[64] This should not surprise us. Professors, no less than other mortals, come with or acquire different quotients of ambition, talent, focus, and energy, and these variations, as much as differing interests or priorities, may explain why the academic workweek and year—and the scholarly products they yield—are not the same for everyone. Productive professors simply spend more time in their studies and labs, take shorter vacations, see less of their friends and families, and get up earlier or stay up later than their colleagues.

Not only are productive faculty rate-busters in research, they are more active in governance and administration, they do as much teaching as their more single-minded teaching colleagues, and, in several key respects, they do it better. First of all, student/teacher ratios in doctoral universities, where one might expect a decline, have not changed from what they were in the 1950s. Nor has the median time spent on teaching and preparation changed. And although the course load of the average teacher has dropped during the century, largely to accommodate revised institutional missions, the load at nearly three-fourths of our colleges and universities, including 55 percent of all four-year institutions, is four or more courses per semester; only at major research universities is the typical assignment four or five courses a year.[65]

Once today's students enter the classroom, they find, across the nation, that research-active professors usually have as many contact hours with students, teach as many introductory courses, teach only undergraduates as frequently, give the same attention and time to students out of class, and use the same labor-intensive teaching methods and evaluations as their pedagogical counterparts who publish less. Characteristically, they also assign more scholarly books and articles and ask more rigorous exam questions than their colleagues. Of thirty studies in the last thirty years that sought to determine the relationship between research and teaching, only one found a conflict; eleven discovered subtle or significant degrees of complementarity and the rest drew blanks.[66] In short, there is virtually no proof—only repetitious hearsay and wishful ideology—that America's professors are in full or even partial flight from teaching and that research is the cause.

Unlike teaching, which is uniquely mandatory, "time spent on research is in large part voluntary." (This alone should make us reject the critics' insinuation that teaching is somehow more noble and moral, less selfish and narcissistic, than research.) But if professors choose to devote themselves to scholarly pursuits and writing, they do not do so at the expense of their students, for two compelling reasons. One is that "a university value system guides the profession and . . . faculty members are aware of prescribed behaviors."[67] The second is that they are convinced as an article of faith and a product of experience that their scholarly interests not only enhance the quality of their teaching and their students' learning but sustain their zest for teaching throughout their careers.

The plain fact is that, over many years, some aspects of teaching—not all of them by any means—tend to wear you out, mostly the repetition, the ageless youth of the student mind, and the reading and laborious editing of student exams and papers. Research, on the other hand, is "less attritional" (though it, too, has its dreary moments) because of its variety and its higher levels of intellectual activity and audience.[68] Professors who are refreshed and challenged regularly by their research tend to bring the passion, intellectual rigor, and moral discipline of the scholarly process into their classrooms, even when the specific subject matter or methods are inappropriate or too recondite for undergraduates.

TEACHING. Compared to the other four fields of faculty folly and malfeasance, critical opinion of the quality of college teaching covers a narrower spectrum and is less marked—but not unmarked—by apocalyptic hyperbole. One former insider purports to expose "the secret shame of *most* universities and colleges": the "studied neglect of the teaching of students," predicated on "a widespread contempt for teaching among teachers." A muckraking journalist adds foolish fuel to righteous ire by titling one chapter "The Crucifixion of Teaching" and claiming that "the academic culture is not merely indifferent to teaching, it is actively hostile to it. In the modern university, no act of good teaching goes unpunished," an allusion to the alleged propensity of colleges and universities to fire (deny tenure to) young faculty to whom they have just given outstanding teaching awards, also known as "the kiss of death."[69]

Most critics, however, worry only that too many professors

have "abandoned" teaching to chase the false god Research, leaving their classes to harried part-timers and "unqualified" graduate teaching assistants (TAS) or brainless audiovisual surrogates. Huge lecture courses, poor advising, and long registration lines also come in for appropriate censure. One of the latest critics to weigh in, a sociological insider, has declared war on what he calls "The Seven Pedagogical Sins": abandonment (of students), (sexual) harassment and exploitation, misrepresentation (trafficking in outdated information), special pleading (indoctrination), default (assuming the worst about students' abilities and making no demands), proud incompetence, and particularistic assessment (favoritism). To add verisimilitude to their dark portraits, he and other critics retail classroom horror stories from their own (limited) knowledge or, more commonly, from published student course guides at select private or large public universities.[70]

The critics' central problem, however, is that no data exist to support generalizations about poor teaching nationwide, for two reasons. The first is that teaching is largely invisible. In its overt form, it takes place privately behind closed doors, and in its essence it occurs in the minds of teachers and students. Indeed, what transpires visibly in the classroom is less important than "what has happened in the professor's mind before he sets foot in [it], and what happens in the students' minds after they have left it and pursued their assignment."[71] The second reason is that, while *poor* teaching is easily recognizable, there is little agreement on what constitutes *good* teaching. There is some consensus on the constituents of good teaching in principle, but when it comes to recognizing good teaching in action, consensus breaks down, for good reason.

Teaching is a very personal transaction between teacher and student, both of whom must be prepared for intellectual synapsis. On the professorial side, the quality of teaching depends most heavily on intellectual mastery of subject and discipline, on imagination (for empathy with one's audience and selection of the best approaches to it), and on personality. No two teachers possess these in the same measure or combination, nor are any two audiences equally receptive to or comfortable with even the best-prepared teacher. And the ubiquitous wild card is classroom climate or mood, which affects every pedagogical encounter.

In order to discover whether America's professors hate teaching and are abandoning their classes, we should first consult the professors themselves. When the Astin survey did that in 1995-96, today's faculties said just the opposite of what the critics are saying about them. Virtually all thirty-four thousand faculty surveyed put being a good teacher at the top of their professional goals; only slightly over half wanted to engage in research. "Opportunities for teaching" was among the top four reasons they gave for choosing an academic career (at 72 percent only slightly below intellectual challenge and freedom). Three-quarters of them said that their *primary* interest lay in teaching, not research. Seventy percent had developed a new course in the past two years. And most remarkable of all, more than a *third* had won an award for outstanding teaching at some point in their career.[72]

Apparently, they did not earn those prizes by sloughing off. Nearly half taught between nine and sixteen hours a week; two-thirds spent between five and sixteen hours preparing to teach and evaluating student work (another 27 percent spent between seventeen and forty-five hours), and more than three-quarters advised or counseled students up to eight hours a week. By contrast, nearly three-quarters spent fewer than eight hours on research and scholarly writing. Only half included research and publishing demands among their top five sources of job stress, and in 1989-90 only half of those felt that research interfered with their *own* teaching.[73] If what they say and what they do are any indication, professors spend the great majority of their time and effort on the teaching side of their jobs.[74]

My own experience in three research universities certainly

bears that out. My colleagues and I invariably attend to our teaching duties and students' needs before turning our attention to our scholarship or writing, only in small part because our unfinished books and articles cannot protest nearly as loudly to our chairperson or dean or on our course evaluations as our students can if we miss class without notice, return papers "late" (like most writers, students expect instant editorial response), or cancel office hours on a whim. Graduate students have access to us year-round and we expect, and are expected, to read their chapters, theses, and dissertations summer or winter. Much of our lunchtime and hallway chat revolves around students, courses, and teaching problems and strategies.

Pedagogical effectiveness is also on the national professoriate's mind, to judge by the increasing variety of their teaching techniques. Far and away the faculty's most important goals for undergraduates are to develop their ability to think clearly and to increase their desire and ability to undertake self-directed learning; neither goal can be realized through rote memorization or passive listening. Since 1989, extensive lecturing has dropped 7 percentage points (to 49 percent) as a method used in all or most courses at the more than four hundred institutions included in the Astin surveys. Appropriately, class discussion is by far the most popular vehicle (68 percent use it), but cooperative learning, independent projects, group projects, computer-aided instruction, and multiple drafts of written work have gained substantial ground in just five years.[75] If these healthy trends continue, we can reasonably expect even more than a third of the intellectual changes that college students typically experience to result directly from their courses and professors.[76]

Not only are the nation's faculties personally and professionally committed to teaching, the quantitative retreat from teaching "exposed" by the critics is largely an illusion. According to the best data we have (from the U.S. Department of Education), college enrollments quadrupled between 1959 and 1993, but the national faculty grew only two and a half times. By 1969, the ratio of students to professors had jumped from less than ten to one to nearly eighteen to one, and it has dropped, very recently, by only two students since then through the use of part-time faculty.[77] Thus, in the last thirty years, relatively fewer professors were obliged to teach considerably more students.

At the same time, three other trends were occurring. One was the accelerated proliferation and specialization of knowledge in the world in general and in the university in particular, which resulted in the curricular ferment and growth we have already examined. The second trend was an extension of the "publish-or-perish" imperative down the Carnegie scale of institutions, sometimes too far and too fast, but overall with a salutary recognition that habitual scholarship is a vital and essential part of the professional obligations of college and university professors.

The third trend was a related pedagogical shift toward more sophisticated, more learning-oriented teaching methods and materials. In the fast-paced age of television, computers, and the Web, Professor Chipses who taught essentially the same courses year after year, who lectured at passive crowds of restless undergraduates, who assigned only textbooks, and who graded on a curve according to (machine-readable) quiz and exam scores were slowly but surely superannuated and accordingly suffered low course enrollments and evaluations, which are as bruising to the professorial ego as harsh book reviews. The explosion of new subjects, new theories and perspectives, and new scholarly publications meant that most disciplines were now deeper, broader, and more reticulate than ever before, and courses therefore required more preparation, management skills, and attention to the eternal problems of student learning. The shift of attention from teaching professor to student learner alone entailed more class discussion, more individualized work with each student, more independent research papers and drafts, more use of scholarly monographs and articles, more assistance from audiovisual aids and computers—in general, more out-of-class time and attention than hitherto. It also meant a serious reallocation of course offerings: in order to make room for more specialized, mid-level lecture courses and more freshman, upper-level, and graduate seminars (which, contrary to the critics, are *not* easier but *harder* to teach than lecture courses), introductory courses were forced to grow in size, though often with numerous "breakout" sections for discussion and evaluation purposes.

To accommodate the masses of new students and to realize the curricular reforms, the professoriate also changed. For many faculties, particularly in research-oriented universities, teaching several courses to large numbers of increasingly diverse students, especially teaching them in the new key, carefully, and well, became ever more difficult. So, in the name of professional integrity and pedagogical quality, they demanded and received some relief, in three forms. First, they taught a course or two less each year. Second, cost-conscious administrations hired greater numbers of part-time or nontenurable adjuncts, instructors, and advanced graduate students to supplement the inadequate numbers of full-time faculty. And, third, senior faculty tended to leave the discussion sections, elementary language, math, and composition classes, science labs, and some of the introductory courses to their junior colleagues, both full- and part-time, while they concentrated their advanced learning and experience on mid-sized, upper-level courses, seminars with individualized research papers, graduate courses, and the occasional introductory lecture course.

We easily forget that all careers, including academic ones, proceed in almost predictable stages and rhythms, and that career-makers have characteristic rights and responsibilities that change with age and status.[78] Since the senior professors, in their turn, had already served in the lower-level courses, they felt little guilt (which the critics would like to impose) over the new division of

247

labor. After all, they might have reasoned, federal judges have clerks, engineers have draftspersons, and physicians have physician's assistants and nurses—all of whom are well-trained professionals in their own right—to help them do their jobs more efficiently, which in turn benefits the public and lowers costs.

In general, when they were not carried to extremes or abused by a few faculty "stars" or prima donnas, these changes have been beneficial to higher education's teaching mission. But the accelerated hiring of part-time instructors (who now constitute 40 percent of our faculties, almost double their numbers in 1970) and the unsupervised deployment of graduate TAs in courses for which they are sometimes not yet qualified to teach are, as the critics allege, a growing shame for both the employees and their students. We needn't worry much about the qualifications of the part-timers because they are either qualified Ph.D.s or ABDs ("all but dissertation" graduate students) who have done the coursework and reading for at least minimal mastery of the discipline; most are dedicated, hard-working, active scholars unlucky in a buyer's market, many of them women. But the frenetic, unstable, ill-supported conditions in which they work should cause concern in both academe and the public.[79]

Although one critic calls them unqualified "children . . . playing at being professors . . . before they are ready," graduate TAs can and should be in the classroom before donning their doctoral robes—as long as they are carefully mentored before and throughout their teaching.[80] If they do not receive adequate training for teaching before they take their degrees, they will begin their first jobs, with full complements of new courses, ill-prepared for the classroom and guaranteed to practice all the novice's mistakes upon their hapless students. A gradual apprenticeship in pedagogy is much preferable.

TAs come in two shapes. Before completing their coursework and taking their comprehensive or qualifying exams, many graduate students serve as graders, discussants, and contact persons in breakout sections of larger, often introductory lecture courses taught by senior professors. Since they are new to the work, these neophytes need a great deal of guidance, optimally in weekly planning sessions with the supervising professor.

The second group of TAs are often awarded their own courses—small introductory lecture courses or upper-level seminars in their specialties—for which they have complete responsibility. Abuses arise either when they have not yet proceeded to ABD status, thus signaling lack of preparation in their discipline, or when they are not given a conscientious faculty mentor to oversee every phase of their teaching.

In my experience, graduate student-teachers are well primed with new knowledge, imaginative in its applications, devoted to their students, and not afraid of hard work, and many of them outscore their seniors on student course evaluations. They are exactly the kind of professors we should want in our classes in the future. One of the professoriate's challenges is to ensure that these initiates continue to regard good teaching as socially valuable and personally fulfilling as good scholarship. This will be no easy task because nonpublishing teachers, even exemplary or prize-winning ones, are not rewarded as well as productive scholar-teachers, for the simple reason that the latter are rarer and their expertise is more marketable in the prestige-and-knowledge economies of academe and the world.[81]

"Teaching," one critic reminds us, "is both one of the hardest and one of the easiest jobs in the world, depending on how conscientiously it is done."[82] If today's faculties do not convincingly and studiously promote to the next academic generation the professional ethic and compelling attractions of teaching, too many of them will come to regard it as an easy task, to be performed grudgingly or carelessly, without dedication, skill, or effort. But they—we—must try to convince them, by our words and our example, that teaching's rewards are intrinsic and pure, that witnessing the flash of understanding in a student's eyes can be as deeply satisfying as our own, that we teach because we must and love to share what we have learned with others, that our perpetually youthful students keep us young while we try to make them older, that teachers work more with the possible future than with the improbable present or the intractable past, that there is a unique and selfless pleasure in teaching to become dispensable. If we can make them see these things, they will have a fighting chance of becoming the kind of teacher-scholars we seek to be (and sometimes are) and of regarding our profession, as many of us do, not only as worthy, rewarding, and socially useful but as a true vocation, the best possible choice for us all.[83]

Notes

1. See, for example, Charles Frankel, *Education and the Barricades* (New York: W. W. Norton, 1968); Roger Rapoport and Laurence J. Kirshbaum, *Is the Library Burning?* (New York: Random House, 1969); Buell Gallagher, *Campus in Crisis* (New York: Harper & Row, 1969); Edward J. Bander, ed., *Turmoil on the Campus*, The Reference Shelf, vol. 42, no. 3 (New York: H. W. Wilson, 1970); Edward Bloomberg, *Student Violence* (Washington DC: Public Affairs Press, 1970); Sidney Hook, *Academic Freedom and Academic Anarchy* (New York: Dell, 1970); Jacquelyn Estrada, ed., *The University under Siege* (Los Angeles: Nash, 1971); K. Ross Toole, *The Time Has Come to Say the Things That Need to Be Said about Campus Violence, the Tyranny of a Minority, the Crusade of the Spoiled Children, the Parental Abdication of Responsibility, and the Lack of Courage, Integrity, and Wisdom on the Part of Our Educational Leaders* (New York: Morrow, 1971); Edward E. Ericson Jr., *Radicals in the University* (Stanford CA: Hoover Institution, 1975).

2. See below, chap. 1, n. 4, for selected titles.

3. Claude Charleton Bowman, *The College Professor in America: An Analysis of Articles Published in the General Magazines, 1890–1938* (Philadelphia: University of Pennsylvania, 1938).

4. Linda J. Sax, Alexander W. Astin, Marisol Arredondo, and William S. Korn, *The American College Teacher: National Norms for the 1995–96 HERI Faculty Survey* (Los Angeles: UCLA Higher Education Research Institute, September 1996), 43.

5. The mis- and underuse of these part-timers is a national tragedy. They love their work so much—as fragmented, frenetic, and undercompensated as it is—that in 1987 89 percent of them would have chosen it again ("Fact File: Faculty Attitudes, Workload, and Earnings, Fall 1987," *Chronicle of Higher Education* [CHE], 7 February 1990, A16). Today, as their numbers expand and their exploitation worsens, their approval rating would undoubtedly be somewhat lower.

6. Peter Costa, *Q & A: Conversations with Harvard Scholars* (Cambridge MA: Harvard University Office of News and Public Affairs, 1991), 97.

7. Charles G. Osgood, *Lights in Nassau Hall: A Book of the Bicentennial: Princeton, 1746–1946* (Princeton NJ: Princeton University Press, 1951), 3.

1. (MIS)UNDERSTANDING ACADEMIC WORK

1. "The Politics of Intervention: External Regulation of Academic Activities and Workloads in Public Higher Education," *Academe* 82, no. 1 (January–February 1996): 46–52.

2. Alexander W. Astin, William S. Korn, and Eric L. Dey, *The American College Teacher: National Norms for the 1989–90 HERI Faculty Survey* (Los Angeles: UCLA Higher Education Research Institute, March 1991), 40; Sax et al., *The American College Teacher, 1995–96*, 33.

3. U.S. Department of Education, *Digest of Education Statistics 1996* (Washington DC: National Center for Education Statistics, 1996), 231 (table 220).

4. Paul Von Blum, *Stillborn Education: A Critique of the American Research University* (Lanham MD: University Press of America, 1986); Bruce W. Wilshire, *The Moral Collapse of the University: Professionalism, Purity, and Alienation* (Albany: State University of New York Press, 1990); Page Smith, *Killing the Spirit: Higher Education in America* (New York: Viking, 1990); Roger Kimball, *Tenured Radicals: How Politics Has Corrupted Our Higher Education* (New York: Harper & Row, 1990); George H. Douglas, *Education without Impact: How Our Universities Fail the Young* (New York: Carol Publishing Group, 1992); Martin Anderson, *Impostors in the Temple* (New York: Simon & Schuster, 1992); Julius Getman, *In the Company of Scholars: The Struggle for the Soul of Higher Education* (Austin: University of Texas Press, 1992); Richard M. Huber, *How Professors Play the Cat Guarding the Cream: Why We're Paying More and Getting Less in Higher Education* (Fairfax VA: George Mason University Press, 1992); Thomas Sowell, *Inside American Education: The Decline, the Deception, the Dogmas* (New York: Free Press, 1993); Jacob Neusner and Noam M. M. Neusner, *The Price of*

Excellence: Universities in Conflict during the Cold War Era (New York: Continuum, 1995); David Damrosch, *We Scholars: Changing the Culture of the University* (Cambridge MA: Harvard University Press, 1995); Cary Nelson, *Manifesto of a Tenured Radical* (New York: New York University Press, 1997); and Michael Lewis, *Poisoning the Ivy: The Seven Deadly Sins and Other Vices of Higher Education in America* (Armonk NY: M. E. Sharpe, 1997), were written by professors or former professors, some for only a short time.

5. "Fact File: Faculty Attitudes, Workload, and Earnings, Fall 1987," A16.

6. Astin et al., *The American College Teacher, 198990*; Sax et al., *The American College Teacher, 1995-96*.

7. Jeffrey L. Sammons, "What Do Professors Do?" *Yale Alumni Magazine and Journal*, December 1979, 22 – 25; Mary Rosenthal Lefkowitz, "'Now Just What Do Faculty Do?'" *Wellesley*, fall 1989, 28 – 29, 42; Allan W. Winkler, "Explaining What Professors Do with Their Time," *CHE*, 15 July 1992, B1 – B2; Winkler, "The Faculty Workload Question," *Change* 24, no. 4 (July/August 1992): 36 – 41; Julia M. Davis, "A Call for Change," *CLA Today* [College of Liberal Arts, University of Minnesota – Twin Cities], May 1993, 2 – 3. For a British perspective, see Jane Wills, "Reflections: Laboring for Love? A Comment on Academics and Their Hours of Work," *Antipode* 28, no. 3 (1996): 292 – 303.

8. *CHE*, 7 February 1990, A16.

9. *CHE*, 16 November 1994, A45. See also "The Work of Faculty: Expectations, Priorities, and Rewards," *Academe* 80, no. 1 (January – February 1994): 35 – 48; Frank Guliuzza III, "Asking Professor Jones to Fix the Crisis in Higher Education Is Getting More and More Expensive," *Academe* 82, no. 5 (September – October 1996): 28 – 32; Beth Anne Shelton and Sheryl Skaggs, "How Faculty Members Spend Their Time: A Closer Look," *Academe* 82, no. 5 (September – October 1996): 16 – 20.

10. See below, chap. 11; John Yemma, "How Profs Vacation," *Boston Globe*, 18 June 1996, 1, 10; Lionel S. Lewis, *Marginal Worth: Teaching and the Academic Labor Market* (New Brunswick NJ: Transaction, 1996), 57 – 58.

11. *CHE*, 7 February 1990, A16; Astin et al., *The American College*

Teacher, 1989 – 90, 40, 41; Sax et al., *The American College Teacher, 1995 – 96*, 33, 34.

12. CHE *Almanac*, 2 September 1996, 3.

13. Astin et al., *The American College Teacher, 1989 – 90*, 40; Sax et al., *The American College Teacher, 1995 – 96*, 33.

14. William Harrison Woodward, *Desiderius Erasmus Concerning the Aim and Method of Education*, Classics in Education, no. 19 (New York: Teachers College Press, 1964), 166 (slightly paraphrased).

15. CHE *Almanac*, 2 September 1996, 3.

16. See below, chap. 9.

17. Michael Rogers Rubin and Mary Taylor Huber, *The Knowledge Industry in the United States, 1960 – 1980* (Princeton NJ: Princeton University Press, 1986), 24 – 25.

18. See below, chap. 3.

19. James Charlton, ed., *The Writer's Quotation Book: A Literary Companion* (New York: Penguin Books, 1981), 27.

20. James O. Freedman, "The Professor's Life," *Dartmouth Alumni Magazine*, February 1991, 14, reprinted in Freedman, *Idealism and Liberal Education* (Ann Arbor: University of Michigan Press, 1996), 99 – 102.

21. Peter J. Markie, *A Professor's Duties: Ethical Issues in College Teaching* (Lanham MD: Rowman & Littlefield, 1994), 5.

2. SCHOLARSHIP RECONSIDERED

1. William G. Bowen and Neil L. Rudenstine, *In Pursuit of the PhD* (Princeton NJ: Princeton University Press, 1992), 32.

2. National Academy of Sciences, *Doctorate Recipients from United States Universities, 1958 – 1966*, NAS Publication 1489 (Washington DC: National Academy Press, 1967), 95 (table 23); National Academy of Sciences, *Summary Report 1991: Doctorate Recipients from United States Universities* (Washington DC: National Academy Press, 1993), 98 (appendix table B-2); the minority figures include foreign nationals on permanent visas as well as native-born Indians, blacks, Hispanics, and Asians.

3. Bernard Berelson, *Graduate Education in the United States* (New

York: McGraw-Hill, 1960), 135, 149, 168, 181; Bowen and Rudenstine, *In Pursuit of the PhD*, 119 (table 6.2), 399 (table G.6-1).

4. Bowen and Rudenstine, *In Pursuit of the PhD*, 21, 61–62.

5. Bowen and Rudenstine, *In Pursuit of the PhD*, 24 (table 2.3); William G. Bowen and Julie Ann Sosa, *Prospects for Faculty in the Arts and Sciences* (Princeton NJ: Princeton University Press, 1989), 47–51.

6. Berelson, *Graduate Education in the U.S.*, 196.

7. James B. Gardner, "Jobs Lag as New Ph.D.s Continue to Increase," *Perspectives: American Historical Association Newsletter* 31, no. 1 (January 1993): 4 (table 5).

8. CHE *Almanac*, 2 September 1996, 20 (1995 Doctorate Recipients); these figures, too, include foreigners on permanent visas.

9. Bowen and Rudenstine, *In Pursuit of the PhD*, 62; Theodore Ziolkowski, "The Ph.D. Squid," *The American Scholar* 59, no. 2 (spring 1990): 182.

10. Bowen and Rudenstine, *In Pursuit of the PhD*, 97–98, 108, 399 (table G.6-1); CHE *Almanac*, 2 September 1996, 20.

11. Howard R. Bowen and Jack H. Schuster, *American Professors: A National Resource Imperiled* (New York: Oxford University Press, 1986), chap. 10; National Academy of Sciences, *Summary Report 1991: Doctorate Recipients*, 74 (appendix table A-3).

12. Sax et al., *The American College Teacher, 1995–96*, 33.

13. Ernest L. Boyer, *Scholarship Reconsidered: Priorities of the Professoriate* (Princeton NJ: Carnegie Foundation for the Advancement of Teaching, 1990), appendix A, table A-29; Carnegie Foundation for the Advancement of Teaching, *The Condition of the Professoriate: Attitudes and Trends, 1989* (Princeton NJ: Carnegie Foundation, 1989), 58 (table 45), 59 (table 46), 67 (chart 18).

14. Douglas Greenberg, *Fellowships in the Humanities, 1983–1991*, ACLS Occasional Paper, no. 18 (New York: American Council of Learned Societies, 1992), 1n. 1, 7, 23 (fig. 1). The recent deep cuts in federal appropriations for the national endowments for the arts and the humanities have raised the award ratios considerably. See also John H. D'Arms, "Funding Trends in the Academic Humanities, 1970–1995: Reflections on the Stability of the System," in *What's Happened to*

the Humanities? ed. Alvin Kernan (Princeton NJ: Princeton University Press, 1997), chap. 2.

15. Greenberg, *Fellowships in the Humanities, 1983-1991,* 5, 8, 9-11, 12, 37 (fig. 15).

16. Clifford Geertz, "Blurred Genres: The Refiguration of Social Thought," *The American Scholar* 29, no. 2 (spring 1980): 165-79, reprinted in Geertz, *Local Knowledge: Further Essays in Interpretive Anthropology* (New York: Basic Books, 1983), chap. 1.

17. James Axtell, "Ethnohistory: An Historian's Viewpoint," in Axtell, *The European and the Indian: Essays in the Ethnohistory of Colonial North America* (New York: Oxford University Press, 1981), chap. 1; Shepard Krech III, "The State of Ethnohistory," *Annual Review of Anthropology* 20 (1991): 345-75. See below, chap. 8.

18. For a thorough and fair-minded guide to the massive literature, see Pauline Marie Rosenau, *Post-Modernism and the Social Sciences: Insights, Inroads, and Intrusions* (Princeton NJ: Princeton University Press, 1992).

19. Advertisements from UMI (Louisville KY) and the Institute for Scientific Information (Philadelphia).

20. James Axtell, "Confessions of a Bibliolater," *Virginia Quarterly Review* 64 (winter 1988): 134-47, and chap. 6 above.

21. James H. Sweetland, "Humanists, Libraries, Electronic Publishing, and the Future," *Library Trends* 40, no. 4 (spring 1992): 782. For more optimistic prognoses, see *Technology, Scholarship, and the Humanities: The Implications of Electronic Information, September 30 – October 2, 1992 . . . Summary of Proceedings* [of a conference sponsored by the American Council of Learned Societies and the Getty Art History Information Program, Irvine CA] (1993), and Pamela Pavliscak, Seamus Ross, and Charles Henry, *Information Technology in Humanities Scholarship: Achievements, Prospects, and Challenges,* ACLS Occasional Paper, no. 37 (New York: American Council of Learned Societies, 1997).

22. Karl J. Weintraub, "The Humanities Scholar and the Library," *Library Quarterly* 50, no. 1 (January 1980): 22-39; Margaret F. Stieg, "The Information of [sic] Needs of Historians," *College and Research Libraries* 42, no. 6 (November 1981): 549-60; Sue Stone, "Humanities

Scholars: Information Needs and Uses," *Journal of Documentation* 38, no. 4 (December 1982): 292-313; Stephen K. Stoan, "Research and Library Skills: An Analysis and Interpretation," *College and Research Libraries* 45, no. 2 (March 1984): 99-109; John M. Budd, "Research in the Two Cultures: The Nature of Scholarship in Science and the Humanities," *Collection Management* 11, no. 3-4 (1989): 1-21; Stephen E. Wiberley Jr. and William G. Jones, "Patterns of Information Seeking in the Humanities," *College and Research Libraries* 50, no. 6 (November 1989): 638-45; Barbara C. Orbach, "The View from the Researcher's Desk: Historians' Perceptions of Research and Repositories," *American Archivist* 54, no. 1 (winter 1991): 28-43; Donald Owen Case, "The Collection and Use of Information by Some American Historians: A Study of Motives and Methods," *Library Quarterly* 61, no. 1 (January 1991): 61-82; Matthew B. Gilmore and Donald O. Case, "Historians, Books, Computers, and the Library," *Library Trends* 40, no. 4 (spring 1992): 667-86; Sweetland, "Humanists, Libraries, Electronic Publishing, and the Future," 781-803; Carla Hesse, "Humanities and the Library in the Digital Age," in Kernan, *What's Happened to the Humanities?* chap. 5.

23. Case, "The Collection and Use of Information by Some American Historians," 78-79; Orbach, "The View from the Researcher's Desk," 35, 38; Wiberley and Jones, "Patterns of Information Seeking in the Humanities," 638, 642; Stoan, "Research and Library Skills," 100, 101, 103; Stieg, "The Information of [sic] Needs of Historians," 554 (table 3), 555.

24. Northrop Frye, "The Search for Acceptable Words," *Daedalus* 102, no. 2 (spring 1973): 17.

25. Mary Ellen Soper, "Characteristics and Use of Personal Collections," *Library Quarterly* 46, no. 4 (October 1976): 397-415.

26. U.S. Department of Education, *Digest of Education Statistics, 1995* (Washington DC: USGPO, 1996), 299 (table 218), 231 (table 221), as of fall 1993.

27. U.S. Department of Education, *Digest of Education Statistics, 1995*, 231 (table 221); Anthony DePalma, "Rare in Ivy League: Women Who Work as Full Professors," *New York Times*, 24 January 1993, 1, 23. See also Lynn Hunt, "Democratization and Decline? The Con-

sequences of Demographic Change in the Humanities," in Kernan, *What's Happened to the Humanities?* 20-21, 25.

28. Logan Wilson, "The Professor and His Roles," in *Improving College Teaching*, ed. Calvin B. T. Lee (Washington DC: American Council on Education, 1967), 105.

29. Everett Carll Ladd Jr., "The Work Experience of American College Professors: Some Data and an Argument," *Current Issues in Higher Education*, vol. 2 (Washington DC: American Association for Higher Education, 1979), 5.

30. Boyer, *Scholarship Reconsidered*, tables A-19, A-20, A-21, A-22; Sax et al., *The American College Teacher, 1995-96*, 34. Since the 1989-90 Astin survey, the hours devoted to research and writing have dropped dramatically, about 7 percentage points in each category (Astin et al., *The American College Teacher, 1989-90*, 41).

31. Sax et al., *The American College Teacher, 1995-96*, 38, 43.

32. Carnegie Foundation, *The Condition of the Professoriate*, 48 (table 35), 49 (table 36), 110 (table 82).

33. Ladd, "The Work Experience of American College Professors," 10 (table 9); Boyer, *Scholarship Reconsidered*, table A-32; Astin et al., *The American College Teacher, 1989-90*, 45 (the 1995-96 Astin survey did not ask the question about the conflict between teaching and research); Peter J. Gray, Robert C. Froh, and Robert M. Diamond, *A National Study of Research Universities on the Balance between Research and Undergraduate Teaching* (Syracuse NY: Center for Instructional Development, Office of Evaluation and Research, Syracuse University, March 1992).

34. Sax et al., *The American College Teacher, 1995-96*, 44.

35. Carnegie Foundation for the Advancement of Teaching, "Change Trendlines: The Payoff for Publication Leaders," *Change* 23, no. 2 (March/April 1991): 27-30.

36. Paul Parsons, *Getting Published: The Acquisition Process at University Presses* (Knoxville: University of Tennessee Press, 1989); Eleanor Harman and Ian Montagnes, eds., *The Thesis and the Book* (Toronto: University of Toronto Press, 1976); Norman Fiering, *A Guide to Book Publication for Historians* (Washington DC: American Historical Asso-

ciation, 1979); Robin Derricourt, *An Author's Guide to Scholarly Publishing* (Princeton NJ: Princeton University Press, 1996); Joseph M. Moxley, *Publish, Don't Perish: The Scholar's Guide to Academic Writing and Publishing* (Westport CT: Greenwood Publishing Group, 1992); Alida Allison and Terri Frongia, *The Grad Student's Guide to Getting Published* (New York, 1992); Beth Luey, *Handbook for Academic Authors*, rev. ed. (New York: Cambridge University Press, 1990).

37. Chester Kerr, "One More Time: American University Presses Revisited," *Scholarly Publishing* 18, no. 4 (July 1987): 213; Sanford Thatcher, "Scholarly Monographs May Be the Ultimate Victims of the Upheavals in Trade Publishing," CHE, 10 October 1990, B2–B3; Herbert S. Bailey Jr., "The Future of University Press Publishing," *Scholarly Publishing* 19, no. 2 (January 1988): 63–69.

38. Dennis P. Carrigan, "Publish or Perish: The Troubled State of Scholarly Communication," *Scholarly Publishing* 22, no. 3 (April 1991): 138; Carolyn J. Mooney, "In 2 Years, a Million Refereed Articles, 300,000 Books, Chapters, Monographs," CHE, 22 May 1991, A17.

39. Carrigan, "Publish or Perish," 137–38; Carolyn J. Mooney, "Efforts to Cut Amount of 'Trivial' Scholarship Win New Backing from Many Academics," CHE, 22 May 1991, A1, A13, A16.

40. Gilmore and Case, "Historians, Books, Computers, and the Library," 673–77, 680–83; Sweetland, "Humanists, Libraries, Electronic Publishing, and the Future," 796–800; Judith Axler Turner, "Enormous Changes in Scholarly Publishing Expected as Result of Advances in Information Technology," CHE, 21 November 1990, A13, A16; Thomas J. DeLoughry, "Professors Report Progress in Gaining Recognition for Their Use of Technology," CHE, 3 March 1993, A19, A21; DeLoughry, "University Presses Try to Ride the Wave of Electronic Publishing," CHE, 27 March 1993, A17–A19.

41. Boyer, *Scholarship Reconsidered*, chap. 2; Joseph M. Moxley and Lagretta T. Lenker, eds., *The Politics and Processes of Scholarship*, Contributions to the Study of Education, no. 66 (Westport CT: Greenwood Publishing Group, 1995).

42. For a critique of Boyer's notions, see Eric J. Ziolkowski, "Slouch-

ing toward Scholardom: The Endangered American College," *College English* 58, no. 5 (September 1996): 568–88.

3. TWENTY-FIVE REASONS TO PUBLISH

1. Boyer, *Scholarship Reconsidered*, chap. 2.

2. Boyer, *Scholarship Reconsidered*, tables A-19, A-20; Carnegie Foundation, *The Condition of the Professoriate*, 47–49 (tables 34–36).

3. Carnegie Foundation, *The Condition of the Professoriate*, 43 (table 30), 50–52 (tables 37–39), 89 (chart 21). Similar results were found in a 1995–96 survey of 33,986 faculty members at 384 colleges and universities conducted by UCLA's Higher Education Research Institute (Sax et al., *The American College Teacher, 1995-96*). The statistics for faculty job satisfaction are found on p. 43.

4. Jacob Viner, "A Modest Proposal for Some Stress on Scholarship in Graduate Training" [1950], *The Long View and the Short: Studies in Economic Theory and Policy* (Glencoe IL: Free Press, 1958), 369–81 at 369.

5. Jaroslav Pelikan, *Scholarship and Its Survival: Questions on the Idea of Graduate Education* (Princeton: Carnegie Foundation for the Advancement of Teaching, 1983), 9; Richard D. Mandell, *The Professor Game* (Garden City NY: Doubleday, 1977), 193; Logan Wilson, *American Academics, Then and Now* (New York: Oxford University Press, 1979), 43.

6. Viner, "A Modest Proposal," 370.

7. Ziolkowski, "The Ph.D. Squid," 193.

8. Theodore M. Benditt, "The Research Demands of Teaching in Modern Higher Education," in *Morality, Responsibility, and the University: Studies in Academic Ethics*, ed. Steven M. Cahn (Philadelphia: Temple University Press, 1990), 93–108 at 106.

9. William G. Bowen, *Ever the Teacher: William G. Bowen's Writings as President of Princeton* (Princeton NJ: Princeton University Press, 1987), 238; Rubin and Huber, *The Knowledge Industry in the United States, 1960–1980*, 24–25.

10. Quoted in J. H. Hexter, "Publish or Perish—A Defense," *Public Interest*, no. 17 (fall 1969): 60–77 at 61.

11. Hexter, "Publish or Perish," 72.

12. Jaroslav Pelikan, "Scholarship: A Sacred Vocation," *Scholarly Publishing* 16, no. 1 (October 1984): 3–22 at 19.

13. Logan Wilson, *The Academic Man: A Study in the Sociology of a Profession* (New York: Octagon, 1942), 186.

14. Quoted in Bowen, *Ever the Teacher*, 248.

15. Wilson, *The Academic Man*, 192, 194. See also Wilson, *American Academics, Then and Now*, 140.

16. Derek Bok, *Higher Learning* (Cambridge MA: Harvard University Press, 1986), 77.

17. Morison retired at 68 and died in 1976. For his post-retirement production, see K. Jack Bauer, "Bibliography of Writings by Samuel Eliot Morison," *North American Society of Oceanic History, Newsletter* 4 (1978): [1–4]. On a smaller, fictional scale, Elizabeth Corbett's Professor Preston was suddenly inspired by retirement from a small New England college to write several accessible books on Greek mythology for a major New York publishing house, which brought him the fame and modest fortune he had missed while teaching (*Professor Preston at Home* [Philadelphia: J. B. Lippincott, 1957]). See also Janice S. Green, "For Retirees, the Life of the Mind Continues," CHE, 9 August 1996, B3.

18. Viner, "A Modest Proposal," 375.

19. Carlos Baker, *A Friend in Power* (New York: Scribner, 1958), 250. Baker's "Enfield University" is patterned after his own Princeton.

20. Quoted in Freedman, "The Professor's Life, Though Rarely Clear to Outsiders, Has Its Rewards—and Its Costs," CHE, 19 February 1986, 92 (also in "The Professor's Life," *Dartmouth Alumni Magazine*, reprinted in *Idealism and Liberal Education*, 99–102).

21. Wilson, *The Academic Man*, 197.

22. Kenneth A. Feldman, "Research Productivity and Scholarly Accomplishments of College Teachers as Related to Their Instructional Effectiveness: A Review and Exploration," *Research in Higher Education* 26, no. 3 (1987): 227–98 at 274–79. See also David S. Webster, "Does Research Productivity Enhance Teaching?" *Educational Record* 66, no. 4 (fall 1985): 60–62; Henry H. Crimmel, "The Myth of the Teacher-Scholar," *Liberal Education* 70, no. 3 (fall 1984): 183–98; and Ian C. Johnston, "Myth Conceptions of Academic Work," *Canadian Journal of Higher Education* 21, no. 2 (1991): 108–16. All of these studies base

"teaching effectiveness" solely on quantified student evaluations, which in turn define teaching almost exclusively as communication and classroom management; the primary *intellectual* basis of course-building, questioning, assignment-making, and evaluation is largely ignored because undergraduates are much less qualified to assess it (Frederick S. Weaver, "Scholarship and Teaching," *Educational Record* 70, no. 1 [winter 1989]: 55–58 at 56). The latest review of the issue finds greater complementarity between teaching and research: John M. Braxton, ed., *Faculty Teaching and Research: Is There a Conflict?* New Directions for Institutional Research, no. 90 (San Francisco: Jossey-Bass, summer 1996).

23. Robert F. Goheen, *The Human Nature of a University* (Princeton NJ: Princeton University Press, 1969), 84–85.

24. Henry Rosovsky, *The University: An Owner's Manual* (New York: W. W. Norton, 1990), 89.

25. Nathan Pusey, "What Makes a College Good?" *The Age of the Scholar* (Cambridge MA: Harvard University Press, 1965), 148. See also "Teaching in the Humanities (Some Criteria of Excellence)," *Ventures: Magazine of the Yale Graduate School* 7 (fall 1967): 13–19 at 16; Sidney M. B. Coulling, "The Role of the Professor in Scholarly Research," in *Library Resources for College Scholars: Transactions of a Conference Held at Washington and Lee University, Lexington, Va., February 14–15, 1980,* ed. Robert E. Danford (Lexington VA, 1980), 27–29 at 29; Nancie L. Gonzalez, "The Professor as Researcher," *National Forum* [Phi Kappa Phi Journal], winter 1987, 7–10 at 10.

26. Ernest L. Boyer, *College: The Undergraduate Experience in America* (New York: Carnegie Foundation for the Advancement of Teaching, 1987), 131.

27. Rosovsky, *The University*, 161.

28. Louis B. Wright, "Teaching and Research," *Association of American Colleges Bulletin* 27 (1941): 75–82 at 76.

29. Wright, "Teaching and Research," 77, 79.

30. Rosovsky, *The University*, 94.

31. Gonzalez, "Professors as Researchers," 7.

32. Boyer, *College*, 131.

33. Pusey, *Age of the Scholar*, 148.

34. Freedman, "The Professor's Life," 92.

35. Rosovsky, *The University*, 87; George Whalley, "'Research' and

the Humanities," in *Studies in Literature and the Humanities: Innocence of Intent*, ed. Brian Crick and John Ferns (Kingston and Montreal: McGill-Queens University Press, 1985), 102–21.

36. Jacques Barzun, "The Scholar Is an Institution," *Journal of Higher Education* 18 (November 1947): 393–400, 445 at 398.

37. Benditt, "The Research Demands of Teaching," 102–3, 107.

38. Benditt, "The Research Demands of Teaching," 100–101; Gonzalez, "Professors as Researchers," 9–10.

39. Pelikan, *Scholarship and Its Survival*, 38.

40. Pelikan, *Scholarship and Its Survival*, 15.

41. Wright, "Teaching and Research," 79.

42. Pelikan, "Scholarship—A Sacred Vocation," 16; Ziolkowski in Bowen, *Ever the Teacher*, 248.

43. Bowen, *Ever the Teacher*, 248–49.

44. Gilbert Highet, *The Immortal Profession: The Joys of Teaching and Learning* (New York: Weybright & Talley, 1976), 64.

45. Coulling, "The Role of the Professor in Scholarly Research," 28; J. Douglas Brown, "Teaching and Research in the University," NEA *Journal* 48, no. 5 (May 1959): 12, 14.

46. Jaroslav Pelikan, *The Idea of the University: A Reexamination* (New Haven CT: Yale University Press, 1992), 94.

47. Hexter, "Publish or Perish," 70–72. See below, 172–73.

48. Bok, *Higher Learning*, 76.

49. "Fact File: Faculty Attitudes, Workload, and Earnings, Fall 1987," A16; Carnegie Foundation, "Change Trendlines: The Payoff for Publication Leaders," 27–30. See Stephen M. Jordan, "What We Have Learned about Faculty Workload: The Best Evidence," in *Analyzing Faculty Workload*, New Directions for Institutional Research, no. 83, vol. 16(3), ed. Jon F. Wergin (San Francisco: Jossey-Bass, fall 1994), 15–23.

50. Mandell, *The Professor Game*, 193, 195, 196; Professor X, *This Beats Working for a Living: The Dark Secrets of a College Professor* (New Rochelle NY: Arlington House, 1973), 64.

51. Pelikan, *Scholarship and Its Survival*, 64.

52. A. N. Whitehead, "Universities and Their Function," in *The Aims of Education and Other Essays* (New York: Macmillan, 1929), 145, 146.

53. For other proponents of faculty scholarship, see Aaron Wildavsky, "The Organization of Time in Scholarly Activities Carried Out under American Conditions in Resource-Rich Research Universities," in *Craftways: On the Organization of Scholarly Work*, 2d enlarged ed. (New Brunswick NJ: Transaction, 1993), chap. 4; Thomas Ehrlich with Juliet Frey, "Research Is Not a Dirty Word," in *The Courage to Inquire: Ideals and Realities in Higher Education* (Bloomington: Indiana University Press, 1995), chap. 3; Robert F. Goheen, "The Ideal of 'The Scholar Teacher,'" *Princeton Alumni Weekly*, 3 June 1960, 16–17, 22; Lawrence Wiseman, "Teaching and Research: Not a Zero Sum Game," *William and Mary Alumni Gazette*, January 1995, 3; J. Douglas Brown, "The Development of Creative Teacher-Scholars," *Daedalus* 94, no. 3 (summer 1965): 615–31; Robert A. McCaughey, "But Can They Teach? In Praise of College Professors Who Publish," *Teachers College Record* 95, no. 2 (winter 1993): 242–57; Mary Renck Jalongo, "On the Compatibility of Teaching and Scholarly Writing," *Scholarly Publishing* 19, no. 1 (October 1987): 49–58; Robert T. Blackburn and Janet H. Lawrence, *Faculty at Work: Motivation, Expectation, Satisfaction* (Baltimore: Johns Hopkins University Press, 1995), chap. 4; Francis Oakley, *Scholarship and Teaching: A Matter of Mutual Support*, ACLS Occasional Paper, no. 32 (New York: American Council of Learned Societies, 1996); Weaver, "Scholarship and Teaching"; Kathryn Mohrman, "The Synergy of Teaching and Research," *AAHE [American Association of Higher Education] Bulletin* 40, no. 7 (March 1988): 12–14; Burton R. Clark, *Places of Inquiry: Research and Advanced Education in Modern Universities* (Berkeley: University of California Press, 1995), 249–52; Ziolkowski, "Slouching toward Scholardom," 568–88; Rae André and Peter J. Frost, eds., *Researchers Hooked on Teaching: Noted Scholars Discuss the Synergies of Teaching and Research*, Foundations for Organizational Science (Thousand Oaks CA: Sage, 1997).

4. ENCOUNTERING THE OTHER

1. James Axtell, "Columbian Encounters: Beyond 1992," *William and Mary Quarterly*, 3rd ser., 49 (April 1992): 336.

2. Phil L. Snyder, ed., *Detachment and the Writing of History: Es-*

says and Letters of Carl L. Becker (Ithaca NY: Cornell University Press, 1958), 134.

3. Reynolds Price, *A Common Room: Essays 1954–1987* (New York: Atheneum, 1987), 377.

4. John Updike, "A Soft Spring Night in Shillington," *The New Yorker*, 24 December 1984, 57.

5. Aimé Césaire, *The Collected Poetry*, trans. Clayton Eshleman and Annette Smith (Berkeley: University of California Press, 1983), 77.

6. *The Complete Works of Montaigne*, trans. Donald M. Frame (Stanford CA: Stanford University Press, 1948), 80, 152, 159.

7. Bowen, *Ever the Teacher*, 151.

8. Peter Brown, "Learning and Imagination," in *Society and the Holy in Late Antiquity* (Berkeley: University of California Press, 1982), 4.

9. Clifford Geertz, "The Uses of Diversity," in *The Tanner Lectures on Human Values VII 1986*, ed. Sterling M. McMurrin (Salt Lake City: University of Utah Press, 1986), 269, 270.

10. Geertz, "The Uses of Diversity," 271.

11. Simon Schama, "Clio Has Problems," *New York Times Magazine*, 8 September 1991, 32.

12. Peter Winch, "Understanding a Primitive Society," in *Religion and Understanding*, ed. D. Z. Phillips (Oxford: Blackwell, 1967), 30.

13. Henri-Irénée Marrou, *The Meaning of History*, trans. Robert J. Olsen (Baltimore: Helicon, 1966), 93.

14. Gerald Early, "Multiculturalism and American Education," *Washington* [Washington University Magazine and Alumni News] 62, no. 1 (spring 1992): 49.

15. José Ortega y Gasset, "The Difficulty of Reading," *Diogenes* 28 (winter 1959): 1–17 at 5.

16. Ortega y Gasset, "The Difficulty of Reading," 15.

17. June Philipp, "Traditional Historical Narrative and Action-Oriented (or Ethnographic) History," *Historical Studies* 20 (April 1983): 339–52 at 350.

18. Clifford Geertz, *The Interpretation of Cultures: Selected Essays* (New York: Basic Books, 1973), 14.

19. Ronald G. Walters, "Signs of the Times: Clifford Geertz and Historians," *Social Research* 47, no. 3 (autumn 1980): 537–56.

20. Clifford Geertz, *Islam Observed: Religious Development in Morocco and Indonesia* (Chicago: University of Chicago Press, 1971), viii.

21. David B. Quinn, ed., *New American World: A Documentary History of North America to 1612*, 5 vols. (New York: Arno Press and Hector Bye, 1979), 2:42, 45.

22. James Axtell, *Beyond 1492: Encounters in Colonial North America* (New York: Oxford University Press, 1992), 45, 47–48.

23. Axtell, *Beyond 1492*, 44, 178–79.

24. H. P. Biggar, ed. and trans., *The Voyages of Jacques Cartier*, Publications of the Public Archives of Canada, no. 11 (Ottawa: F. A. Acland, 1924), 134–35.

25. Axtell, *Beyond 1492*, 45–52.

26. Barbara W. Tuchman, *Practicing History: Selected Essays* (New York: Alfred A. Knopf, 1981), 60.

27. John H. Elliott, *National and Comparative History. An Inaugural Lecture Delivered before the University of Oxford on 10 May 1991* (Oxford: Clarendon, 1991), 5.

28. I have shamelessly lifted this paragraph from Axtell, *Beyond 1492*, 9, with the express consent of the author.

29. Inga Clendinnen, *Aztecs: An Interpretation* (Cambridge: Cambridge University Press, 1991), 1, 4, 284.

30. Benedict de Spinoza, *Tractatus Politicus* (1670), intro., sec. 4, quoted in Brown, *Society and the Holy in Late Antiquity*, 21.

31. Marc Bloch, *The Historian's Craft*, trans. Peter Putnam (New York: McGraw-Hill, 1953), 143.

32. Quoted in Anthony Pagden, "*Ius et Factum*: Text and Experience in the Writings of Bartolomé de Las Casas," *Representations* 33 (winter 1991): 149.

33. Thomas L. Haskell, "Objectivity Is Not Neutrality: Rhetoric vs. Practice in Peter Novick's *That Noble Dream*," *History and Theory* 29, no. 2 (1990): 129–57 at 132, 134.

34. George Whalley, ed., *A Place of Liberty: Essays on the Government of Canadian Universities* (Toronto: Clarke, Irwin, 1964), 166. See also Gordon N. Ray, "The Idea of Disinterestedness in the University," *The Graduate Journal* 8 (1971): 295–309.

35. Edwin Tribble, ed., *A Chime of Words: The Letters of Logan Pearsall Smith* (New York: Ticknor & Fields, 1984), 20.

36. George Steiner, "Knights of Old," *The New Yorker*, 26 May 1986, 104; Pelikan, *The Idea of the University*, 18.

37. James Axtell, "History as Imagination," in *Beyond 1492*, 4-22. See also Partha Mitter, "Can We Ever Understand Alien Cultures? Some Epistemological Concerns Relating to the Perception and Understanding of the Other," *Comparative Criticism* 9 (1987): 3-34.

38. Whitehead, *The Aims of Education*, 145.

39. A. Bartlett Giamatti, *A Free and Ordered Space: The Real World of the University* (New York: W. W. Norton, 1988), 49, 299.

40. T. S. Eliot, "Little Gidding" (lines 239-42) in *Four Quartets* (London: Faber and Faber, 1959), 59.

5. WHAT MAKES A UNIVERSITY GREAT?

1. David S. Webster, *Academic Quality Rankings of American Colleges and Universities* (Springfield IL: C. C. Thomas, 1986).

2. Clark Kerr, "The New Race to Be Harvard or Berkeley or Stanford," *Change* 25, no. 5 (May/June 1991): 8-15 at 10.

3. Kerr, "The New Race," 8; CHE *Almanac,* 2 September 1996, 3. A recent ranking of research universities, based solely on their per capita "creation of new knowledge," finds more movement in and out of the top fifty positions, particularly among public universities (Hugh Davis Graham and Nancy Diamond, *The Rise of American Research Universities: Elites and Challengers in the Postwar Era* [Baltimore: John Hopkins University Press, 1997]).

4. Webster, *Academic Quality Rankings*, 153-54.

5. Weaver, "Scholarship and Teaching," 56.

6. Harold W. Dodds, former President of Princeton, observed that "Research ability is a function of certain segments of the personality and can be appraised with some detachment, whereas teaching ability is more a function of the whole personality" (*The Academic President— Educator or Caretaker?* [New York: McGraw-Hill, 1962], 143).

7. Hexter, "Publish or Perish," 172-73, 61, 72. See below.

8. Frederick Rudolph, *Mark Hopkins and the Log: Williams College, 1836-1872* (New Haven CT: Yale University Press, 1956), vii.

9. Bowen, *Ever the Teacher*, 298 (1986 Annual Report, on Libraries).

10. CHE *Almanac,* 2 September 1996, 31.

11. Webster, *Academic Quality Rankings*, chap. 15; Webster, "America's Highest Ranked Graduate Schools, 1925-1982," *Change* 15, no. 4 (May/June 1983): 14-24; Marvin L. Goldberger, Brendan A. Maher, and Pamela Ebert Flattau, eds., *Research-Doctorate Programs in the United States: Continuity and Change* (Washington DC: National Academy Press, 1995); Denise K. Magner, "Doctoral Judgments," CHE, 22 September 1995, A20, A32-33.

12. Rosovsky, *The University*, chap. 2.

6. CONFESSIONS OF A BIBLIOLATER

1. In reading Nicholas Basbanes's *A Gentle Madness: Bibliophiles, Bibliomanes, and the Eternal Passion for Books* (New York: Henry Holt, 1995), I was heartened to discover that classmate and future world-class collector Louis Brodsky was equally miffed—with more reason—when his two-hundred-volume collection of and on William Faulkner placed second.

8. BETWEEN DISCIPLINES

1. *Ethnohistory* began publication in 1954 under the auspices of the Ohio Valley Historic Indian Conference. In 1965 the sponsoring association was incorporated as the American Society for Ethnohistory.

2. James L. Axtell, ed., *The Educational Writings of John Locke: A Critical Edition with Introduction and Notes* (Cambridge: Cambridge University Press, 1968), chap. 3.

3. J. G. A. Pocock, *Politics, Language and Time: Essays on Political Thought and History* (New York: Atheneum, 1971); James Tully, ed., *Meaning and Context: Quentin Skinner and His Critics* (Princeton NJ: Princeton University Press, 1988), esp. chaps. 2-6.

4. John Locke, *Two Treatises of Government*, ed. Peter Laslett (Cambridge: Cambridge University Press, 1960); Laslett, *The World We Have Lost* (London: Methuen, 1965).

5. Bernard Bailyn, *Education and the Forming of American Society* (Chapel Hill: University of North Carolina Press, 1960), 14.

6. Werner Jaeger, *Paideia: The Ideals of Greek Culture*, 2d ed., 3 vols., trans. Gilbert Highet (New York: Oxford University Press, 1945);

Lawrence Cremin, *American Education: The Colonial Experience, 1607–1783* (New York: Harper & Row, 1970).

7. James Axtell, *The School upon a Hill: Education and Society in Colonial New England* (New Haven CT: Yale University Press, 1974), xi–xii.

8. Philip Bagby, *Culture and History* (Berkeley: University of California Press, 1959); David Bidney, *Theoretical Anthropology*, 2d ed. (New York: Columbia University Press, 1967).

9. George D. Spindler, ed., *Education and Culture: Anthropological Approaches* (New York: Holt, Rinehart & Winston, 1963); George F. Kneller, *Educational Anthropology: An Introduction* (New York: Wiley, 1965).

10. Robert Redfield, *The Little Community* (Chicago: University of Chicago Press, 1960), 30, 59; *Human Nature and the Study of Society: The Papers of Robert Redfield*, vol. 1, ed. Margaret Park Redfield (Chicago: University of Chicago Press, 1962), 49.

11. Arnold van Gennep, *The Rites of Passage*, trans. Monika B. Vizedom and Gabrielle L. Caffee (Chicago: University of Chicago Press, 1960).

12. A. Irving Hallowell, "American Indians, White and Black: The Phenomenon of Transculturalization," *Current Anthropology* 4 (1963): 519–31.

13. James Axtell, "The White Indians of Colonial America," *William and Mary Quarterly*, 3d ser., 32 (January 1975): 55–88; also in Axtell, *The European and the Indian*, chap. 7.

14. James Axtell, "A North American Perspective for Colonial History," *The History Teacher* 12 (August 1979): 549–62.

15. Richard M. Dorson, "Ethnohistory and Ethnic Folklore"; Wilcomb E. Washburn, "Ethnohistory: History 'In the Round'"; David A. Baerreis, "The Ethnohistoric Approach and Archaeology"; and Nancy Oestreich Lurie, "Ethnohistory: An Ethnological Point of View" appeared in *Ethnohistory* 8 (winter 1961): 12–92; the comments of Eleanor Leacock, John C. Ewers, and Charles A. Valentine followed in the summer 1961 issue (pp. 256–80).

16. William Sturtevant, "Anthropology, History, and Ethnohistory," *Ethnohistory* 13, nos. 1–2 (winter–spring 1966): 1–51; Robert M.

Carmack, "Ethnohistory: A Review of Its Development, Definitions, Methods, and Aims," *Annual Review of Anthropology* 1 (1972): 227–46; Bruce G. Trigger, "Ethnohistory: Problems and Prospects," *Ethnohistory* 29, no. 1 (winter 1982): 1–19; Trigger, "Ethnohistory: The Unfinished Edifice," *Ethnohistory* 33, no. 3 (summer 1986): 253–67; William N. Fenton, "The Training of Historical Ethnologists in America," *American Anthropologist*, n.s., 54 (1952): 328–39; Fenton, "Ethnohistory and Its Problems," *Ethnohistory*, 9, no. 1 (winter 1962): 1–23; Fenton, "Field Work, Museum Studies, and Ethnohistorical Research," *Ethnohistory* 13, nos. 1–2 (winter–spring 1966): 71–85.

17. Toronto, 1969 (1st ed., Saint John NB: Tribune, 1937). See also Bruce G. Trigger, "Alfred G. Bailey—Ethnohistorian," *Acadiensis* 18, no. 2 (spring 1989): 3–21.

18. New York, 1970.

19. Philadelphia, 1955; New York, 1967.

20. For Fenton's career and bibliography (1935–82), see the *festschrift* in his honor, *Extending the Rafters: Interdisciplinary Approaches to Iroquoian Studies*, ed. Michael K. Foster, Jack Campisi, and Marianne Mithun (Albany: State University of New York Press, 1984), particularly 1–12 and 401–17.

21. James Axtell, "Ethnohistory: An Historian's Viewpoint," *Ethnohistory* 26, no. 1 (winter 1979): 1–13 at 2; also in Axtell, *The European and the Indian*, 4–15 at 5.

22. Fenton, "Ethnohistory and Its Problems," 11.

23. The first volume, *The Invasion Within: The Contest of Cultures in Colonial North America*, was published in 1985 (New York: Oxford University Press). *American Encounter: The Confluence of Cultures in Colonial North America* and *The European Presence: The Conflict of Cultures in Colonial North America* are to follow.

24. Melville J. Herskovits, *Acculturation: The Study of Culture Contacts* (New York: J. J. Augustin, 1938); Ralph Linton, ed., *Acculturation in Seven American Indian Tribes* (New York: D. Appleton-Century, 1940), chaps. 8–10; George Devereux and Edward M. Loeb, "Antagonistic Acculturation," *American Sociological Review* 8 (1943): 133–47; Homer G. Barnett et al., "Acculturation: An Exploratory Formulation,"

The Social Science Research Council Summer Seminar on Acculturation, 1953, *American Anthropologist*, n.s., 56 (1954): 973-1002; Edward M. Bruner, "Cultural Transmission and Cultural Change," *Southwestern Journal of Anthropology* 12 (1956): 191-99; Edward H. Spicer, "Types of Contact and Processes of Change," in *Perspectives in American Indian Culture Change* (Chicago: University of Chicago Press, 1961), chap. 8; Nancy O. Lurie, "Culture Change," in *Introduction to Cultural Anthropology: Essays in the Scope and Methods of the Science of Man*, ed. James A. Clifton (Boston: Houghton Mifflin, 1968), 275-303; Amado M. Padilla, ed., *Acculturation: Theory, Models and Some New Findings*, AAAS Selected Symposium 39 (Boulder CO: American Association for the Advancement of Science, 1980).

25. Axtell, "Ethnohistory: An Historian's Viewpoint," 2; also in Axtell, *The European and the Indian*, 6.

26. Rhys Isaac, *The Transformation of Virginia, 1740-1790* (Chapel Hill: University of North Carolina Press, 1982), 323-57 at 324; Geertz, *The Interpretation of Cultures*, chap. 1; Philipp, "Traditional Historical Narrative and Action-Oriented History," 339-52.

27. Redfield, *The Little Community*, chaps. 1-10.

28. Ronald G. Walters, "Signs of the Times: Clifford Geertz and Historians," 552-56; Rhys Isaac, "On Explanation, Text, and Terrifying Power in Ethnographic History," *Yale Journal of Criticism* 6, no. 1 (spring 1993): 217-36; Jean-Christophe Agnew, "History and Anthropology: Scenes from a Marriage," *Yale Journal of Criticism* 3, no. 2 (spring 1990): 29-50.

9. EXTRACURRICULUM

1. On the perils of expert witnessing, see Lawrence Rosen, "The Anthropologist as Expert Witness," *American Anthropologist* 79, no. 3 (September 1977): 555-78. For coverage of the trial, see Paul Brodeur, *Restitution: The Land Claims of the Mashpee, Passamaquoddy, and Penobscot Indians of New England* (Boston: Northeastern University Press, 1985), most of which appeared originally in *The New Yorker*; Francis G. Hutchins, *Mashpee: The Story of Cape Cod's Indian Town* (West Franklin NH: Amarta Press, 1979), a clear and fair-minded treatment by the de-

fense's historical expert, mostly from the documents collected and presented by the plaintiff; James Clifford, "Identity in Mashpee," *The Predicament of Culture: Twentieth-Century Ethnography, Literature, and Art* (Cambridge MA: Harvard University Press, 1988), 277-346, by an anthropologist who attended the trial; and Jack Campisi, *The Mashpee Indians: Tribe on Trial* (Syracuse NY: Syracuse University Press, 1991), a hard-hitting critique by the Mashpees' anthropological expert.

2. But see fellow colonialist Joseph J. Ellis, "Whose Thomas Jefferson Is He Anyway?" *New York Times*, 16 February 1997, H35, and Paul Boyer, "Dealing with the Media Circus: Confessions of a 'Cult Expert,'" CHE, 18 April 1997, B4-B5.

CONCLUSION

1. Barry R. Gross, "The University and the Media: *Apologia Pro Vita Sua* with a Defense of Rationality," in *Higher Education under Fire: Politics, and the Crisis of the Humanities*, ed. Michael Bérubé and Cary Nelson (New York: Routledge, 1995), 126-48 at 134.

2. Robert Suro, "More Spent Building Prisons than Colleges, Study Finds," *Washington Post*, 24 February 1997, A8.

3. U.S. Department of Education, *Digest of Education Statistics 1996*, 187 (table 179); CHE *Almanac*, 2 September 1996, 3.

4. Adam Ulam, *The Fall of the American University* (New York: Library Press, 1972); Wilshire, *The Moral Collapse of the University*; Bill Readings, *The University in Ruins* (Cambridge MA: Harvard University Press, 1996).

5. Clark Kerr, *The Uses of the University* (Cambridge MA: Harvard University Press, 1963), chap. 1.

6. Hanna Holborn Gray, "Some Reflections on the Commonwealth of Learning," AAAS *Science and Technology Policy Yearbook 1992* (Washington DC: American Association for the Advancement of Science, 1992), 229-38 at 236.

7. Giamatti, *A Free and Ordered Space*, 50.

8. Ronald A. Smith, *Sports and Freedom: The Rise of Big-Time College Athletics* (New York: Oxford University Press, 1988); John R. Thelin, *Games Colleges Play: Scandal and Reform in Intercollegiate Athletics*

(Baltimore: Johns Hopkins University Press, 1994); Murray Sperber, *College Sports, Inc.: The Athletic Department vs. the University* (New York: Henry Holt, 1990); Gary D. Funk, *Major Violations: The Unbalanced Priorities in Athletics and Academics* (Champaign IL: Human Kinetics, 1991); Amy Shipley, "Most College Funding Goes to Men's Sports," *Washington Post*, 29 April 1997, E1, E5; Thelin and Lawrence L. Wiseman, "Fiscal Fitness? The Peculiar Economics of Intercollegiate Athletics," *Capital Ideas* 434 (February 1990): 1–12; Thelin and Wiseman, "The Future of Big-Time Intercollegiate Athletics," *Planning for Higher Education* 19 (winter 1990–91): 18–27.

9. Anne Matthews, "Hazing Days," *New York Times Magazine*, 3 November 1996, 50–51; Matthews, *Bright College Years: Inside the American Campus Today* (New York: Simon & Schuster, 1997), 80–108; Colman McCarthy, "Campus Choice: Hit the Books or Hit the Bottle?" *Washington Post*, 20 November 1995, D5.

10. Matthews, *Bright College Years*, 30.

11. Matthews, *Bright College Years*, 30–31.

12. "Tuition: A Special Report," CHE, 30 May 1997, A11–A19; Rene Sanchez, "Colleges' Failure to Resolve Funding May Bar Millions from Attending, Study Finds," *Washington Post*, 18 June 1997, A3; CHE *Almanac*, 2 September 1996, 27.

13. Erik Larson, "Why Colleges Cost Too Much," *Time*, 17 March 1997, 46–53; Tom Morganthau and Seema Nayyar, "Those Scary College Costs," *Newsweek*, 29 April 1996, 52–68; Louis Menand, "Everybody Else's College Education," *New York Times Magazine*, 20 April 1997, 48–49; Daniel S. Cheever Jr., "Tomorrow's Crisis: The Cost of College," *Harvard Magazine*, November–December 1992, 40–46; Neil L. Rudenstine, "The Grand Experiment," *Harvard Magazine*, January–February 1993, 39–43; Charles T. Clotfelder, *Buying the Best: Cost Escalation in Elite Higher Education* (Princeton NJ: Princeton University Press, 1996); Robert M. Dunn Jr., "Tuition 101: A Primer for Parents," *Washington Post*, 1 April 1990, C2; Clotfelder, Ronald G. Ehrenberg, Malcolm Getz, and John J. Siegfried, *Economic Challenges in Higher Education*, National Bureau of Economic Research Monograph (Chicago: University of Chicago Press, 1991); Bowen, *Ever the Teacher*, 527–43; Ernest Benjamin, "A Faculty Response to the Fiscal

Crisis: From Defense to Offense," in Bérubé and Nelson, *Higher Education under Fire*, 52-72. For a conservative view, see George Roche, *The Fall of the Ivory Tower: Government Funding, Corruption, and the Bankrupting of American Higher Education* (Washington DC: Regnery, 1994).

14. Sowell, *Inside American Education*, chaps. 5-7; Dinesh D'Souza, *Illiberal Education: The Politics of Race and Sex on Campus* (New York: Random House, 1991); "Identity Politics and Campus Communities: An Exchange," in Bérubé and Nelson, *Higher Education under Fire*, 305-67; "Race on Campus," *New Republic* (spec. iss.), 18 February 1991; Angela Browne-Miller, *Shameful Admissions: The Losing Battle to Serve Everyone in Our Universities* (San Francisco: Jossey-Bass, 1996).

15. Ben Gose, "Duke May Shift Grading System to Reward Students Who Take Challenging Courses," CHE, 14 February 1997, A40 (the proposal did not pass); James B. Twitchell, "Stop Me before I Give Your Kid Another 'A,'" *Washington Post*, 4 June 1997, A23; Valerie Strauss, "Seeking to Slow College Grade Inflation," *Washington Post*, 12 June 1997, A1, A17; Craig Lambert, "Desperately Seeking Summa," *Harvard Magazine*, May-June 1993, 36-40; Gose, "Efforts to Curb Grade Inflation Get an F from Many Critics," CHE, 25 July 1997, A41.

16. Sax et al., *The American College Teacher, 1995-96*, 41; Astin et al., *The American College Teacher, 1989-90*, 44.

17. John K. Wilson, *The Myth of Political Correctness: The Conservative Attack on Higher Education* (Durham NC: Duke University Press, 1995), xv, 1; Charles J. Sykes, *The Hollow Men: Politics and Corruption in Higher Education* (Washington DC: Regnery, 1990); Kimball, *Tenured Radicals*; D'Souza, *Illiberal Education*; Richard Bernstein, *Dictatorship of Virtue: Multiculturalism and the Battle for America's Future* (New York: Random House, 1994); Paul Berman, ed., *Debating P.C.: The Controversy over Political Correctness on College Campuses* (New York: Doubleday, 1992); Paul Lauter, "'Political Correctness' and the Attack on American Colleges," in Bérubé and Nelson, *Higher Education under Fire*, 73-90; Jeffrey Williams, ed., PC *Wars: Politics and Theory in the Academy* (New York: Routledge, 1995).

18. Wilson, *The Myth of Political Correctness*, 2, 10-12, 26-29; Ellen Messer-Davidow, "Dollars for Scholars: The Real Politics of Humanities Scholarship and Programs," in *The Politics of Research*, ed. E. Ann

Kaplan and George Levine (New Brunswick NJ: Rutgers University Press, 1997), 193-233; Messer-Davidow, "Manufacturing the Attack on Liberalized Higher Education," *Social Text* 36 (fall 1993): 40-80.

19. Wilson, *The Myth of Political Correctness*, 3, 6.

20. Wilson, *The Myth of Political Correctness*; Lauter, "'Political Correctness' and the Attack on American Colleges"; Berman, *Debating P.C.*, chaps. 2, 5.

21. Wilson, *The Myth of Political Correctness*, 8; Catherine R. Stimpson, "New 'Politically Correct' Metaphors Insult History and Our Campuses," CHE, 29 May 1991, A40. The NEXUS database "hits" for "political correctness" in 1996 were down to 5,827; "politically correct," however, was holding its own at 9,114 hits, down slightly from 10,995 in 1994. (Thanks to William Cooper of the Marshall-Wythe Law Library for consulting NEXUS for me.)

22. Francis Oakley, "Ignorant Armies and Nighttime Clashes: Changes in the Humanities Classroom, 1970-1995," in Kernan, *What's Happened to the Humanities?* 63-83; Oakley, "Against Nostalgia: Reflections on Our Present Discontents in American Higher Education," in *The Politics of Liberal Education*, ed. Darryl J. Gless and Barbara Herrnstein Smith (Durham NC: Duke University Press, 1992), 267-89; Arthur Levine and Jeannette Cureton, "The Quiet Revolution: Eleven Facts about Multiculturalism and the Curriculum," *Change*, January/February 1992, 25-29; "Change Trendlines: Signs of a Changing Curriculum," *Change*, January/February 1992, 50-52; Alberta Arthurs, "The Humanities in the 1990s," in *Higher Learning in America, 1980-2000*, ed. Arthur Levine (Baltimore: Johns Hopkins University Press, 1993), 259-72; "Engaging Cultural Legacies," *Liberal Education* (spec. iss.), 77, no. 3 (May/June 1991); Lawrence W. Levine, *The Opening of the American Mind: Canons, Culture, and History* (Boston: Beacon Press, 1996); William Casement, *The Great Canon Controversy: The Battle of the Books in Higher Education* (New Brunswick NJ: Transaction, 1996); Russell Jacoby, *Dogmatic Wisdom: How the Culture Wars Divert Education and Distract America* (New York: Doubleday, 1994); Henry Louis Gates Jr., *Loose Canons: Notes on the Culture Wars* (New York: Oxford University Press, 1992); L. Robert Stevens, G. L. Seligmann, and Julian Long, eds., *The Core and the Canon: A National Debate* (Denton: University of

North Texas Press, 1993); Martha C. Nussbaum, *Cultivating Humanity: A Classical Defense of Reform in Liberal Education* (Cambridge MA: Harvard University Press, 1997).

For conservative complaints about the new curriculum, see Allan Bloom, *The Closing of the American Mind: How Higher Education Has Failed Democracy and Impoverished the Soul of Today's Students* (New York: Simon & Schuster, 1987); Bernstein, *Dictatorship of Virtue*; Sykes, *The Hollow Men*; Kimball, *Tenured Radicals*; D'Souza, *Illiberal Education*; James Atlas, *Battle of the Books: The Curriculum Debate in America* (New York: W. W. Norton, 1990); Lynne V. Cheney, *Telling the Truth: A Report on the State of the Humanities in Higher Education* (Washington DC: National Endowment for the Humanities, 1992); John M. Ellis, *Literature Lost: Social Agendas and the Corruption of the Humanities* (New Haven CT: Yale University Press), 1997.

23. Rosenau, *Post-Modernism and the Social Sciences*; Steven Best and Douglas Kellner, *Postmodern Theory: Critical Interrogations* (New York: Guilford Press, 1991).

24. John R. Searle, "Is There a Crisis in American Higher Education?" *American Academy of Arts and Letters Bulletin* 46 (January 1993): 24–47 at 41; Michael Geyer, "Multiculturalism and the Politics of General Education," *Critical Inquiry* 19, no. 3 (spring 1993): 499–533; Douglas, *Education without Impact*; Gordon C. Winston, "The Decline in Undergraduate Teaching: Moral Failure or Market Pressure?" *Change* 26, no. 5 (September/October 1994): 9–15; Francis Oakley, *Community of Learning: The American College and the Liberal Arts Tradition* (New York: Oxford University Press, 1992); Gerald Graff, *Beyond the Culture Wars: How Teaching the Conflicts Can Revitalize American Education* (New York: W. W. Norton, 1992); Henry H. Crimmel, *The Liberal Arts College and the Ideal of Liberal Education: The Case for Radical Reform* (Lanham MD: University Press of America, 1993).

25. Matthews, *Bright College Years*, 31.

26. Matthews, *Bright College Years*, 26, 31, 54; CHE *Almanac*, 2 September 1996, 3, 14, 17, 22; Menand, "Everybody Else's College Education," 48–49.

27. CHE *Almanac*, 2 September 1996, 9.

28. Searle, "Is There a Crisis in American Higher Education?" 29;

"Change Trendlines: Signs of a Changing Curriculum," 52. See also Richard H. Brodhead, "An Anatomy of Multiculturalism," *Yale Alumni Magazine*, April 1994, 45-49 at 45.

29. Whitehead, *The Aims of Education*, 10.

30. Brodhead, "An Anatomy of Multiculturalism," 49.

31. W. B. Carnochan, *The Battleground of the Curriculum: Liberal Education and American Experience* (Stanford CA: Stanford University Press, 1993), 114 (my emphasis); Frederick Rudolph, *Curriculum: A History of the American Undergraduate Course of Study since 1636* (San Francisco: Jossey-Bass, 1977), xxi, 1.

32. Rudolph, *Curriculum*, 3, 5, 7.

33. *Addresses at the Inauguration of Charles William Eliot as President of Harvard College, Tuesday, October 19, 1869* (Cambridge MA: Sever & Francis, 1869), 62.

34. *CHE Almanac*, 2 September 1996, 9.

35. Herbert Lindenberger, "On the Sacrality of Reading Lists: The Western Culture Debate at Stanford University," in *The History of Literature: On Value, Genre, Institutions* (New York: Columbia University Press, 1990), 148-62; Atlas, *Battle of the Books*; Carnochan, *The Battleground of the Curriculum*; Casement, *The Great Canon Controversy*; Peter Shaw, *The War against the Intellect: Episodes in the Decline of Discourse* (Iowa City: University of Iowa Press, 1989).

36. Jerry L. Martin, *The Shakespeare File: What English Majors Are Really Studying* (Washington DC: National Alumni Forum, December 1996); Carolyn J. Mooney, "Study Finds Professors Are Still Teaching the Classics, Sometimes in New Ways," *CHE*, 6 November 1991, A1, A22; John K. Wilson, "Come Not to Bury Shakespeare; He Lives," *CHE*, 14 February 1997, B6; Oakley, "Ignorant Armies and Nighttime Clashes," 63-83; "Change Trendlines: Signs of a Changing Curriculum," 50-51.

37. Rudolph, *Curriculum*, 4, 11-13; Rudolph, "The Neglect of Students as an Historical Tradition," in *The College and the Student*, ed. Lawrence E. Dennis and Joseph F. Kauffman (Washington DC: American Council on Education, 1966), 47-58; James McLachlan, "The Choice of Hercules: American Student Societies in the Early 19th Century," in *The University in Society*, ed. Lawrence Stone (Princeton NJ: Princeton University Press, 1974), 2:449-94; Laurence Biemiller,

"Generations of Students Learned Oratory and Debate in 2 Literary Societies," CHE, 7 March 1997, B2; Thomas S. Harding, *College Literary Societies: Their Contribution to Higher Education in the U.S., 1815–1876* (New York: Pageant, 1971).

38. Christopher Shea, "The Latest Salvo in the Culture Wars Comes in a History of the College Curriculum," CHE, 6 September 1996, A22– A23 at A22; Levine, *The Opening of the American Mind*, 21.

39. Richard Hofstadter and Walter P. Metzger, *The Development of Academic Freedom in the United States* (New York: Columbia University Press, 1955), 487–89 at 487. In 1915, the AAUP's founding statement was co-signed by presidential representatives of the Association of American Colleges; by 1990, 140 professional organizations had endorsed its principles. Ralph S. Brown and Jordan E. Kurland, "Academic Tenure and Academic Freedom," in *Freedom and Tenure in the Academy*, ed. William W. Van Alstyne (Durham NC: Duke University Press, 1993), 325–55 at 326.

40. Smith, *Killing the Spirit*, 116, 122; Charles J. Sykes, *ProfScam: Professors and the Demise of Higher Education* (Washington DC: Regnery, 1988), 137.

41. Hofstadter and Metzger, *The Development of Academic Freedom*, 487, 488.

42. Commission on Academic Tenure in Higher Education, *Faculty Tenure* (San Francisco: Jossey-Bass, 1973), 75.

43. Lewis, *Poisoning the Ivy*, 6; Henry Rosovsky, *The University: An Owner's Manual* (New York: W. W. Norton, 1990), 210–11; Brown and Kurland, "Academic Tenure and Academic Freedom," 328.

44. Thomas L. Haskell, "Justifying the Rights of Academic Freedom in the Era of 'Power/Knowledge,'" in *The Future of Academic Freedom*, ed. Louis Menand (Chicago: University of Chicago Press, 1996), 43–90 at 54. In 1915, the AAUP noted that the "responsibility of the university teacher is primarily to the public itself, and to judgment of his own profession" ("General Declaration of Principles," in *American Higher Education: A Documentary History*, ed. Richard Hofstadter and Wilson Smith [Chicago: University of Chicago Press, 1961], 2:860–78 at 866).

45. Louis Menand, "The Trashing of Professionalism," *Academe* 81,

no. 3 (May-June 1995): 16-19 at 18. At its founding in 1915, the AAUP declared that it is "unsuitable to the dignity of a great profession that the initial responsibility for the maintenance of its professional standards should not be in the hands of its own members" (Hofstadter and Smith, *American Higher Education*, 2:872).

46. Haskell, "Justifying the Rights of Academic Freedom," 47 (emphasis removed).

47. Denise K. Magner, "Beyond Tenure," CHE, 21 July 1995, A13, A16; William G. Tierney, "Academic Community and Post-Tenure Review," *Academe* 83, no. 3 (May/June 1997): 23-25; Richard Edwards, "Can Post-Tenure Review Help Us Save the Tenure System?" *Academe* 83, no. 3 (May/June 1997): 26-31. In 1994, Eugene Arden polled sixty-three provosts and academic vice presidents about their institutional reviews of tenured faculty: 72 percent regularly reviewed them (40 percent annually); one-third were observed by other faculty in their classrooms; 85 percent were evaluated semesterly by students (Arden, "Is Tenure 'Obsolete'? An Opinion and a Survey," *Academe* 81, no. 1 [January-February 1995], 38-39).

48. Short-term contracts do not appear to give institutions any more flexibility in practice than does tenure; in fact, they may give considerably less. In 1971, 87 percent of the institutions without tenure renewed more than 90 percent of their faculty term contracts. By contrast, only 56 percent of colleges with tenure awarded it to more than 80 percent of their candidates; 25 percent awarded tenure to fewer than 70 percent (Commission on Academic Tenure, *Faculty Tenure*, 223 [table 4], 225 [table 5]).

49. U.S. Department of Education, *Digest of Education Statistics, 1996*, 231 (table 220); Brent Staples, "The End of Tenure?: When Colleges Turn to Migrant Labor," *New York Times*, 29 June 1997, sec. 4, 14; Robin Wilson, "Scholars Off the Tenure Track Wonder If They'll Ever Get On," CHE, 14 June 1996, A12-A13; Judith M. Gappa and David W. Leslie, *The Invisible Faculty: Improving the Status of Part-Timers in Higher Education* (San Francisco: Jossey-Bass, 1993); Roger G. Baldwin, Jay L. Chronister, Ana Esther Rivera, and Theresa G. Bailey, "Destination Unknown: An Exploratory Study of Full-Time Faculty off the Tenure Track," *Research in Higher Education* 34, no. 6

(1993): 747-61; Baldwin and Chronister, "Full-Time Non-Tenure-Track Faculty," NEA *Higher Education Research Center Update* 2, no. 5 (September 1996): 1-4.

50. Astin et al., *The American College Teacher, 1995-96*, 40.

51. Fritz Machlup, "In Defense of Academic Tenure," AAUP *Bulletin* 50 (summer 1964): 112-24, reprinted in Matthew W. Finkin, ed., *The Case for Tenure* (Ithaca NY: Cornell University Press, 1996), 9-26 at 19-21; Richard B. McKenzie, "In Defense of Academic Tenure" (1996) (available on the World Wide Web: gsm.uci.edu/mckenzie/tenure.html), 1-13 at 2, 13; Albert Rees, *The Salaries of Ph.D.s in Academe and Elsewhere*, Princeton University Industrial Relations Section Working Paper, no. 286 (Princeton NJ, June 1991), cited in Sita Nataraj, "Work and Pay in Academe" (B.A. honors thesis in economics, College of William and Mary, May 1997), 50; Denise K. Magner, "Increases in Faculty Salaries Fail to Keep Pace with Inflation," CHE, 3 July 1997, A8, quoting Linda A. Bell.

52. H. Lorne Carmichael, "Incentives in Academics: Why Is There Tenure?" *Journal of Political Economy* 96, no. 2 (1988): 453-72; McKenzie, "In Defense of Academic Tenure," 6, 11.

53. Nataraj, "Work and Pay in Academe," 93-95; McKenzie, "In Defense of Academic Tenure," 10-11.

54. Machlup, "In Defense of Academic Tenure," 22. For other arguments in favor of tenure, see Arthur Raines, "Tenured and Untouchable . . . As Faculty Ought to Be," *Washington Post*, 3 December 1996, A15; James E. Perley, "Tenure Remains Vital to Academic Freedom," CHE, 4 April 1997, A48; George B. Chapman, "There Are Lots of Good Reasons for Tenure," *Washington Post*, 20 January 1990, A17; Brenda Miller Power, "The Danger Inherent in Abusing Academic Freedom," CHE, 20 June 1997, A52; Finkin, *The Case for Tenure*; Menand, *The Future of Academic Freedom*; Andrew Oldenquist, "Tenure: Academe's Peculiar Institution," in *Morality, Responsibility, and the University: Studies in Academic Ethics*, ed. Steven M. Cahn (Philadelphia: Temple University Press, 1990), 56-75; Bardwell L. Smith and Associates, eds., *The Tenure Debate* (San Francisco: Jossey-Bass, 1973); Bowen and Schuster, *American Professors*, 235-44; Rosovsky, *The University*, 177-212; Mary W. Gray, "Colleges Need It," *Washington Post Education*

Review, 27 July 1997, 1, 5; Edward Shils, "Academic Freedom and Permanent Tenure," *Minerva* 33 (spring 1995): 5-17, reprinted in Shils, *The Order of Learning: Essays on the Contemporary University* (New Brunswick NJ: Transaction Press, 1997), chap. 9.

55. Smith, *Killing the Spirit,* 7; Sykes, *ProfScam,* 101-2, 257 (quoting Chester Finn's confident estimate); Anderson, *Impostors in the Temple,* 85.

56. Anderson, *Impostors in the Temple,* 85.

57. Anderson, *Impostors in the Temple,* 84; Smith, *Killing the Spirit,* 197; Jacques Barzun, *Begin Here: The Forgotten Conditions of Teaching and Learning* (Chicago: University of Chicago Press, 1991), chap. 12; Sykes, *ProfScam,* 103, 104.

58. Sykes, *ProfScam,* 257, 258; Smith, *Killing the Spirit,* 198, 304.

59. James S. Fairweather, *Faculty Work and Public Trust: Restoring the Value of Teaching and Public Service in American Academic Life* (Boston: Allyn & Bacon, 1996), 30; Robert A. McCaughey, *Scholars and Teachers: The Faculties of Select Liberal Arts Colleges and Their Place in American Higher Learning* (New York: Conceptual Litho Reproductions, 1995); McCaughey, "But Can They Teach? In Praise of College Professors Who Publish," 242-57; Oakley, *Scholarship and Teaching,* 6-8; Kenneth P. Ruscio, "The Distinctive Scholarship of the Selective Liberal Arts College," *Journal of Higher Education* 58, no. 2 (March/April 1987): 205-222; Ziolkowski, "Slouching toward Scholardom," 568-88.

60. Astin et al., *The American College Teacher, 1995-96,* 29, 34, 37. The data on book publishing can be misleading because scientists and many social scientists typically publish articles rather than books.

61. Haskell, "Justifying the Rights of Academic Freedom," 44, 47. Although a small minority of journal articles, particularly in the sciences, are apparently never read, or at least never cited, by anyone other than their authors, "it would be difficult, if not impossible, to separate the dross from what is valuable before work was introduced to the scholarly or scientific community" (Lewis, *Marginal Worth,* 69 n. 7).

62. Robert W. Beard, "On the Publish-or-Perish Policy," *Journal of Higher Education* 36, no. 8 (November 1965): 455-59 at 457.

63. Lewis, *Marginal Worth,* 57-58, citing a 1991-92 survey of thirty-five hundred academics by the Carnegie Foundation for the Advancement of Teaching.

64. Lewis, *Marginal Worth*, 57–58; Oakley, *Scholarship and Teaching*, 4–5.

65. Lewis, *Marginal Worth*, 6, 28, 29; Fairweather, *Faculty Work and Public Trust*, 27.

66. Braxton, *Faculty Teaching and Research*, 5–14, 84–85 (table 9.1).

67. Lewis, *Marginal Worth*, 56; Anna V. Shaw Sullivan, "Teaching Norms and Publication Productivity," in Braxton, *Faculty Teaching and Research*, 15–21 at 19.

68. Hans A. Schmitt, "Teaching and Research: Companions or Adversaries?" *Journal of Higher Education* 36, no. 8 (November 1965): 419–27 at 426; Brand Blanshard, "'For One Who Is Liberally Educated, Life Is Far Too Short,'" *Yale Alumni Magazine*, October 1975, 13–15 at 13.

69. Anderson, *Impostors in the Temple*, 45, 46 (my emphasis); Sykes, *ProfScam*, 54; Sowell, *Inside American Education*, 205–6; Scott Heller, "Teaching Award: Aid to Tenure or Kiss of Death?" CHE, 16 March 1988, A14. Only a few well-publicized denials of tenure to award-winners at major *research* universities have given rise to the "kiss of death" theme; no one reports the hundreds of awardees who do receive tenure.

70. Anderson, *Impostors in the Temple*, 49, 53; Lewis, *Poisoning the Ivy*, chap. 3.

71. Sowell, *Inside American Education*, 219, 223.

72. Sax et al., *The American College Teacher, 1995–96*, 29, 32, 38, 40.

73. Sax et al., *The American College Teacher, 1995–96*, 33, 34; Astin et al., *The American College Teacher, 1989–90*, 45.

74. From the college side, teaching is also number one. A 1987 U.S. Department of Education survey of twenty-five hundred department chairpersons found that 75 percent rated "teaching quality" their top priority in hiring new faculty; 90 percent said that teaching quality was a key factor in tenure decisions. Research universities, understandably, gave priority to research ability (Lewis, *Marginal Worth*, 30).

75. Sax et al., *The American College Teacher, 1995–96*, 12 (table 7), 13 (table 8).

76. This is a high rate of influence; psychosocial changes are only marginally attributable to the academic program or its professorial purveyors. The majority of all changes are affected by peers, general and

college cultural environments, and normal maturation. Ernest T. Pascarella and Patrick T. Terenzini, *How College Affects Students: Findings and Insights from Twenty Years of Research* (San Francisco: Jossey-Bass, 1991), 556–85.

77. U.S. Department of Education, *Digest of Education Statistics 1996*, 175 (table 168), 227 (table 216); Ernest Benjamin, "Improving Teaching: Tenure Is Not the Problem, It's the Solution," *Footnotes* [American Association of University Professors] (fall 1997): 4–6 at 4 (table 1).

78. Roger G. Baldwin and Robert T. Blackburn, "The Academic Career as a Developmental Process: Implications for Higher Education," *Journal of Higher Education* 52, no. 6 (1981): 598–614; Baldwin, "Faculty Career Stages and Implications for Professional Development," in *Enhancing Faculty Careers: Strategies for Development and Renewal*, ed. J. H. Schuster, D. W. Wheeler, and Associates (San Francisco: Jossey-Bass, 1990), 20–40; Peter J. Frost and M. Susan Taylor, eds., *Rhythms of Academic Life: Personal Accounts of Careers in Academia*, Foundations for Organizational Science (Thousand Oaks CA: Sage Publications, 1996); Blackburn and Janet H. Lawrence, *Faculty at Work: Motivation, Expectation, Satisfaction* (Baltimore MD: Johns Hopkins University Press, 1995); Bennett M. Berger, *Authors of Their Own Lives: Intellectual Autobiographies of Twenty American Sociologists* (Berkeley: University of California Press, 1990).

79. See above, n. 49.

80. Anderson, *Impostors in the Temple*, 49, 53, 64–65, 71, 76.

81. Lewis, *Marginal Worth.*

82. Sowell, *Inside American Education*, 202.

83. James M. Gustafson, "Professions as 'Callings,'" *Social Service Review* 56, no. 4 (December 1982), 501–15; Pelikan, "Scholarship: A Sacred Vocation," 5–22; Mark R. Schwehn, "The Academic Vocation: 'Specialists without Spirit, Sensualists without Heart,'" *Cross Currents* 42 (1992): 185–99.

Index

Scargill, Daniel, 107, 108
scholar-athletes: college, 115, 118, 120–22; and confidence, 134; postgraduate, 115–16, 118–19; and school, 102, 115, 118, 119–20, 124–25; self-fashioning of, 122–24; social relations of, 124–25; and time management, 127–28
scholars, attributes of good, 60–61
scholarship: and athletics, 126–29; habitual, 52, 53, 60, 63, 246; types of, 46–47, 49; as vocation, 55. *See also* research
seminars, 10
"Sesame Street," 168
Shakespeare, William, 105, 225
Shorter, Frank, 128
Shubow, Larry, 151
Simon, Scott, 154
Skinner, Quentin, 137
Skinner, Walter J., 150, 153, 154
Sloane, Alfred P., Foundation, 91
Smith, Logan Pearsall, 83
Social Science Research Council (SSRC), 57, 90–91
Society of American Historians, 91
sororities, xi, 214
Spindler, George, 139
Spinoza, Benedict de, 82
Stadacona (Indian town), 79
Sterling Memorial Library (Yale), 104–5, 106
Stonehill, C. A., & Co., 107, 108, 109
student-athletes. *See* scholar-athletes
student/faculty ratios, 215, 246
students: and course evaluations, 12, 54, 89, 170, 217, 249, 261 n.22, 267 n.6, 279 n.47; diversity of, 215–16, 224; and extracurricula, 96, 226; of great universities, 91–92, 95–96; honors, 14; minority, 222; numbers of, 8, 224, 245–46; profile of, 221–22; and substance abuse, 214; as unprepared, 214; writing deficiencies of, xi. *See also* graduate students
Sturtevant, William, 141
substance abuse, student, 214

summer schools, 7, 196
Sundown, Chief Corbett, 158

Tarkington, Booth, 101–2
teachers, attributes of good, 60–61, 66
teaching, 8: audiovisual aids in, 12, 247; awards, 89; classroom, 4; criticized, 242–43; as difficult to assess, 54, 243–44; evaluations, 12, 54, 89, 217, 249, 261 n.22, 267 n.6, 279 n.47; extra-classroom, 13, 15–16, 148, 162–63, 165; goals of, 9, 66, 71; graduate, 14–15, 245; and learning, 58; loads, 31, 67, 241, 244, 247; methods, 245, 246–47; portfolios, 90; preparation for, 11, 248; as professional goal, 244, 282 n.74; and research, 42, 43, 58–66, 90, 240–42; and status, 55–56; student-led, 13
teaching assistants (TAs), xii, 15–16, 215, 248–49
technology, 4, 215, 247. *See also* computers; libraries: technology in
television, professors and, 164, 165, 167–69
tenure: and administrative flexibility, 231–32, 279 n.48; criticisms of, 226–27; duration of, 227, 228; economic arguments for, 232–34; goals of, 226; probation for, 230–31, 234, 239, 282 n.69; and publication, 50; as revocable, 229
theses, 14. *See also* dissertations
Thornton's, 104
tobacco, Indian uses of, 78, 79
track and field, JLA and, 118–19, 120, 127–28, 130; and coaches, 127, 128, 132; and Harvard-Yale select team, 108, 118, 132–33; and Oxford-Cambridge select team, 108, 119, 132–33
transculturalization, 140
Trigger, Bruce, 141, 205
Trinity College, Cambridge, 117
trustees, of great universities, 96–97
Tuchman, Barbara, 80
Tupi Indians, 72
Tureen, Tom, 151

Also by James Axtell

The Educational Writings of John Locke:
A Critical Edition

The School upon a Hill: Education and
Society in Colonial New England

Indian Missions: A Critical Bibliography
(with James P. Ronda)

The European and the Indian: Essays
in the Ethnohistory of Colonial North
America

The Indian Peoples of Eastern America:
A Documentary History of the Sexes

The Invasion Within: The Contest
of Cultures in Colonial North America

After Columbus: Essays in the
Ethnohistory of Colonial North America

Beyond 1492: Encounters in Colonial
North America

The Indians' New South:
Cultural Change in the Colonial South-
east